PATRICIAN IN POLITICS

1.

SHERRY PENNEY

PATRICIAN IN POLITICS

Daniel Dewey Barnard

of

New York

National University Publications
KENNIKAT PRESS ● 1974
Port Washington, N.Y. ● London

Library of Congress Catalog Card No. 74-77652
ISBN: 0-8046-9067-7

Manufactured in the United States of America

Published by
Kennikat Press Corp.
Port Washington, N.Y./London

To Mike and Jeff

CONTENTS

		Preface	xi
Chapter	I	New England Yankee	3
Chapter	II	Apprentice Politician	21
Chapter	III	Man of Letters: Critic of Reform	37
Chapter	IV	Patrician in the State Assembly	55
Chapter	V	Up the Political Ladder: U.S. Congress	67
Chapter	VI	Anti-Abolition Whig	93
Chapter	VII	Gentleman Abroad	113
Chapter	VIII	Danger of Disunion	133
Chapter	IX	A Man of Principle	157
		Notes	163
		Bibliography	183
		Index	203

ILLUSTRATIONS

1. Daniel Dewey Barnard. From *American
   Whig Review, (AWR)* May, 1848   frontispiece
2. Hamilton Fish. From *AWR,* December, 1848   20
3. Washington Hunt. From *AWR,* March, 1849   20
4. Thurlow Weed. From Collection Albany Institute
   of History and Art (AIHA)   20
5. Robert Winthrop. From *AWR,* March, 1848   20
6. Daniel Webster. From *AWR,* July, 1846   33
7. Henry Clay. From *AWR,* January, 1845   33
8. Millard Fillmore. From *AWR,* October, 1848   33
9. John Quincy Adams. From *AWR,* May, 1845   33
10. An 1812 view of what is now Main Street in
    Rochester. From *History of Monroe County,*
    1877   34
11. Residence of E. Henry Barnard, Mendon, Monroe
    County. From *History of Monroe County,* 1877   35
12. Daniel Barnard's residence, One Elk Street, Albany.
    From Albany Room Collection, (ARC)
    Harmanus Bleeker Library, Albany   36
13. View of Albany, 1830. From ARC   53
14. Albany Medical School, formerly the Lancastrian
    School, Eagle Street. From AIHA   54
15. Albany Female Seminary, Engraving by Edwin
    Forbes. From AIHA   64

ILLUSTRATIONS

16. Albany Academy, Academy Park. From AIHA   65
17. State Street, Albany, about 1845, by James
    Wilson. From AIHA   66
18. Albany Capitol, 1806, Lithograph by Henry Walton.
    From AIHA   92
19. Albany City Hall, Lithograph by August Knoller.
    From AIHA   111
20. Second Saint Peter's Episcopal Church. From AIHA 112
21. Crossing the Hudson on ice in 1856. The scene
    looks across the river from the East Albany station
    of the Hudson River Railroad. From ARC   131
22. Pearl Street Theater, Albany. From AIHA   132
23. Mansion House, Albany, a popular hotel.
    From ARC   155
24. Congress Hall Hotel, Albany, 1815-1878. From
    ARC   156
25. Old Elm Street. Corner State Street and North
    Pearl in 1849, Albany. From ARC   161

ACKNOWLEDGMENTS

Many persons have helped me in the preparation of this study, and I would like to acknowledge their assistance. The idea of doing research on the conservative wing of the New York Whig party grew out of conversations with Dr. Arthur Ekirch, Jr. and Dr. Catharine Newbold of the History Department at the State University of New York at Albany. Dr. Newbold has provided not only helpful advice throughout every step of the research and writing but encouragement and inspiration as well. Dr. Ekirch made many suggestions in the early part of the research and subsequently read the entire manuscript, offering numerous constructive comments. The manuscript also was strengthened by the helpful suggestions of Dr. Donald Liedel and Dr. Harry Price.

Friends who have done me the favor of critically reading the manuscript are Linda Hanneman, Dr. Marshall Lapp, and Dr. James Livingston.

A special word of thanks must go to Mrs. John DeWitt Peltz of New York City, who allowed me to use the private collection of Barnard papers in her possession.

I am also indebted to Marguerite Mullinneaux of the Harmanus Bleeker Library and Kenneth MacFarland of the Albany Institute for their assistance in securing photographs of nineteenth century Albany.

A number of other persons at the following libraries and depositories were very helpful: the Union College Library; the

Interlibrary Loan Office of the State University of New York at Albany, especially Elizabeth Salzer; the New York State Library; the Manuscript Division of the Library of Congress; the National Archives; the New York Public Library; the New York Historical Society; the Harmanus Bleeker Library in Albany; the University of Rochester Library; the Harvard University Library; the Historical Society of Pennsylvania; and the Massachusetts Historical Society. Mr. Arthur Detmers of the Buffalo Historical Society assisted me in securing photocopies of the Barnard-Fillmore correspondence while the Fillmore Papers were in the process of being microfilmed; and Dr. Charles Snyder made available to me the Barnard-Fillmore correspondence in the Fillmore Collection at Oswego.

Special thanks must be given to my typists Arliss Nygard and Annie Sweet for their intelligent corrections and time. To Mike and Jeff, I give my love and thank them for being cheerful while their mother rewrote the numerous drafts. Finally, I thank my husband Murray for his suggestions, support, and sense of humor.

PREFACE

American society in the antebellum period was beset with numerous tensions. Forces making for nationalism contended with those of sectionalism. Industrial development resulted in social and economic dislocations. Intellectual ferment was widespread. Reform sentiment swept the country: antislavery societies were formed; the first women's rights convention was held; peace societies were organized and communal living arrangements were attempted. Some Americans advocated the cause of temperance, while others pushed for educational and prison reforms. The country found itself involved in war with Mexico, and as a result of the vast amount of territory acquired took up the cry of manifest destiny.

Because American history is usually written from the vantage point of the major figures of an era, these tensions have often been studied as seen by such "giants." Yet there were numbers of people who resisted not only the war but the sweeping tide of reform as well, and the reactions of people outside the mainstream are significant in demonstrating how deep were the strains operating throughout the society. One such figure was the New York intellectual and political figure, Daniel Dewey Barnard (1796–1861), who represented New York in Congress for four terms and was later appointed United States Minister to Berlin under the Fillmore administration.

In his political career Barnard was a lifelong supporter of the

Clay brand of Whiggery. He was an economic and political nationalist who believed in positive action by the federal government for the good of society. The United States Constitution was his guide, and he was a staunch defender of protective tariffs, federally sponsored internal improvements, and a national bank. However, his nationalistic outlook ran aground over federal interference with slavery, and he favored state sovereignty in regard to the peculiar institution. In addition, Barnard never accepted the newer politics of the nineteenth century with its appeals for mass support, whether advocated by Whigs or Democrats. Rather he continued to favor the older paternalistic and patrician approach in which gentlemen stood for office.

Barnard was an outspoken critic of the Mexican War and called it an executive war—a war of the President's "own seeking." He was an antiabolitionist at a time when most Whigs were flirting with antislavery and the Republican Party. He fought against temperance and legislation to benefit laborers and the poor, and failed to support the women's rights movement. He pronounced a scathing indictment on Jacksonian Democracy and all those associated with it. He believed that government by the Jacksonians would bring chaos to an otherwise orderly society and cause widespread social and economic upheaval.

Political activity provides only a partial picture of Barnard's role in nineteenth century America. As a scholar and literary figure he delivered over twenty lectures during the 1830's, 40's, and 50's. In these he outlined his beliefs in the importance of education, the duty of the scholar toward society, and the inevitability of progress. His philosophy was grounded in his own brand of conservatism, the central theme of which was a belief in determinism and the desirability of slow evolutionary change as opposed to radical reform movements. He never accommodated himself to the vast amount of social change which stirred the country in the nineteenth century nor made peace with the reform sentiment.

Barnard was optimistic about the future of his country until mid-century, when he predicted that if the Republicans were elected, disunion would follow. During the decade of the fifties his efforts were directed toward persuading his fellow citizens of the impending "dangers of disunion." He opposed the Conscience Whigs of the North and pleaded for no interference with slavery in Southern states because if slavery were left alone, it would eventually disappear. He asserted that the country should stand by the compromises of the Constitution.

Barnard was born to wealth, educated in the classical tradition, and reared as a strict Protestant. His life exemplifies the dilemma of a man, personally conservative, when confronted with the problems of a rapidly changing society. In rejecting not only the Conscience Whig approach to slavery but also the professional politics of the era, Barnard provides a striking contrast to the prevailing political climate. An examination of Barnard's philosophy and his role as one of the chief spokesmen of the conservative viewpoint sheds new light on political, social, and intellectual life in this period, adds to an understanding of the dissension and eventual split within the Whig Party, and aids in evaluating the complex issues that led to the Civil War.

PATRICIAN IN POLITICS

Chapter I

NEW ENGLAND YANKEE

Arriving in Washington, D.C., late in November, 1827, the newly elected Congressman from Rochester reflected with pride over the past few years of his life. Now just thirty-one, he had begun his active political career only two years before and was about to enter the House of Representatives as the first delegate from the district which included Monroe and Livingston counties. A firm believer in the guiding hand of Providence, he felt blessed that so much success had come his way. He not only wanted to be in Congress but felt that he should be. A man of ability and dedication from a respectable background, he was the kind of representative that the people needed.[1]

Daniel Dewey Barnard's roots were planted deep in New England soil. Born into a well established family in 1796, while his parents were residing temporarily in Sheffield in Berkshire County, Massachusetts, he was named in honor of his mother's brother, Daniel Dewey, a judge of the Supreme Court of Massachusetts. Barnard's great-grandfather, a man of means who was born and educated in England, came to America and settled in Hartford, Connecticut, early in the eighteenth century. Soon after, he married Sarah Williams, and the couple subsequently had five children. Barnard's grandfather, Ebenezer Barnard, Sr., their last son, was born in 1727. He rose to prominence as a merchant and ship owner in Hartford and also served as a captain in the Revolutionary War. Barnard's father, Timothy, was born in 1756. He received a practical education in business from his father and, like him, was a soldier in the Revolutionary War, serving from 1776 to 1782. Beginning his service as a drum major, he became a sergeant and later a major in the commissary department. After the conclusion of the war, Timothy married Phoebe Dewey in 1784. To them were born five children. Daniel was their third child and second son.[2]

Barnard's early years were spent on the family farm near Hartford. He received little formal schooling, but education and learning were held in high regard by his parents, who encouraged him to pursue scholarly interests. His mother spent much time reading the Bible to him, and from her he learned basic skills in reading and writing. When he was twelve, his parents moved to the small settlement of Mendon, New York, not far from Rochester. In 1809 western New York was a frontier area, with Rochester numbering fewer than five hundred persons. In the 1790's Ebenezer Barnard Jr. had purchased over 5,000 acres of land in the Mendon vicinity, and Barnard's father was now attracted to the area because of the availability of land for farming and for speculation. The Barnards, like many New Englanders moving to the western frontier of New York, took with them their habits of frugality and enterprise. Barnard's father purchased a farm already under cultivation located about a mile west of Mendon village. He combined farming, land speculation, and civic and legal activities. He was the first postmaster, with headquarters in his residence, and also served as a judge in Ontario County. When the first town meeting was held in Mendon in April, 1813, he served as chairman and was later chosen as one of the two commissioners of school funds.

Barnard irregularly attended the Mendon frame school, which was erected in 1810, and also continued to read and study on his own. In addition, he worked on his father's farm. Since he was a frail child and frequently troubled by sickness, more of his time was spent on literary pursuits than on farm work. At an early age Barnard, influenced by his father's business transactions involving land sales, became interested in the law. A little more than a year after moving to New York, Barnard began working in the County Clerk's office at Canandaigua.

At fourteen years of age he began to act as Deputy Clerk of
the county, often with full charge of the office. Because of the
time spent reading law, Barnard no longer took an active part
in the operation of the farm, but for his brothers and sisters
the farm remained the central focus. Within five years the Barnards
were recognized throughout the area as a family of "honest,
reputable farmers."[3]

Barnard's education assumed a more formal character when
his parents sent him to Lenox Academy in Berkshire, Massachusetts, to study Greek, Latin, mathematics, and natural
philosophy in order to prepare for college. After a year at Lenox
he entered Williams College as a sophomore in 1815. Barnard
was a serious minded and mature young man and the scholarly
life was attractive to him. He enjoyed reading the classics and
worked to develop his own skills as an orator. His endeavors
were rewarded, and at commencement he delivered an original
poem and received honors for scholarship. He was one of a
class of twenty-one young men who received the Bachelor of
Arts degree in 1818.[4]

After graduation Barnard returned to Rochester and worked
as a clerk in a law office. A land boom followed the close of
the War of 1812, and many young lawyers established their practices in Rochester in order to take advantage of the highly specula-
tive climate there. In 1820, the village of Rochester had a population of 1,502 with only six lawyers. In the period from 1821
to 1827 the number of lawyers increased to twenty-seven, including Barnard. After being admitted to practice as an attorney before
the Supreme Court of the state in 1821, Barnard devoted full
time to the law. Fees from a practice almost entirely in land
transactions provided the main source of his income. While the
majority of his clients were from Rochester and the surrounding
areas, one more distant was his uncle, Ebenezer Barnard, who,
though continuing to reside in Hartford, speculated in land in
western New York. Barnard collected debts owed to his uncle
and handled land sales and the payment of taxes due on New
York lands for him. As the work load increased, Robert Brecken-
ridge joined Barnard and assisted in the practice.

Lawyers, including Barnard, who were forced to travel more
than thirty miles on difficult roads to county seats in Canandaigua

or Batavia to handle the increasing volume of legal transactions, were desirous of establishing a county seat at Rochester. Barnard went to Albany during the legislative session in the winter of 1821 to lobby for a bill which would create the county of Monroe. His efforts, along with those of the other lawyers accompanying him, were successful, and in February a bill was passed to establish a new county out of portions of Genesee and Ontario counties. Barnard's father benefited from the project too by becoming an associate judge and one of the first judicial officers of Monroe County.[5]

In addition to his work in law and politics, Barnard, by the time he was twenty-three, had begun to formulate the philosophy which would guide his personal and political career. Much of this he outlined in a letter to his uncle Ebenezer Barnard. Because his parents had instilled in him a deep respect for the principles of the Protestant faith, a respect for tradition and stability, and a belief in the necessity of hard work, he was concerned about economic security and status. Barnard had little sympathy for the poor classes in society and believed that by strict attention to duty and frugal living most people could prosper. He stressed the necessity of a life grounded in the essentials of a sound education and a strong religious faith. He praised the habits of honesty, reliability, and sobriety and was unsympathetic to those who responded to their emotions rather than to their intellects. However, he realized that many people were not inclined to lead frugal and regular lives. Such people needed guidance and should be educated so that they would not hinder the progress of society. Therefore he favored a political system in which those with a stake in society would make the decisions concerning the direction it should take.

The depression of 1819 strengthened many of his ideas. Land hunger had been a causative factor in the depression, and although Barnard favored the use of credit in order to facilitate trade and business, he concluded that greater regulation of the economic system was needed. He blamed the depression on the desire of many to get rich without working and on the easy credit policies of the states. Barnard was particularly distressed that as a result of the depression creditors stood to lose money. In the final analysis, however, he predicted that the depression might have a healthy effect on the total economic picture because it would force people to curtail expenses and live frugally.[6] Barnard believed in the emergent economic nationalism of the post-1812 period, and the principles which were to guide him in politics were based largely on those of Henry Clay. Throughout his life, Barnard maintained that positive governmental action based on Constitutional authority should guide the progress of society.

In his own life Barnard saw himself as the kind of enlightened public leader who would work for the public interest. He was pleased when he was appointed District Attorney for Monroe County in 1825—an appointment which he received in part because of his efforts in creating the county and also because of his father's influential position as a judge. The following year he was also appointed one of the four examiners for education in the county.

During this period Barnard made the acquaintance of the young editor and proprietor of the Rochester *Telegraph,* Thurlow Weed. Through their mutual interest in politics, a limited friendship began to develop.[7] Barnard was not a particularly social person apart from his political colleagues, and most of his relationships were limited to his family circle.

However, when he met Sarah, the daughter of Henry G. Livingston, a man of means and a descendant of Robert G. Livingston, the First Lord of Livingston Manor, he was ready to consider marriage. Her father, like Barnard's, had been a patriot in the Revolutionary War. Barnard admired her domestic skills, and the romance which developed had the approval of both families. Their courtship was brief, and on July 23, 1825, at St. Luke's Episcopal Church in Rochester, they were married in a formal ceremony.

The young couple made their home in Rochester, where Barnard could continue his legal and political activities. Their daughter Cora was born two years later. Barnard was a devoted father and husband and commented often about his immediate family in his business correspondence.[8]

Shortly after his marriage Barnard's name began to be mentioned as a possible candidate for elective office. He presented an attractive public image, and early in 1826 the supporters of John Quincy Adams selected him as their candidate for the congressional seat from Monroe and Livingston counties. Many factors operated in his favor. He had a reputation as a highly successful lawyer, he had gained valuable experience as District Attorney, and he had shown an interest in the civic affairs of the community. In addition, his support of positive governmental action in the economic sphere was popular to the many prospective entrepreneurs in the fast growing Rochester area. Barnard was willing to be the candidate, but wrote to his uncle that he would not actively seek the office. However, when the party managers urged him to accept the nomination, he complied. He thus set a precedent he would follow for the rest of his life, desiring office but waiting to be sought by the party.

During the months of the campaign, Barnard was put forth as an Adams man and as one who would serve the best interests of the area. He achieved a strong success at the polls in his first bid for elective office, defeating his opponent, Enos Pomeroy, by 372 votes. In addition, he led the Adams candidate for Governor in Monroe County by 98 votes and in Livingston County by 3 votes. He would join twenty-one other Adams men in the group of thirty-four Congressmen from New York.[9]

The area Barnard was to represent was centered in Rochester, which had grown from a frontier outpost to a leading town in western New York. By 1826 the city had a population of 7,669, while Monroe County numbered about 39,000. Rochester was a booming manufacturing center, with iron works, flour mills, and cotton, wool, footwear, and furniture factories among its leading industries. Livingston County, with a population of 23,860, was largely an agricultural area devoted to sheep raising and wheat growing.

When he arrived in Washington for the opening session of the Twentieth Congress in 1827, Barnard took lodging in a boarding house near the Capitol. An early acquaintance and fellow boarder was Congressman Edward Everett from Massachusetts, and the two men developed a friendship which lasted until Barnard's death. As a result of the election of 1824, political parties were in a state of flux. Barnard identified himself as an Adams supporter and indicated that he was not a Federalist. He heartily approved of Adams' recommendations for federally sponsored internal improvements and the encouragement of home industry.

In his first term in Congress, Barnard served as a minority member on the Committee on Public Expenditures. In this capacity, he continued to support Adams. Although not the most active member of the Twentieth Congress, he was praised for his eloquence and debating skills by many, including President Adams, Edward Everett, and Silas Wright, a fellow New Yorker but political opponent.[10]

In his first term as an elected representative, Barnard spoke out on three major issues: slavery, the tariff, and internal improvements. Soon after Congress met in December, 1827, it had to deal with the complex question of the status of slaves. Were they persons or were they property? Under debate was the claim of Marigny D'Auterive, the owner of a slave who had been impressed into labor by federal troops at New Orleans during the War of 1812. D'Auterive submitted a request for $200, claiming that his slave Warwick had suffered injury that impaired his ability to work. A bill was introduced to settle the claim, and debate dragged on through January and into February.

Barnard opposed the claim and on February 7 delivered an impassioned speech before the House. He considered the legal question of impressment of private property into public service and whether the evidence showed that this slave went into the service by impressment or by contract with his master. He conceded that the services of the slave were contracted for but argued that this did not justify the claim. Although admitting that slaves were property and that private property could be taken for public use provided there was compensation, Barnard considered slaves a special kind of property.

> . . . we deceive ourselves if we imagine them to be property in the same sense in which the ox and horse are property. . . . I hold them to be always property, and always persons, and that they are entitled to certain civil rights . . . they are reasonable human beings . . . they are men, always men; absolutely men. . . .

Barnard concluded that the life of the slave was the property of Him who gave it and not of the master. Therefore, a slave could not be impressed into war service against his will and a master must not use his slave so as to do violence to his human qualities. Barnard's central thesis, developed from his legal background and knowledge of English law, was that where the slave qualities of property and humanity collided, the quality of humanity must be paramount. He argued that a master could not compel a slave to put his life in jeopardy in the defense of the country. Since Warwick had been so compelled, there was no justification for the claim.

Many of Barnard's ideas toward the black race were outlined in this speech, and although the speech had antislavery overtones, he extended his argument to praise colonization societies and applauded their effort to remove the African race from the United States. The very existence of colonization societies was to him proof of the humanity of the slave. Were there no distinction between slaves and other property, there would be no need for colonization societies. No one would colonize unwanted cattle but would simply kill them. Barnard revealed his own indecision and ambiguity as to the best means of dealing with the black man when he elaborated on the institution of slavery. While he looked forward to colonization of free Negroes, he found little to criticize in the institution of slavery, finding a slave to be generally a "passive being . . . in the habit of passive obedience. . . ." Barnard believed that "slaves in this country [were] universally treated by their masters with the utmost humanity and kindness." Although he was against the claim of D'Auterive and considered slaves to be men, Barnard did not believe slavery to be morally wrong. He was careful to point out that he intended no hostility towards the South or the institution of slavery.

Of the speakers who followed Barnard, Northern men generally spoke against the claim and those from the South supported the argument of William Brent of Louisiana, who contended that slaves definitely were property. The bill favoring the claim was defeated by a slim margin when it was recommitted to the Committee on Claims. Barnard's speech was credited with having had a strong influence in the defeat.[11]

On the tariff issue Barnard's stand was more definite. Like many others in Northern and Northeastern states, he was aware of the increasing importance of manufacturing in the decade of the twenties. With this had come a growing concern for protection.

By 1820 the capital investment in manufacturing was estimated at $75,000,000, and in 1826 the three states with the highest investments were Pennsylvania with $30,000,000, New York with $28,000,000, and Massachusetts with $26,000,000. In the Nineteenth Congress there had been much discussion of the tariff, and a woolens bill providing for an increased tariff on manufactured wool had passed the House only to lose in the Senate by the deciding vote cast by Vice President John C. Calhoun. Following this defeat the advocates of protection in and out of Congress began to meet and pass resolutions favoring an increased tariff.

In New York there was sentiment in both parties for protection, and delegates were selected to attend a convention devoted to protection to be held in Harrisburg, Pennsylvania, in the summer of 1827. The convention, which included delegates from the Eastern, Middle Atlantic, and New England states, did not confine itself solely to wool and woolens but also recommended higher duties for the aid of agriculture and for the manufacturers of cotton, hemp, flax, iron, and glass.

Tariff proposals came before Congress when it met for the first session in December, 1827, and were one of the main subjects of debate through April of 1828. In March a bill recommending some increased duties, especially on many of the raw materials which were needed in manufacturing, was presented to the House by the Committee on Manufacturers. The committee majority was composed of antitariff men; however, the chairman of the committee, Rollin Mallary of Vermont, was an Adams man and had been a strong supporter of increased protection at the Harrisburg Convention. He therefore spoke in opposition to the bill of his own committee and argued for higher duties on woolen goods to protect woolen manufacturers. He moved an amendment to make the committee's bill conform more closely to the protective proposals of the Harrisburg Convention in regard to wool.

It was to be expected that Barnard would favor increased protection as Rochester was a fast growing manufacturing center and meetings favoring protection had been held in the area prior to the Harrisburg Convention. In addition, there was strong tariff sentiment throughout the state of New York, and resolutions had been adopted by the New York legislature and sent to the

Congressional committee requesting further protection for both the growers and manufacturers of wool.

Barnard had not been one of the delegates to Harrisburg, but he was sympathetic to the recommendations of the convention favoring aid to encourage wool growing and additional protection for the manufacturers of woolen cloth. Because of his constituency he was concerned for both the grower and manufacturer and pointed out that there was an erroneous impression that the interests of the wool grower and woolen manufacturer were distinct. Barnard saw the grower and manufacturer as dependent upon each other. On March 17, 1828, he addressed the House in a lengthy speech in favor of Mallary's amendment and in opposition to the bill of the committee majority. His remarks indicated his strong support for the protective principle. As had Mallary, Barnard stressed the general benefit to the entire nation of a protective policy. He believed that a monopoly of the domestic market should be given to the home manufacturers and pointed out that the monopoly demanded for woolens was already enjoyed by the manufacturers of such things as boots and shoes. Barnard supported Mallary's amendment because he wanted to see the manufacturer protected not only by higher duties on woolen goods but also by lower duties on raw wool. Importing wool at low cost would aid the manufacturer and need not be injurious to the grower because the farmers were concerned with other grades of wool. Barnard was conscious of the thirty million dollar figure attached to the value of sheep and land in New York and desired a bill that would please his constituents whether they were wool growers or manufacturers. Above all he wanted to see the United States become a manufacturing country, and he believed that this could be accomplished only by a general protective policy.[12] When the vote was taken, however, the Mallary amendment was rejected by 80 to 114. A number of additional amendments offered by Mallary and others relative to duties on wool and woolens were supported by Barnard but all to no avail.

The editor of *Niles Weekly Register,* which favored the tariff, expressed concern for the repeated rejections of the amendments. It appeared to him that Southern members of the House in combination with Jackson antitariff forces had succeeded in making the tariff so unpalatable that many New England tariff men would vote against it. However, the bill passed the House by 105 to 94, with Barnard and Mallary voting in favor. It passed the Senate, with Southerners opposing and those from Middle and Western states favoring it. The vote of New England was split.[13] The act as passed satisfied no one. Southerners who had hoped for defeat of the entire measure were distressed that it passed. Protectionists were not satisfied either. They were pleased by the increased duties on textiles, iron, molasses, and hemp, but with the high duties on raw wool retained, the act fell far short of the protection sought for the manufacturer of woolens. Barnard had been a reluctant supporter of the bill, and at a later date would work for changes in the tariff.

One of President Adams' recommendations to the Twentieth Congress had been the appropriation of money to continue the Cumberland Road. Debate on the appropriation took place in the second session, which met from December of 1828 to March 3, 1829. The debate centered not only on appropriations but also on the broader question of federal support for internal improvement projects. Opponents argued that the enumerated powers of the government were limited and rejected the idea that the power to construct roads and canals belonged to the federal government. Advocates of internal improvements, including Barnard, consistently supported the exercise of power by the federal government to build roads, improve harbors, and construct canals.

In February a bill providing for the preservation and repair of the Cumberland Road came before Congress. Barnard delivered a bold and forthright address both favoring the bill and outlining his support for the general policy of internal improvements and, even more important, explaining his nationalistic view of the government. He found the authority for federal government sponsorship of internal improvement projects in the Constitution, especially in the power of Congress over territories. To those who opposed the bill because of fear that it would go far in establishing the supremacy of the federal government and destroying state sovereignty, Barnard answered that the power would be exercised only with the consent of the individual state legislatures. However, he could not visualize consent being withheld as the road was clearly in the interest of the nation. It was ". . . a vascular system by which the blood at the center could be thrown into the extremities.'' Barnard's support of federal internal improvements placed him in a somewhat difficult position. On the one hand, he wanted to reassure the South that a favorable stand on internal improvements did not lead to a centralizing of all power and hence a threat to slavery; yet his support of nationalistic policies carried with it an obvious dislike for the idea of state sovereignty. He reminded those who advocated such sovereignty that in the United States persons were not only citizens of a sovereign state but were also " . . . and equally, the citizens of a sovereign United States, owing obedience and allegiance to both Governments. . . .'' Barnard insisted that the Cumberland Road benefited not only the people in the particular states involved but the entire Union. In addition, he suggested that the federal government must be protected in the exercise of its power against state encroachments. He accused his opponents of making war upon the federal government and of trying to weaken it in the legitimate exercise of its power. In Barnard's thinking, the government had the power to charter a bank, pass tariff legislation, and fund internal improvements. He concluded that the ''never slumbering spirit'' which ''hovered'' about trying to prevent the government from taking action in areas of legitimate concern was dangerous to the well-being of the country.

Debate on the Cumberland matter continued into March, when two separate bills were passed. One provided for the continuation of the road, and the other for its preservation and repair. Barnard voted for both bills, and the supporters of internal improvements could claim a victory.[14]

Barnard's first term in Congress coincided with the closing years of the administration of John Quincy Adams, with whose policies he generally agreed. In this time Barnard's position as a supporter of both a protective tariff and internal improvements became clear. He applauded the positive use of national power, and he castigated those who stood in the way of the exercise by the government of what he considered to be its rightful powers as stated in the Constitution. He pleaded with proponents of state sovereignty to acknowledge that there was no threat when the government exercised powers granted in the Constitution. In his speech against the D'Auterive claim he assured Southern representatives that he in no way opposed the South or the institution of slavery because slavery was sanctioned and protected by the Constitution. He loved the Union above all, and his central concern was that of reassuring the South that empowering Congress to enact a tariff or sponsor internal improvements did not imply power to interfere with slavery.

The Barnards enjoyed Washington, and the young and pretty Sarah Barnard was a favorite in society. Barnard noted that Mrs. Adams treated her as if she were her own daughter. However, Sarah was in frail health and in February of 1829 she contracted a severe cold which steadily became more serious. Barnard wrote to her grandfather during the second week of February: ". . . I do not allow myself to think of losing her. I should be distracted if I did." Throughout February Sarah's condition failed to improve and on March 2, she died. The Barnards had been married less than four years and Sarah's death shattered Barnard, who wrote to his brother that he was "a solitary" and "miserable man," adding ". . . nobody knows and can ever know how precious she was to me."[15]

After the death of his wife and the close of the session, Barnard returned to Rochester, where he arranged to have a couple live with him to keep house and care for his infant daughter Cora. He was devoted to Cora and at times refused to keep social engagements in order to remain with her. He wrote to the child's great-grandfather, ". . . it seems agreed on all hands that she is one of the sweetest and most intelligent children in the world. She exhibits already many of the excellent characteristics of her mother. . . ."[16]

The death of his wife was one important factor influencing Barnard's immediate political future. Another was the Anti-Masonic movement, which had its beginnings in western New York in September of 1826 with the alleged abduction of William Morgan. Morgan was a stonemason who was disappointed when he was not readily received into the Masonic order upon his arrival in Batavia, New York. Possibly for revenge, he wrote the *Illustrations of Masonry* to divulge the secrets of the order and arranged for its publication by the *Batavia Advocate*. This action angered Masons, and Morgan was abducted and never heard from again. His publisher, David Miller of Batavia, charged that members of the fraternity had kidnaped and murdered Morgan. Several Masons suspected as participants in the abduction were indicted. During the subsequent series of trials, the denunciation of Masonry continued.[17]

Barnard was not a Mason but neither did he support the Anti-Masonic movement. He was District Attorney and campaigning for his first term in Congress when the disappearance occurred, but the event had little effect on his election. However, in the heated emotional climate which ensued, Barnard was identified as one sympathetic toward Masonry because as District Attorney he refused to prosecute Masons unless there was substantial evidence. He believed that persons accused of crimes should not be convicted on insufficient evidence simply because passions were running high. Barnard resigned as District Attorney shortly after his election to Congress, then permitted himself to be hired as one of the defense attorneys for several of the men accused of participating in the alleged abduction. In the summer of 1827, before he began his term in Congress, between Congressional sessions, and again after the conclusion of his service in March of 1829, he assisted the other lawyers in preparing the defense.

Since the most active businessmen in the area were Masons and many were acquainted with Barnard through legal transactions, he was personally sympathetic to those accused. However, he was also convinced that those he defended had not been actual conspirators but were simply acquainted with some who had previously been tried and convicted. During the trials tension ran high throughout the community, and Barnard recognized that the excitement connected with the case made it difficult for the defendants to obtain a fair hearing. In preparing arguments for the case he contended that guilt had to be firmly established and based much of the defense on the lack of evidence against his clients. In spite of the general unfavorable attitude toward Masonry, acquittal was secured for all his clients.[18]

The Anti-Masonic movement which grew out of the "Morgan episode" had a profound effect on New York politics. Barnard opposed the political implications of Anti-Masonry. By contrast Thurlow Weed took advantage of the situation by attaching dislike of Masonry to President Jackson, who was a Mason. He also attempted to depict Masonry as an aristocratic order, placing it in opposition to the farming class in western New York. Weed saw the Anti-Masonic movement as the basis for a new political coalition which would bring together Adams men and Anti-Masons against the forces of Jackson. He, along with fellow New Yorkers and political aspirants William H. Seward and Francis Granger, became instrumental in uniting the various elements opposed to Masonry into a political party. During the winter of 1827 at meetings held throughout western New York opposition was voiced against Masons as political candidates. By the spring of that year the Rochester area had become the center of Anti-Masonry. Throughout the year Anti-Masonic feeling spread rapidly and additional meetings were called to support Anti-Masonic candidates for the state legislature. Weed convinced Timothy Childs, a Rochester lawyer, to become the Anti-Masonic candidate for the Assembly, and Childs was elected in November. Weed continued his efforts to unite Adams men and Anti-Masonic elements, and in 1828 he began editing the *Anti-Masonic Enquirer* in Rochester to support the cause.[19]

Many former Adams men were now active in the Anti-Masonic movement but Barnard, refusing to be associated with a political coalition based on Anti-Masonry, remained aloof. He would not support the effort in part because he opposed a one-issue party and did not want to see the emotion of the times used for political purposes, but also because many of his clients among the wealthy citizens of the community were Masons. He continued to support Adams on the national level, at the same time working against Weed's efforts to unite Adams men and Anti-Masons. However, Weed was highly successful in organizing a new political alliance based on opposition to Masonry, thus placing Barnard in a difficult position as the election of 1828 approached. Although he was the incumbent for the Congressional district of Monroe and Livingston counties, not to be an Anti-Mason in Rochester was almost certain to ensure defeat even though the Anti-Masons and Barnard alike supported Adams.

Weed, convinced that Timothy Childs, who had been elected to the Assembly in 1827 by a majority of 1,700 as an Anti-Mason, would be the strongest candidate for Congress, urged him to run. Differences over Anti-Masonry resulted in the first of what would be a long series of clashes between Barnard and Weed. Because of Barnard's sympathy toward Masons as District Attorney and his rejection of political Anti-Masonry, Weed would not support him for reelection. Barnard was acutely aware of the difficulty he faced because many voters who had voted for him as an Adams man in 1826 when Anti-Masonry had not been an issue were now sympathetic to the movement and to Childs. In October several supporters of Adams who, like Barnard, had not joined the Anti-Masons convinced him that he should seek reelection as an Adams man. He questioned such advice, replying, however, that he could not "consistently refuse his consent to become a candidate," but he would not actively seek the office.[20] Weed lashed out at Barnard's candidacy, writing that even the "most extravagant vanity and egoism" could not anticipate victory and that Barnard's sole purpose was to block a win by the Anti-Masonic candidate. Criticizing Barnard's lack of action as District Attorney, Weed accused him of "waving the crimsoned flag of Free Masonry over our heads."[21]

An underlying reason for Barnard's decision to remain in the running was his intense dislike of the Democratic nominee. He had always been a strong anti-Jackson man and now took to the public forum to attack Jackson. Barnard predicted in a speech to the citizens of Rochester that the country would be ruined if Jackson were to win. In attempting to persuade the electorate not to vote for Jackson, Barnard criticized Jackson's private life and his lack of qualifications for the office and argued that Jackson's election would "endanger the settled policy of the country in the protection of manufacturers."[22]

In November, Barnard was swamped, receiving only 678 votes from his own county of Monroe and an additional 449 in Livingston. Childs won the election with a total of 6,521 votes. The result demonstrated that neither Barnard's opposition to Anti-Masonry nor his anti-Jackson stand carried much weight in 1828.[23]

Barnard's political career was over for the time. With Jackson and the Democrats now in control of the government, he prepared to observe the political process from afar. In his thinking a political party should be morally sound, stand on the Constitution and laws of the land, and favor protection and internal improvements. For the present he had no party since many Adams men had gone into the Anti-Masonic Party in New York, thereby weakening the National Republican Party. His position was not unique, and he would eventually find a place in the Whig Party.

2.

3.

4.

5.

Chapter II

APPRENTICE POLITICIAN

Barnard resumed his law practice at the conclusion of his term in Congress, and during 1830 devoted more time to literary pursuits. In March he declined an offer to serve again as District Attorney for Monroe County, pleading ill health and lingering grief over the loss of his wife. In spite of his defeat for reelection to Congress in the wake of the Anti-Masonic movement, he was still a respected member of the community, and his reputation as an eloquent speaker which he had earned in Congress was beginning to spread. The address which he delivered at the July Fourth celebration in Rochester was an emotional oration in support of the principles embodied in the Declaration of Independence. In October, Barnard allowed his name to be put on the ballot as one of three National Republican candidates for the state Assembly from Monroe County. However, he was certain he would not be successful and, as in the previous election, Monroe County elected Anti-Masons to office.[1]

Barnard decided that in order to overcome his grief, regain his health, and await a more favorable political climate, he would embark on a European tour. As part of his preparations, he asked Jared Sparks, the historian, to recommend places to visit in France, Italy, and England. Sparks responded with letters of introduction and information on sightseeing and asked Barnard in return to obtain for him permission to use the French archives.[2]

On December 1, Barnard sailed on the packet ship *Sully* from

New York bound for France. He was depressed when he left New York but hoped that the six months' vacation would improve his health and aid him in overcoming his sorrow. He found the early days of the sea voyage monotonous and gloomy, and he wondered whether he could find the relief he sought. After the first week of travel his impressions softened. He enjoyed in particular the "sumptuous dinners" and found many of his companions to be quite agreeable. By the time he arrived in France, he was rested and in good spirits.[3]

While on his European tour, Barnard wrote over forty letters for the Rochester *Republican*. These accounts of the places he visited and of his impressions concerning European society and politics were published in the paper in installments.[4] Reform and revolution were the order of the day in Europe in the 1830's, and Barnard's letters contained many observations indicating that he was acutely aware of their significance.

He first visited France, which still bore the marks of the July Revolution. His hotel in Paris was in the central part of the city facing the Rue St. Honoré, which had been a scene of bloodshed during the recent revolution. Barnard thought that there was no better way to understand history than to visit the scenes of major events, and as he looked reflectively out his hotel window, he concluded that the aftermath of the revolution had been beneficial. Some reforms had been instituted in order to make the monarchy under the Citizen King Louis Philippe more acceptable to the people. The franchise had been extended and press censorship curtailed. Barnard favored the resulting constitutional monarchy because he believed it preserved substantial liberty without giving way to radical democracy of the Jacksonian variety. He thought that the friends of freedom ought not to ask for more.

Barnard found the French industrious and noted that many of them had progressed from tenants to the ownership of their land. He compared them to "yankees" like himself and was pleased that they had been able to effect a change in their economic status. His observations of the French strengthened his belief that each individual played a major role in achieving his own success.

In writing to Sparks to inform him that permission to use

the archives had been granted, Barnard shared with the historian thoughts which revealed much of his own philosophy. He predicted that the European governments were not disposed toward war because with war came a "march of the people toward liberal principles."[5] He was very unsympathetic toward the "growing spirit of republicanism" and believed that the French people were not in a "moral condition" which fit them for complete self-government since they were a "nation of atheists" and "free institutions cannot exist where the virtues of personal religion are wanting."

Barnard found European cities, especially Paris, to be "disgusting scenes of human degradation" with "masses of flesh packed together." While the contrast between the poverty and misery of some and the "pomp and splendor" of others bothered him, he was indignant about the fact that until recently there had been no such thing as a sidewalk in Paris. He preferred the "pomp and splendor" for himself and his letters of introduction gave him access to some of the titled, professional, and scholarly people in European society. Just before leaving Paris, he attended a "select ball" held at the French opera for the benefit of the poor. His description of the event in one of his letters to the *Republican* stated that he was "benevolent enough to go" and that he had thoroughly enjoyed himself. Six thousand guests attired in splendid finery attended; the hall was hung with velvet and light was provided by a hundred chandeliers. King Louis Philippe and his Queen were the honored guests.

At the end of January Barnard left Paris for a more agreeable climate and visited Marseilles, Avignon, and Nice before taking a steamer to Rome. He marveled at the "wonders of painting, sculpture and architecture" of Italy, but again the contrast of extreme wealth and poverty bothered him. The display of wealth seemed almost always in direct proportion to the sum of poverty and misery. He did not like the rigid class system of European society and believed that the poor could and should do something to improve their situation.

Barnard was a lifelong Episcopalian, and, influenced in part by the growing tide of anti-Catholicism in the United States, brought to Europe with him an aversion to the religion. The atmosphere in Rome was particularly distasteful to him. He wrote that worship was offered more to the Pope than to the Deity and that the "attempt at display and pomp" was not enough to save the whole scene from being "both contemptible and disgusting." He was appalled that the churches were uniformly dedicated to some saint, "rarely" to God. However, Catholicism in Italy was more repugnant to him than it was in the United States. He thought that it had been "purified" somewhat in crossing the Atlantic and consequently released of some of the absurdities and superstitions which characterized it in Rome.

Barnard was bothered almost as much by Italian morals as by Italian religion. He was distressed to learn that in the cities many husbands and wives had lovers and that this behavior was "open" and "notorious." When he found an exception, he praised it, stressing the importance of pure affection between husbands and wives and the "cultivation of the domestic virtues."

En route to Austria from Italy, Barnard found himself observing first hand some of the revolutionary activities. At Terni where he stopped, thousands of republicans demonstrated in front of his hotel and occupied the surrounding area. The Italian rulers requested assistance from Austria, whose army advanced into the area and compelled a republican retreat. The struggle between the forces of liberty and autocracy made a strong impression on Barnard, and he voiced the opinion that the despotic governments in Europe would be forced to make some concessions to their opponents. He hoped that the final solution would be in the direction of constitutional monarchy.

Barnard's travels took him to Switzerland and back briefly to Paris. After Paris he spent a few days in England before returning home. He was critical that the worst features of the English feudal system, primogeniture and entail, had been retained "with obstinancy." He predicted violence if economic and political reforms were not instituted by constitutional means.

Barnard enjoyed the leisurely voyage back to the United States and returned to Rochester in July after an absence of almost seven months.[6] His European tour had reinforced many of his previously held opinions. Although he was bothered by the poverty in many cities, he did not become more sympathetic to those so afflicted in the United States. He continued to believe that hard work and frugal living were the answer to getting ahead.

The European experience strengthened his belief in instituting cautious reforms to avoid a complete overthrow of the established system. For France the best hope was a constitutional monarchy in which the people had some rights but were guided by a king. A further result of his trip was an intensified, lifelong intolerance of the Catholic Church. Some four years before Samuel F. B. Morse published his *Foreign Conspiracy,* Barnard seemed to entertain suspicions of a papist plot similar to those which Morse would express. The trip did accomplish the purposes for which it was undertaken—those of improving his health and providing some relief from his grief.

Upon returning to Rochester, Barnard resumed his law practice and took a renewed interest in politics. His distaste for Anti-Masonry hindered him from becoming involved as a candidate, and for the next few years his political activity centered around serving as a frequent delegate to conventions and speaking at political functions. The New York convention of National Republicans held in June, 1831, adopted resolutions recommending Henry Clay for the Presidency. Barnard did not attend the convention, but supported its action since he firmly believed in the Clay principles as spelled out in the American System. Barnard was appointed a delegate from Monroe County to the National Republican Convention which met in Baltimore in December and nominated Clay for President. He was confident that Clay was the man to beat Jackson.[7]

Barnard's fear of Jacksonian politics had increased after Jackson's successful bid in 1828, and in the months preceding the election, Barnard continued to pronounce a scathing indictment on Jackson and on all that was associated with Jacksonian democracy. In February, 1832, after the Senate had rejected Jackson's nomination of Martin Van Buren as United States Minister to England, a meeting was held in Rochester to support the Senate action. Barnard played a major role in drafting resolutions which stated in part that the Senate deserved the thanks of the country and was exercising a legitimate constitutional power in withholding its consent to the nomination. As principal speaker at the meeting, Barnard showed once again that his idea of the role of the political figure was formed in terms of the older Federalist concept. He rejected turning politics over to the new breed of party managers whose rhetoric sympathized with the common man. His contempt for the party of Jackson echoed forth:

> I do not object to a party based on principles but I can have no fellowship with a party which is bottomed on the science of numbers . . . whose effective force is more physical than human . . . which does not permit the rank and file to hold opinions except as they are furnished to them.[8]

The implications were clear. The National Republican party was composed of educated men who gave careful thought to party policy. The Democratic Party, however, appealed to the still uneducated masses and encouraged them to be blind followers.

In July, 1832, Barnard was one of three delegates from Monroe County to the state convention of National Republicans which met at Utica. The convention supported Henry Clay and John Sergeant for President and Vice President and Francis Granger for Governor. Many Anti-Masonic candidates were renominated for state offices. The convention resolutions contained in an address to the people of the state were critical of Jackson, particularly of the bank veto. Criticism also centered on Jackson's interpretation of the Presidency. Because of his failure to support nationalistic economic policies, Jackson was accused of construing the Constitution to make the government a "mere confederacy" of independent states. In contrast to Jackson, Clay received laudatory praise. Barnard moved the adoption of the address and accompanying resolutions and spoke for almost three quarters of an hour in defense of the anti-Jackson sentiments of the convention. This time he attacked the states' rights implications of the Democratic philosophy and Jackson's lack of qualifications for the office of President. According to Barnard, Jackson's only qualification was that he had been the military hero at New Orleans and that was as good as no qualification at all. In addition, he angrily attacked Jackson's removal of office holders and use of the spoils system. Jackson's extreme partisanship aroused Barnard's ire as he called Jackson "the nominal head of a band of party politicians who do as much as they can for themselves and as little as possible for their country." In an attempt to defeat Jackson, Barnard supported the National Republicans as they joined forces with the Anti-Masons; both parties supported Granger for Governor while dividing the electoral ticket between delegates for Clay and William Wirt, the Anti-Masonic candidate.[9]

Shortly before the election Barnard addressed another anti-Jackson meeting in Rochester. Again Jackson was severely indicted for exercising powers which were "unknown to the Constitution, inconsistent with its provisions and beyond its authority." Coming in for particular denunciation was Jackson's use of the veto. Barnard argued that Jackson used the veto as a legislative power while its only justification was as "a check . . . on extraordinary measures" where the Constitution might be violated. He concluded that only if Jackson were defeated would the Constitution and the country be saved.[10]

The election results confirmed Barnard's worst fears as Jackson was reelected and William L. Marcy, the Democratic candidate, was elected Governor of New York. New York sent thirty Jackson men to Congress, and the Democratic Party scored an overwhelming victory not only in New York but in the rest of the country as well.[11]

Shortly after the election Barnard moved from Rochester to Albany, where he made his home for the rest of his life. His political future had come to an impasse in the heavily Anti-Masonic Rochester area, and Albany, where Anti-Masonic sympathy was not so strong, offered a better opportunity. As the seat of state government it was an ideal place to further future political ambitions. In addition, Barnard had become acquainted with one of Albany's prominent and wealthy young women, Catharine Walsh. After a brief courtship Barnard and Miss Walsh were married in mid-November of 1832, an event which was discussed throughout the social circles of the city.[12]

This second marriage to a wealthy young woman also enhanced Barnard's own social and economic position. His bride's father, Dudley Walsh, had immigrated to the United States from Dublin. After establishing himself in Albany he founded the general merchandising firm of Walsh and Staats to deal in domestic products, imports, and landed property. The business, with headquarters in Albany and branch offices in New York City, was highly successful. In addition to business activities, Walsh was President of the Bank of Albany and a local philanthropist. Upon his death in 1816, Catharine had inherited a substantial estate.[13]

Connections through his wife's family aided Barnard in setting up his own lucrative law practice in Albany, and he was soon recognized as one of the eminent members of the profession. His clients were usually business and professional men and those with substantial property holdings. Much of his work involved drawing up wills and securing probate settlements.[14]

When Barnard arrived in Albany in 1832, it was a city of some prominence, with an aristocratic and conservative climate. Its population numbered 24,209 in 1830 and by 1832 had reached 26,000. The Albany County census for 1830 put the county population at 53,520 out of a state population of 1,919,404. In addition to being the seat of government the city was a leading center of trade and education. Manufacturing establishments included a steam planing and plaster mill, a stove factory, a brush factory, and factories to make iron hollow ware, ale, and malt. Among educational institutions were the Female Academy, Female Seminary, Classical School, Library, Albany Institute, Albany Academy, and Young Men's Association.[15]

Barnard and his wife settled into the elegant residence at 1 Elk Street which Dudley Walsh had built in 1795. It was located in one of the most exclusive sections of the city, opposite Academy Park and within a short walking distance of the Capitol, the City Hall, and Albany Academy. The house had been used as the Governor's mansion by Enos Throop, who had filled out the gubernatorial term of Martin Van Buren when he resigned to become Jackson's Secretary of State in 1829. It was the Governor's mansion again from 1851 to 1853 for Washington Hunt while Barnard was serving abroad.[16]

With his new wife Barnard made a home once again for his daughter Cora, now five years old. In 1835 a second child was added to the family when another daughter, Sarah, was born. In spite of the seven years difference in age, the two sisters became very close, and Cora took great delight in teaching the younger sister to knit, crochet, and draw. The Barnards spent most of their winters in Albany, where they were prominent on the social scene and active in civic affairs. They enjoyed visiting the theater, dinners with friends, and attending public lectures. They made occasional trips to New York City and Washington, D.C. Summers the house was usually closed for the season and the family frequented Saratoga Springs, Lebanon

Springs, Sharon Springs, and Newport, Rhode Island. Barnard continually suffered from poor health and found the "watering places" a source of benefit to his frail constitution.[17]

Barnard very quickly became involved in political affairs in Albany, and in October of 1833 was appointed one of five delegates from the second ward to the Anti-Jackson National Republican County Convention held at New Scotland, south of Albany. In the mid-term elections the Jackson ticket was successful in New York.[18]

However, Barnard's anti-Jackson activity continued, and in March of 1834 he took part in an Albany meeting of those opposed to the currency policies of the Democrats. A resolution was drafted to the effect that the current financial distress in the country was caused by the removal of deposits from the Bank of the United States. It was agreed to send delegates to Washington to voice a protest at the government's action. Barnard was selected as one of twenty delegates and assisted in drawing up a memorial which placed the blame for the financial situation in the country on the President. Reporting for the Committee on Memorials Barnard exclaimed:

> . . . borrowers are distressed because they cannot borrow and lenders because they dare not lend . . . . the great evil under which the country now groans . . . [is] *the derangement of the currency.*

He then addressed the meeting in support of the Memorial.[19]

Late in March the delegates journeyed to Washington and subsequently reported back to the citizens of Albany. Barnard acted as spokesman for the group. His report voiced pessimism concerning the efforts of the group. While desiring a central banking system, he believed the measures of the Executive were likely to be sustained for the sake of party unity. The only remedy he could suggest was the ballot, and he urged that all efforts be made to defeat Jackson men in the next election.[20]

Because of its resounding defeat in 1832 the National Republican Party had largely disintegrated. The Anti-Masonic Party never became a significant national organization, and by 1834 former National Republicans and Anti-Masons along with men opposed to Jackson for a variety of reasons began to coalesce. A new political alliance adopting the name Whig emerged. Many who became Whigs had been, like Barnard, Clay National Republicans. Other prime movers in the New York movement were the former Anti-Masons Thurlow Weed, William Henry Seward, Francis Granger, and Millard Fillmore. Whigs tended to favor positive governmental action, and at the national level they generally supported a tariff, internal improvements, and a bank. In New York, Whigs pushed for aid to canals, railroads, and education. The majority of them were sympathetic toward reform.[21]

Because of his anti-Jackson sentiments, Barnard was an early Whig supporter, and addressed one of the first Whig meetings held in Albany, in April, 1834. His speech was no less critical of Jackson and his policies than earlier ones. After Jackson's removal of deposits the Senate had passed a resolution declaring that the President had exceeded his powers under the Constitution. Jackson responded with a written Protest in which he denied that either house of Congress had any right to the opinions embodied in the resolution. Barnard challenged the position of the President, arguing that absolute and unqualified control over public money belonged exclusively to Congress. He lashed out at what he called Jackson's attempt to extend the power of the executive branch beyond Constitutional limits. Again he urged voters to use the ballot in an effort to save the country.[22]

Barnard's political activity increased during the fall, when he was selected as the Whig candidate for Congress from the Congressional district which included the city and county of Albany. He made Jackson's bank policies the chief national issue in his campaign. He was termed the "bank candidate for Congress" by the Albany *Argus,* a leading Democratic paper. However, his campaign speeches centered on local issues as well. In October he gave an impassioned speech in which he condemned the Democratically controlled legislature for attempting to influence Albany city politics. The legislature had passed a law which changed the time of holding charter elections from October of 1834 to May of 1835, with the incumbent officials, the majority of whom were Democratic, to continue in office in the interim. Barnard charged that this action amounted to legislative appointment in lieu of an election. He argued that since the elected term of the incumbent officials was over in the fall of 1834, it was the right of the citizens of Albany to elect new officials

then. He called the legislative act the "result of a cool determination, by a political party, to retain and enjoy power. . . ."

Barnard's highly charged remarks were denounced by the
Argus, which now labeled him and his supporters as nullifiers
because they called into question an act of the legislature. Barnard
denied the charge of nullifier by pointing out that he was calling
for adherence to constitutional provisions and the right to vote
whereas Southern nullifiers defied the Constitution.[23]

The Whig Albany *Evening Journal* carried a strong endorse-
ment of Barnard. At this time the paper was edited by Thurlow
Weed, who had moved to Albany in 1830. Barnard and Weed
temporarily put aside past differences, and Weed's paper praised
Barnard as more worthy, capable, and "more devoted to the
Constitution and laws" and "less obedient . . . to the behests
of party discipline" than the Democratic candidate. Furthermore,
Barnard was a scholar, an eloquent speaker, and one who was
honest, firm, and patriotic. Weed advised Whigs to work for
Barnard's election.[24]

Barnard's opponent, Gerrit Lansing, was Albany born and
an unwavering supporter of Jackson. He was the incumbent Congressman, completing his second term, and he had been a strong
opponent of the Bank of the United States. The *Argus* praised
not only his stand on economic affairs, but his long career within
the area in contrast to the recently arrived Barnard. The result
of the November election was a disappointment to Barnard and
the Whigs. The Democrats swept the state and Albany County.
The official canvass of Albany County gave Barnard a total of
4,521 to Lansing's 4,944 votes. Seward was defeated by William
L. Marcy for Governor in Albany County by the narrow margin
of 4,917 to 4,888.[25] While the Whigs did not win, the election
totals showed the growing strength of the new party which had
just entered its first campaign. The defeat seems not to have
been a personal rebuke to Barnard, who was running against
a popular incumbent, but rather an indication that the Democratic
Albany Regency simply could not be beaten in 1834 by the
challenge of the newly formed Whig Party.

For the next few years the Whigs continued their efforts to
build a viable party. What the party needed was a strong candidate
to oppose the Jackson nominee in 1836. Weed was an early

supporter of William H. Harrison, believing he might be a strong vote getter because of his military record, and in September of 1835 a Harrison meeting was held at the Capitol in Albany. It was followed in December by a Harrison convention of the city and county of Albany. Barnard, because he continued to favor Henry Clay as the strongest Whig candidate, was not active in these meetings, but by the winter of 1836, he, too, had become a supporter of Harrison. He was a delegate to the Harrison State Convention which met in February in Albany and was one of five men named to draft the address to the people. Resolutions supporting Harrison for President and Francis Granger of New York for Vice President were adopted. In the convention address Jackson was accused of attempting to appoint "his successor," Van Buren's qualifications for the office of President were called into question, and fear was expressed that he would simply carry on the politics of Jackson. In drafting the address, Barnard, who had criticized Jackson as a mere military hero, attempted to show that Harrison's qualifications transcended the military. Harrison was hailed as eminently qualified for the office due to his varied public service. Even more ironic was the praise given to Harrison as an advocate of the rights of the common people since Barnard was never one to favor extending rights to the masses.[26] While Barnard was not comfortable with the broadened party approach, he momentarily gave in to the game of politics played by Weed as a means of improving the chances for his own political future. He worked for the election of Harrison and shared Weed's concern for finding a winner for the Whigs.

During the spring and summer, county conventions in support of Harrison were held throughout New York. Barnard was a delegate to the one held in Albany County and was appointed to a committee to invite Harrison to visit Albany.[27] Adopting many of the techniques of their opponents, the Whigs held rallies and worked hard for their candidate but to no avail. Van Buren was elected President and Marcy was reelected Governor. During 1837 things would begin to change for the Whigs, and Barnard would again become a successful candidate. In the meantime, in addition to political activities, Barnard continued to preach his philosophy of personal conservatism based on a belief in the inevitability of progress and the need for positive governmental action in the national interest.

6.

7.

8.

9.

10.

11.

12.

Chapter III

MAN OF LETTERS: CRITIC OF REFORM

Barnard renewed his career as a public speaker in 1831 at the age of thirty-five, and for the next several years enjoyed the dual role of man of letters and political figure. During the 1830's and 1840's he addressed numerous college and literary audiences at campuses and educational institutions throughout New York and New England. Unlike his political speeches, in which he addressed the masses of people at huge rallies, his literary addresses were given to audiences composed of educated men and women much like himself and rarely to farmers, laborers, or uneducated groups. He outlined his views on politics and education, emphasizing the role of the scholar and his responsibility to society, the necessity for widespread education, and the part played by citizens in the democratic process.

In a period of famous orators Barnard seemed to pattern his speaking primarily after that of Henry Clay, not only in ideas but to some extent in style as well. He was a stirring and eloquent speaker with a scholarly and poetic style. Yet Barnard put his audiences at ease with little difficulty. Political and philosophical ideas were blended with simple examples from everyday living. Numerous facts were used to buttress his arguments and, like Clay, Barnard was fond of citing historical examples. As was typical in the period, his orations were lengthy, often running well over two hours. As a result of his style and scholarly bearing his reputation as an orator spread throughout the area, and in a very short time lecturing became almost a second profession.

In September of 1831, shortly after returning from Europe, Barnard addressed the literary society at his own college, Williams. His thesis was that commencement was only the beginning of education and that graduates must realize that graduation did not in itself produce accomplished scholars. The purpose of college was rather to lay the foundations of scholarship; learning came "only of toil and study." Barnard mixed his comments on education with observations of conditions in the United States and clung to his opinion about the gains to be accrued from hard work. Anyone who would make an honest effort could get ahead and such a thing "as pauperism [was] scarcely known except under the visitations of Providence . . ." due to the abundance of land in the United States.[1] In several later addresses he frequently returned to the difference between education and learning and warned young scholars not to consider themselves learned when they were in truth only educated. Similarly, the theme of the Protestant ethic of work was to recur in many orations.

Between 1833 and 1835 Barnard began to outline his personal and political philosophy in his orations. The influences of his stern and orthodox Christian upbringing, his family's social and economic position, and his own legal training produced in him a cautious attitude toward change and innovation. Because he feared that Jacksonian ideas and the new mass politics would prevail, his thinking became more conservative as the years passed. He was acutely aware of the vast amount of social change taking place around him, and he tried to delineate ways of dealing with the many complex problems society faced.

Barnard held a deterministic view of the world and of man's place in it. God had created the universe and subsequently designed an overall plan for its operation based on the principles of uniformity and certainty. He found God's laws or the laws of nature manifest in the operation of the universe. Education was necessary to determine man's place in the scheme, to bring him into communion with nature, to make him acquainted with her laws and able to put himself in harmony with them. Barnard admitted that it was no easy task to become acquainted with the laws of nature, but he was optimistic that any person could attain the goal through a combination of book learning and practical experience. Without the benefits of education, man would not always do what was best for himself or for society; however, with the knowledge gained through education man would understand society and his place in it.[2]

Since Barnard saw himself as a scholar who had achieved an understanding of the laws of nature, he felt bound to share it with others through his voice and pen. His reputation as a scholar and speaker continued to grow, and in 1833 he was made an honorary member of the Phi Beta Kappa chapter at Union College. In 1835 he was awarded the degree of Doctor of Laws from Geneva College, and ten years later he received the same award from Columbia. In 1837 he was selected to give the Phi Beta Kappa oration at Union College. In an eloquent and stirring address he elaborated upon his personal philosophy, outlining the task facing the scholar and delineating his own views on the principle of equality. Barnard believed that the most important feature of the American political system was that of equality. However, like Alexis de Tocqueville he worried about excesses of democracy and equality. Barnard preferred a limited equality and lashed out at those who wanted to sweep away all differences in society. He decried the attempt

> . . . to bring all the distinctive qualities of the human character to a [common] level . . . by depressing those which are . . . noble, and exalting such as are . . . low. . . . God has made men to differ in intellectual endowment, as in stature and aspect . . . some among them are always fitted for high employment and great affairs, and many are not.

Opposing what he felt to be the current tendency toward a leveling in society, he pointed out that the principle of equality as stated in the Declaration of Independence was not intended to mean an equality of "levelling radicalism" [sic] or that all men had an equal share in the administration of affairs. At the same time, he championed the principle of equality of opportunity. In fact, he stated that by equality he meant that there should be equality of opportunity, politically and economically, not that all men could or should reach the same level of attainment. He viewed with disdain the popular doctrines of Jacksonian democracy and the Jacksonian attempt to broaden the base of government to include the masses. He was enough of a realist not to oppose outright universal manhood suffrage although his preference was that voters be educated males who owned property. He did not favor attempts to expand the electorate by admitting blacks, women, or recent immigrants, and he applauded the fact that the number of qualified voters was limited. However, he accepted the principle of majoritarian rule, as did most Whigs, believing in popular education as a means of upgrading the population as a whole. He thereby hoped to see the society move forward. Given the safeguard of an educated electorate, he was optimistic about the principle of political equality, concluding". . . it is entirely practicable to bring this excellent, democratic principle into actual, common, and, in time, universal use."[3] Blending democracy and education would foster the patrician system which he preferred whereby the people selected those among them of superior training or intellect to make the laws or at least to advise those who made the laws. He felt that he was well qualified for such a position.

In an era when the American faith in progress was widely accepted, Barnard became a leading exponent of a conservative interpretation of the idea of progress. He was a firm believer in the principle that man's position on earth was capable of vast improvement. Addressing the literary society at the University of Vermont, he declared ". . . progression, improvement, lies at the very foundation of his [man's] being." But while progress was inevitable it had to come through slow evolutionary changes, and the scholar or literary man should provide the leadership which would guide society in the right direction—better he than the politicians who "plot and plunder" for their party. Addressing a similar group at Rutgers, Barnard proclaimed that it was up to the educated men to save the country from the fates of dishonest politicians and deluded masses.[4]

In his address at Rutgers he advised literary men to enter politics. Ideally, however, he preferred that they aim at higher service; they should "govern the governors, and rule the rulers." Their influence should come from their voice and pen. Because he always feared turning political affairs over to the party professionals, he looked to the scholar to counteract this trend. The scholar should lead in the formation of public opinion and thereby public policy. Barnard's own political experience reflected his adherence to these principles. He repeatedly stated that he was a reluctant candidate for office. Yet his correspondence reveals that he struggled in his own mind with what his role should be in politics. He wanted to serve, but preferred being sought and asked to serve. He did not want to stoop to trafficking after office or playing the political game in order to obtain a nomination because he never considered himself of "that class of politicians." Yet at times he was willing to sidestep principle to push his own political career because the party leaders, rather than seeking him out, ignored him. And it was evident that once he was elected to office, he enjoyed the decision making and leadership role.[5]

One of the political goals which Barnard steadfastly supported was that of economic nationalism. His support for positive action by the government grew out of his theory of progress, as was evidenced in a speech delivered before the Mercantile Library Association of New York in December, 1838. Barnard entitled the address "Commerce as Connected with the Progress of Civilization," and he developed the idea that from the time of creation, mankind had been tending toward excellence. He then related commerce to the predetermined plan of progress: "Commerce always has been . . . now is, and always must be . . . most closely connected with the progress of human improvement." Since commerce furthered progress, support of positive national economic policies became one of Barnard's chief aims.[6]

Although Barnard believed in the inevitability of progress, he admitted that the road was not smooth. One primary obstacle in the way was that there had been and would continue to be attempts by various classes to subvert the truth for their own advantage. He singled out for scorn, men—religious, political and literary—who attempted to sway the popular mind. Coming in for particular criticism was the Catholic Church for encouraging the worship of saints and relics instead of emphasizing the simple Christianity of the Bible. Political men, too, perverted the truth to their advantage by making unrealistic promises to the electorate in order to win office. Even literary men were not free from attempts at exploiting the truth, particularly those who chose to advance their ideas through newspapers. The only hope for reversing the trend toward perversion of the truth was in the elevation of the popular mind. The people must be educated until they were capable of forming sound judgments, and the scholar should aid them in this endeavor.[7] Throughout the 1830's Barnard continued to advocate his doctrine of progress through slow evolutionary change and the necessity of educating the people so that they would select the most desirable men to lead them.

Barnard took a more conservative approach in a biographical tribute to Stephen Van Rensselaer delivered in 1839. Praising Van Rensselaer's conservatism, Barnard expressed his concern that the spirit of reform was gaining supporters daily. He feared that the deep foundation upon which society was grounded would be destroyed and the moral fiber of the society "utterly dissipated."[8] Barnard saw dissent as having a constructive role in society and emphasized the need for a real debate on issues. Out of debate and discussion came a new synthesis; therefore, the view of the conservative as well as that of the reformer was needed in a free society.

Fearing that the conservative viewpoint was being ignored, the elevation of conservatism became the dominant theme of addresses in the 1840's. Barnard now argued that the leaders should not only guide progress but should keep stable values alive by encouraging resistance to change and by fighting the tendency in the public consciousness to unsettle fixed opinions. In 1845 Barnard delivered one of his most important addresses, *Social and Popular Repose,* to a group at the University of the City of New York. What he desired was " . . . enough of settled and solid opinion on fundamental questions, to keep the body of the public mind at ease and at rest, to keep society firm. . . ."

Barnard expressed disdain for attempts to call into question what he considered to be "fixed" institutions in society: the Christian religion, especially Protestantism, and representative democracy under a written constitution. To Barnard it was obvious that men were better off with Christianity and democracy than any other religious or political form. Therefore, the people should be instructed to support these institutions rather than question them. He deprecated all sectarian reformers who advocated Judaism, Mohammedanism, or Mormonism, as well as those who attempted to form socialistic or communistic societies. Similarly he criticized those who wanted further changes in the governmental system in the United States, particularly those who thought that the government was too far removed from the people. Opinions of that sort were destructive and led only to perpetual agitation. He feared that the chief danger in the political system was not in its structure but in that "fit and proper persons may not always be selected for important public station."

Barnard's emphasis on stability looked to constant progress but very slow change. He continually revealed his own inner tensions as an elistist confronted with widespread social change. He never identified himself as a transcendentalist but he was influenced by the movement. He supported Ralph Waldo Emerson's idea of self-reliance and the unlimited possibilities of the individual. Yet he worried about the implications of widespread individualism and rejected the philosophical anarchism implicit in transcendental thought. Rather than rapid widespread change or violent upheaval, he asked that there be no changes simply for the sake of change and advocated the more conservative approach of amending the Constitution if changes became necessary.[9]

In a Phi Beta Kappa address entitled *Man and the State,* given at Yale in 1846, Barnard again stated his disapproval of the appeals to the popular mind by agitation about reform. He feared that reform attempts would lead the people to reject the existing institutions, and he again called on the educated classes to instill a respect for such institutions. According to Barnard, national morality consisted of respecting the rights of other men, and for this there had to be respect for constituted authority and established law. It was essential for the state to assure the rights of personal safety, property, and contract. He concluded his speech with the words:

Would we had more patriotism, and fewer Patriots;
Would we have more reform, and fewer Reformers;
Would that my countrymen were let alone, to enjoy and improve all the superior advantages of their most eligible position.[10]

Barnard continually grappled with the reform sentiment in the country but was never able to accommodate himself to it. His final address of a philosophical nature was given at a convocation at Trinity College in 1848. In *The Social System* Barnard launched a vitriolic attack on all the festering sores of reform which he believed were coming to a head and urged respect for the established order. As he witnessed the growing hyperemotionalism of the public temper and the general feeling of instability, he called for adherence to the stable institutions: the family, the church, and the state. Barnard, the rationalist, lawyer, and scholar, saw inherent dangers in social anxiety and criticized those who advocated changes in these institutions. He praised, in particular, "the remarkable completeness and perfectness of our political organization." He wanted the issues raised by the Mexican War to be put aside and urged compassion between the North and South. There was no need for dissatisfaction because the people in both areas were American in character and the differences between the sections were not substantial.[11]

In some of his addresses Barnard departed from broad philosophical topics to deal with more specific subjects. In 1843 he was invited to address the American Institute, an organization devoted to the promotion and encouragement of home industry. In his speech he outlined his support of economic nationalism and criticized the laissez-faire doctrines of Adam Smith. As a Clay and Adams nationalist, he continually called for positive government intervention in the economy by the establishment of tariffs, internal improvements, and a national bank. He argued that positive action in the economic sphere would foster the progress of society in an orderly direction by providing open opportunity.[12]

Barnard was also a political nationalist. In two addresses, one on the life of James Madison and one in honor of the Fourth of July, he stressed nationalism and justified his own support of the federal system. Barnard preferred the Madison of the Federalist Papers and played down the Madison of the Virginia and Kentucky Resolutions because he had no use for the doctrine of nullification. He praised the federal system as outlined in the Constitution, and like the founders he preferred a middle course between the extremes of monarchy and radicalism. In particular, he emphasized that the founders had intended the United States government as a republic and not a democracy. They had purposely set up a representative democracy and had not advocated a "government of brute numbers."[13]

Barnard's attitude toward reform grew out of his philosophical determinism and belief in slow evolutionary change. Calling reformers radicals and believing that they were determined to restructure the natural order in society, he opposed most humanitarian reforms. However, he was a staunch advocate of educational reform because he looked to education as a bulwark against violent social change. In addition, he believed that education was indispensable to the successful operation of a democratic system. Voters must be educated in order to make wise choices on issues and candidates. Speaking at the Albany Institute in 1836, he argued that education should be a prime responsibility of the state government and a matter of public policy. He called for increased state funding for common schools to raise the standards of education and for an increase in teacher salaries. In addition, he warned that under no circumstances should education become involved in party politics or religion. Barnard thought that the administration of the educational system should be in the hands of literary men. Included in his broad plan of reform was the suggestion that academies occupy a middle place between the primary schools and colleges and that the better academies be upgraded into colleges. Furthermore, he recommended the immediate establishment of a state university. He was aware that such reforms would come only with additional state aid, and he urged literary men to push for reform of the entire educational system.[14]

Barnard's central principle was that widespread education would help eliminate the necessity for further reform because it would provide an increased awareness of God's plan, instilling in people an understanding of the differences that were bound to exist among men, and disseminating information on the opportunities which existed in society. Education would act as a means of social control by inculcating desirable values and, therefore, would engender respect for the established order and institutions. Believing that reform efforts which interfered with the natural progress of society were useless or worse, Barnard looked to education as the means of preserving the status quo. Yet agitation for reform continued all around him. The sweeping tide of reform was a substantial vexation to a man committed to slow evolutionary change, and with the exception of educational and some types of economic reform, Barnard closed his mind to the reform sentiments associated with women's rights, abolition, state relief for the poor, trade unionization, abolition of the capital penalty, and temperance.

Barnard's views on women's rights were expressed in addresses to the graduates of the Albany Female Seminary in his position as President of the Board of Trustees. His ideas on education for women reflected his view of the place of women in American society and demonstrated that he had no sympathy with the women's rights movement. He saw the purpose of education for women as one of giving them access to the refinements of life and of making them good wives and mothers. Therefore, he approved of education in literature, art, music, and modern languages for women but did not consider them to be serious students. He warned that the female mind would be damaged by intensive study and competitive examinations. Since he believed that the function of women in society should be limited to their role within the family, he argued against training women to enter the professions of law, medicine, and the ministry. He had no sympathy with demands for expanded legal rights for women and reminded the females in his audiences that the condition of women had shown considerable improvement since the days of antiquity, and they need not ask for more.[15]

In his first term in Congress Barnard had expressed approval of colonization societies while also taking the mildly antislavery position of calling for a recognition of slaves as men. His flirtation with antislavery was brief, and after 1830, he moved farther and farther from his original stand. For the rest of his life he criticized antislavery agitation, and as a member of the New York Colonization Society, he turned more and more to the support of colonization as the best means of dealing with the black race. Barnard, although an economic nationalist, was steadfast in support of states' rights in regard to slavery.

Barnard's views on slavery and abolition were in accord with the sentiments expressed at an Albany antiabolition meeting in

September, 1835. The call for the meeting came from leading
Democrats, William L. Marcy, Erastus Corning, and John A.
Dix, but participants included both Democrats and Whigs. Barnard, along with twenty other men representing both parties,
was appointed to the committee on resolutions. Resolutions passed
advocated using the Constitution for the adjustment of all questions dealing with slavery and put the institution in the states'
right context which Barnard favored. The relationship of master
and slave was held to be a matter whose determination belonged
to the people of each state since the general government had
no control over the domestic institutions of the states. Any attempt
by the general government to interfere would violate the compromises of the Constitution and endanger the Union. Slavery was
an evil forced upon the young republic by the mother country
and neither New York nor any of the other states was responsible
for it. Those states burdened with slavery should be allowed
to select the time and prescribe the mode of emancipation.[16]

As the years passed Barnard became more adamant in his
criticism of abolition efforts. In the late forties he became a
Cotton Whig because he feared that the slavery issue would have
a divisive effect not only on the Whig Party but on the entire
nation. Such sympathies were common among men like Barnard
who held a high regard for property rights and whose interests
were tied to the commercial interests of the nation. However,
while many other New Yorkers, especially within the Whig Party,
moved to an antislavery position, Barnard came more and more
to that of an energetic antiabolitionist. From the late forties until
his death he saw slaves less as men and more as property, and
as his fear of a widespread agitation over slavery grew, he became
more and more sympathetic to the South.[17]

In 1849 he summed up his attitude on slavery in an inflammatory
pamphlet, *Whig or Abolition?* His theme was that the Whigs
should have nothing to do with antislavery because they were
a national party embracing both Northerners and Southerners.
Under no circumstances would he countenance interference with
slavery in the states where it existed, and he expressed approval
that the Wilmot Proviso left slavery alone in the South. Attempts
to make abolition the primary issue for the Whigs were termed

acts of "madness," and Barnard pleaded for calm reasoning and patience and "no political war on the local institution of domestic slavery."[18]

Barnard, the antiabolitionist, spoke out vigorously in the New York Assembly and on the stump on a number of measures and issues relating to other reforms of the day. While serving in the Assembly in 1838, he argued that providing special legislation for the poor was unnecessary because the poor were "quite as happy as the rich." He advocated teaching the poor to emulate the rich in their habits of learning and their comforts. He opposed the leveling concept and attacked the Democratic Party for "professing the sentiments of a strong and destructive radicalism." He described these as sentiments which looked to the "prostration" of some of the most useful institutions of the United States and the "supposed natural hatred of the poor towards the rich as the means of levelling distinctions among men . . . which exist by the appointment of God himself."[19]

Barnard opposed the growing labor movement. Since he saw a harmony of interest among the groups in society, he believed that differences between capital and labor could be solved by bringing the two groups together to talk, reason, and discuss mutual problems. He deplored the attempt of laborers to organize and accused them of thereby fostering a hostile attitude toward their employers. Barnard viewed labor and capital as natural friends and desired the capitalists to make the business decisions because what was good for business would naturally be good for labor. Nothing would be gained by protests on the part of labor.[20]

In the area of penal reform Barnard defended capital punishment during his term in the New York Assembly on the ground of "high public necessity." Responding to the argument that by capital punishment the community took a life which would never be restored, he answered that this was also the case when a man was imprisoned, because the years in prison would never be given back to him. Barnard believed that capital punishment was a proper means for dealing with those who deviated from the norm in society. He did favor investigation of prison conditions but was not an advocate of any specific prison reforms.[21]

Barnard was no friend of the prohibition movement. The New

York prohibition law adopted in 1855 on the model of the Maine law he called unconstitutional. His statement on the question published in the Albany *Evening Journal* pointed out that enforcement of the law would constitute an attack on private property and would set a precedent for government take-over of other kinds of private property. Since liquor in the hands of persons was private property, the government should protect rather than take it away. In addition, Barnard argued that drinking was a habit that could not easily be changed by legislation.[22] Here again his views were akin to transcendentalism in that he put the emphasis on man's autonomy and self-control as the best answer to human improvement. He contended that legislative power should be limited to matters public in character and affecting the whole community and should not deal with the private sphere.

Barnard's lack of sympathy for reform, his defense of the rights of property, and his preference for individual autonomy were reflected in his part in the antirent dispute in New York. The dispute began with the death of Stephen Van Rensselaer in 1839 and the settlement of his estate. As the owner of the Manor of Rensselaerswyck, the Patroon had sold his land in fee to tenants but had reserved to himself some of the old feudal powers, such as mineral extraction, control over streams that operated mills, and the right to one-quarter of the purchase price on every land sale. He had been a generous landlord and had not enforced all these provisions, but he provided in his will that the back rents of approximately $400,000 be applied toward the payment of his debts. The tenants were outraged when they learned the terms of the will and protested not only against paying the rents but against the whole manorial system and the aristocratic style in which Van Rensselaer had lived. Stephen Van Rensselaer IV, one of the heirs, was not so generous as the Patroon had been and determined to collect the back rents. The dispute continued during several years of unsuccessful efforts to collect. By 1844 the antirent movement culminated in an attack by farmers throughout eastern New York on the entire leasehold system.[23]

Barnard was an executor of the will. The amount of rent he and his coexecutors collected was minimal in the face of organized tenant resistance. With his admiration for the Patroon and his disgust at the lack of respect for the right of property and contract, throughout the continuing struggle he remained a consistent supporter of the landlord position. Like James Fenimore Cooper, whom he read and admired, Barnard took the unpopular side in the case.

Barnard outlined his views in an article published in the *American Whig Review* in 1845. At this time he was the chief political contributor to this conservative Whig journal and addressed a limited audience composed for the most part of men much like himself. He likened the antirent struggle to Dorr's rebellion in Rhode Island in 1842 and feared that the whole country was being exposed to "public licentiousness." He carefully outlined the legality of the landlord position, pointing out that the purchasers or tenants had received free deeds to the soil in return for agreeing to a perpetual annual payment. He found this situation in which there had been a *"concerted, practical repudiation"* of these rents and of the obligation of contract to be disgusting. That the tenants based their claim less on legal grounds than on an objection to indebtedness for land in any form was utterly repugnant to him. He blamed the growing restlessness on the agrarian spirit engendered by Jacksonian democracy and a misunderstanding of the idea of equality. The farmers contended that paying rent for land was inconsistent with democratic institutions. Barnard predicted that if this dangerous experiment in agrarianism were allowed to persist, widespread ruin would follow.

When the antirenters banded together to resist the state authorities, violence resulted. Barnard believed that Governors William Bouck and William H. Seward should have taken sterner measures and somehow forced the antirenters to pay. He decried the fact that in spite of "insubordination," "acts of violence," and threats to property tending to overthrow all "social order," the public officials had refused to insist that contracts be respected. Barnard seemed to worry that there would be a demand for a division of property, and he warned the antirenters that they could not escape from meeting lawful contracts because there were too many men of property in the country to allow the repudiation of debts. Contracts were inviolate; failure to keep them threatened not only private property but the whole fabric of society. Barnard stated that the poor should be content in their poverty, and fulfill their contracts, and if they were truly deserving, their situation would improve. He concluded:

> God help the poor, if they must needs add hatred, and envy, and malice, and strife, to the necessary evils of poverty. . . . Let them try what virtue there is in gentleness and contentment . . . the honest fulfillment of just contracts is what is required of them, and without which all sympathy with them is only an insult and a curse.[24]

Barnard's lack of sympathy for reform was combined with a belief that the literary man should serve the community not only in politics but also as a community leader. In his own life Barnard gave this kind of service as a trustee of Albany Medical School, Albany Female Seminary, and St. Peter's Episcopal Church.

Barnard was one of the early supporters for the establishment of a medical college in Albany and was a member of the original Board of Trustees in 1838. He continued on the Board for over a decade and in 1840 was elected President, a position which he held until October, 1850, when he resigned after his appointment as Minister to Prussia.[25]

His lifelong interest in education was manifested in his support of education for young men and women. He served as President of the Board of Trustees of the Albany Female Seminary for several years and participated in planning curriculum and administering examinations as well as delivering frequent addresses to the graduates. He was also a supporter of the Albany Young Men's Association, an organization which encouraged youths to debate, attend lectures, and utilize the library.[26]

Barnard, a defender of Protestant Christianity, was prominent in the affairs of the parish of St. Peter's from 1840 until his death. He was one of the prime movers in the effort to build a new church building and spoke at its consecration in October of 1860, seven months before his death.[27]

Barnard developed a social, political, and economic philosophy which enabled him to live with the rapid social change in society. In the light of the few accomplishments of reform in this period, his concern over the destruction of institutions seemed out of

proportion to reality. However, because he believed the rhetori
of the Age of Jackson, his fears intensified over the years. Hi
vision of the good society was one in which there was ope
opportunity and in which reasonable changes could be made whil
tested institutions were not hastily discarded. Man was perfectibl
as was society and, therefore, progress was inevitable and nee
not be hurried. He believed in the American system of a democra
tic republic and did not want to see it fail because men pushe
its principles of individualism and equality to their outer limits

Barnard, the man of letters, the lecturer, the defender of property, and the critic of radical reform remained also a politica
figure. To see how his personal philosophy affected his year
of public service, it is necessary to examine his career in the
New York State Assembly and his further service in Congress.

13.

14.

Chapter IV

PATRICIAN IN THE STATE ASSEMBLY

Soon after Martin Van Buren assumed the duties of President, the country was hit by a severe depression which lasted almost five years. Many banks and businesses closed, prices fell, and an estimated one third of the working class was out of jobs within the first year. Dissatisfaction was widespread and there were fierce bread riots in New York. In May of 1837 New York banks suspended specie payments. The Whigs blamed Jackson and the Democrats for the depression, and the resulting crisis worked to the benefit of the Whig Party.

The New York Whigs were optimistic about their chances for success in the state elections in the fall of 1837. Not only was the Democratic Party suffering from the effects of the panic but it had to deal with internal power struggles as well. Capitalizing on these factors the Whigs made the economy the dominant issue in the campaign and promised financial relief if elected. Barnard's reputation as a scholar and lecturer, his successful law practice, and his support of positive governmental action in the economy again made him a likely choice as a political candidate for the Whigs. Weed backed Barnard as a candidate for the Assembly, praising particularly his support of government intervention in the economy. Early in October Barnard, Paul Settle, and Edmund Raynsford were selected as the three Whig nominees for the Assembly from the city and county of Albany. The opposition paper, the *Argus,* noted that the three would be hard to beat.[1]

Barnard capitalized on the public unrest resulting from the depression by appealing directly to the economic interests of the voters. Van Buren came in for strong criticism as the heir of the Jacksonian tradition, and Barnard blamed the Democrats for the entire financial distress in the United States. He promised to work for governmental intervention in the economy in order to correct the problems caused by the depression.[2]

Barnard led his fellow Whig Assembly candidates from the Albany area to victory and outdistanced the Whig candidate for State Senator in the county. The Whigs swept the state, gaining 101 of the 128 Assembly seats and six of the eight Senate districts.[3]

The Assembly which opened January 2, 1838, was composed for the most part of farmers, with a scattering of lawyers, merchants, and manufacturers. In his message to the legislature the Democratic Governor William L. Marcy called the suspension of specie payments by New York banks a public calamity. He recommended passage of a general banking law, legislation providing for the enlargement of the Erie Canal, and educational reform. Luther Bradish, a leading Whig and acquaintance of Barnard's, was elected Speaker of the Assembly. Barnard was appointed Chairman of the Committee on Colleges, Academies, and Common Schools.[4] Financial issues dominated the debates in 1838; Barnard, in spite of being a first-year Assemblyman, did not hesitate to speak out on measures which interested him.

The first order of business in the Assembly after its organization was an attempt to repeal a law which prohibited the circulation of bank-note currency in denominations under five dollars. It had been passed in 1835 by the Democratically controlled legislature, which, in line with its hard-money policies, favored a specie-note currency over a bank-note currency. Barnard, one of the principal speakers calling for repeal of the law, presented supporting petitions from Albany citizens. As an economic nationalist, he argued that the state had been derelict in its duty to assure an adequate money supply. Because New York banks could not issue small bills, foreign bills of dubious value were circulating and causing financial distress to many. Barnard opposed an exclusive specie currency, arguing that a sound banking system and financial security included both convertible paper and specie.[5] Repeal passed in the Assembly, ninety-nine to twenty-seven, but the Senate, still under Democratic control in spite of the substantial Whig gains, refused to concur. However, in a compromise, the small-bill law was suspended for two years.[6]

In February the Whig-controlled Assembly attacked the subtreasury plan of Van Buren. A select committee, to which Barnard was appointed, drew up resolutions voicing opposition to be forwarded to Washington. Barnard expressed the sentiments of the committee when he criticized the United States government for its failure to perform what he called one of its most indispensable duties—that of providing a sound national currency of uniform value. Barnard never doubted that the federal constitutional power to regulate trade between the states imposed the duty of providing a paper currency. The subtreasury, he objected, by taking money out of banks would reduce the money supply. The government money in the independent treasury, he argued, would in fact be controlled by the executive, thus giving the President what Barnard considered extended and unwarranted power and limiting the power of the people through their elected representatives in Congress to influence policy making. Instead of the government being republican and popular, the subtreasury would push it in the direction of an empire or despotism. Barnard called on his colleagues to realize that only Congress had power over the —"treasures of the nation." His views were shared by many, and at the conclusion of the debate, the resolutions condemning the subtreasury passed easily by a vote of eighty-seven to eighteen.[7]

In mid-March one of the most historic bills of the session, the General or Free Banking Bill, came up for discussion. Despite support for free banking in New York in one form or another since 1825, banking had largely become a monopoly awarded on the basis of political favoritism. The charge of favoritism was strengthened by the many charters granted by the Democratic legislatures of 1834 and 1835. An antimonopoly movement had developed within the Democratic Party itself, and now the Whigs took up the issue of free banking. As one of the early supporters of free banking legislation, Barnard was a member of the select committee which drew up the bank bill. He favored an impartial law that would permit any group meeting legal requirements to enter banking. Believing that the instituting of banks was a necessity and a duty of government, he called their creation the "establishment of public agencies, by means of which the government has undertaken to discharge the duty of furnishing and regulating the currency." The bill drawn up by the committee was generally in line with Barnard's thinking. It provided that any person or association could start a bank without securing special legislation. Providing that it began with a capital of $100,000, the bank could issue notes against a deposit of public stocks or a combination of at least half stocks and real estate. However, Barnard did not support all the provisions of the committee bill. Although he favored the intent to remove banking from political control and favoritism, he objected that the bill did not offer sufficient safeguards against undue expansion. He proposed an amendment to require all banks to limit issues to five times the average amount of specie on hand. He also questioned the inclusion of the real estate clause, noting that the use of property as security worked only as long as public confidence lasted. He advocated provisions for inspection of banks and recommended as the ideal "a regulated and uniform currency, at all times convertible, and limited in volume to the true wants of business. . . ."[8]

In replying to objections to his amendments by Democrats and Whigs alike, Barnard reiterated his belief that "all experience demonstrated that the tendency of paper money to undue expansion could never be counteracted but by the exaction of a specie basis." However, his amendment requiring banks to keep on hand in specie an amount equal to twenty per cent of the paper issue was rejected, as was his subsequent amendment providing a fifteen per cent rate. Barnard voted against the bill, which passed the Assembly without his amendments by a vote of eighty-six to twenty-nine. Then the Assembly and Senate agreed on a compromise bill which provided for twelve and one half per cent as the proportion of specie to circulation, so Barnard's efforts had not been entirely in vain. The Free Banking Law democratized banking and established a model for future legislation by taking banking away from special interest groups.[9] Barnard's support of a bank law with safeguards against overexpansion was consistent with his belief in the need for government intervention in the economy to foster equal opportunity. Although his amendments were more conservative than the original bill, he demon-

strated his concern for securing a law which met the needs of
an expanding economy without contributing at the same time
to uncontrolled inflation. He also showed that he held one of
the most sophisticated views of the economic realities of the
times of any man in his party, by anticipating the needs of a
growing society in terms of increased population, commercial
activities, and capital expenditures.

Financial issues were not Barnard's only concern. In January
of 1838 his Committee on Colleges, Academies, and Common
Schools became involved in a church-state controversy. Education
in New York during this period was dominated by the Protestant
churches, and the King James Version of the Bible was in common
use in the public schools, partly, at least, to acculturate the immigrant population. Such Protestant influence was resented by the
Catholics. William Griffin came to the Assembly with a petition
from several upstate Catholic parents, including himself, requesting that the legislature enact a law prohibiting prayer, Bible
reading, and other religious exercises in schools which received
public money. He argued that such practices enforced particular
religious opinions at public expense and could lead to a union
of church and state. The petition was referred to Barnard and
his committee.[10]

Barnard, influenced by his Yankee Protestant background, had
always been strongly anti-Catholic, and he urged the committee
to refuse to advocate the requested law. The committee concurred
and instructed him, as chairman, to report unfavorably on the
petition to the Assembly. In his remarks Barnard skirted the
Protestant-Catholic issue and argued the case on the basis of
the relationship of church and state. He defended prayer and
Bible reading because he believed that a majority of the parents
wanted religious exercises in schools. Since state law left determination up to local school districts, in places where the practices were observed the wishes of the parents were being followed.
He extended his remarks to make a strong defense of prayer
and Bible reading. He noted that schools should provide both
intellectual and moral instruction and that the Bible was an excellent textbook ". . . indispensable to a good system of popular
instruction." It was particularly important to use the Bible to
teach morality because in order to make such instruction effective

it had to be according to the best code of morals known—that contained in the Bible. Although Barnard made a point of decrying the idea of a union of church and state, he glossed over the real problem involved and ignored the Protestant domination of the schools. He concluded that there was no justification for a complaint because no particular religion was being taught. He supported religious freedom, defined as man's professing whatever religious faith he pleased or in rejecting all religions, but he maintained that this freedom was not invaded when the morals of the Bible were taught in public schools. Barnard never resolved the inconsistency in his thinking which on the one hand called for religious freedom and separation of church and state, and on the other saw nothing wrong with Protestant influence in the public schools. Yet his recommendation was accepted in the Assembly by an almost unanimous vote of 120 to 1, and no law was passed to prevent prayer and Bible reading.[11]

In 1836 in a forceful speech delivered at the Albany Institute, Barnard had called for statewide educational reform and for greater state responsibility for education. In the Assembly in 1838 he had occasion to repeat his request. Congress had authorized the deposit of the federal surplus with the several states, with New York receiving a total sum of $4,014,520. Governor Marcy recommended that the proceeds from this fund be used for education, and during March the Assembly considered his recommendation. The subject was referred to Barnard's committee, which agreed with the Governor's recommendation.

At the core of the committee report, which bore the imprint of Barnard's thinking, was a comprehensive evaluation of the entire system of education in the state and an affirmation that the state had the primary responsibility in providing education. The committee wanted first priority given to upgrading the common schools. One method proposed to accomplish this was to raise salaries to a minimum of fifteen dollars per month for male teachers and ten dollars for females. It was suggested that the procedure by which the money in the school fund was allocated solely on the basis of the number of children in a district be altered to provide proportionately more money to school districts which increased teachers' salaries than to those which did not. Other recommendations were: 1) consolidation of districts, especially for high schools, 2) additional funds for private academies from the state, 3) the establishment of district libraries throughout the state under partial state responsibility, 4) separation of the office of Secretary of State from that of Superintendent of Common Schools, and 5) the immediate establishment of a State University.[12]

The bill Barnard introduced based on the committee recommendations was considered throughout March and into April. There was little disagreement in either the Assembly or Senate with the fundamental purpose of upgrading education, but there were wide differences on the means. Defeated were proposals for consolidation of high school districts and a separate office of Superintendent of Common Schools. The common school fund continued to be apportioned on the basis of population and teacher salaries were not uniformly raised to the levels requested, nor was the State University established. However, the recommendations for increased funds for common schools and academies and for the establishment of district libraries under partial state responsibility were incorporated into the bill as passed by both houses. New York State thus determined that the proceeds of the federal surplus should be appropriated for the purpose of education.[13]

Barnard's enthusiasm for education helped to secure the passage of some of the committee recommendations, and his forthright support of education was perhaps his greatest achievement in the session of 1838.

Some of his other recommendations came to fruition later. Steps were taken to consolidate high schools districts in 1853, and in 1854 the office of Secretary of State was separated from that of Superintendent of Common Schools with the creation of the office of Superintendent of Public Instruction. Finally, in 1867 New York made a significant step in the direction of a system of free public education with the abolition of the rate bill system, and the state reaffirmed the principle for which Barnard had fought that it had the primary responsibility for education.[14]

There was considerable interest in the state at this time for the enlargement of the Erie Canal, and petitions were presented early in the Assembly calling for positive action. Whigs, including Barnard, favored using the credit of the state for greater expansion.

and an Erie Canal Bill was drawn up in accordance with the Whig view. The Democrats were not outright opponents of internal improvement projects but preferred that further expenditures for canals come out of surplus revenue or taxes. Whig Assemblyman Samuel B. Ruggles, an enthusiastic advocate of canal expansion, led the fight for the bill in the Assembly. Barnard, agreeing with Ruggles and defending Whig policy, called for recognition that internal improvements, especially the Erie Canal, were of benefit to all the people in the state. Responding to Democratic opponents who argued that such expansion would undoubtedly entail additional taxation, Barnard maintained that the people of New York wanted internal improvements and were ready and willing to pay for them.[15]

There was substantial agreement in the Assembly on the Whig bill, and on the final vote only three dissenting votes were cast. The law as enacted provided for the speedy enlargement of the Erie Canal and $4,000,000, to be borrowed on the credit of the state, was appropriated for the purpose.[16]

Barnard's four months in the Assembly were busy ones. In addition to his support of economic legislation, educational reform, and expanded internal improvements, he handled numerous claims and petitions for Albany constituents. Unlike his support of educational and banking reform, he opposed proposals for penal reform and relief for the poor. Likewise he did not back an effort to send resolutions to Congress asking for abolition of slavery and the slave trade within the District of Columbia and requesting that no state in which slavery existed be admitted to the Union. In March of 1838 he also opposed efforts to speed up the Assembly's business by setting an early morning meeting time of 9:30. Barnard's opposition seemed to stem from his fear that the Assembly would resemble a factory and Assemblymen, common laborers. Arguing for retention of a flexible meeting time, he pointed out that many members were involved outside the Assembly hall in committee hearings, investigations, and meetings with constituents. A required meeting time of 9:30 or earlier might well interfere with these other duties and would require members to ''sit here as long as human nature can endure.'' A lively discussion ensued, but the matter was laid on the table and the meeting time was not changed.[17]

Late in April the session adjourned after meeting 107 days and passing 332 laws. The Whig paper, the Albany *Evening Journal,* found particularly worthy its actions in regard to the enlargement of the Erie Canal, the General Banking Law, suspension of the small-bill law, and the law which provided that surplus revenue be used for education. Barnard's service in the Assembly was praised, but some of Weed's doubts about Barnard as a representative of the people which were to become much clearer at a later date were again apparent after his first term in the Assembly. Weed wrote: ". . . he errs, we think, in attempting to make human nature what it ought to be, instead of endeavoring to make the best of it, as it is."[18]

Weed's comment on Barnard as a representative of the people also shed some light on the recurring problem that Barnard was to have within the Whig Party. Barnard's basic philosophy governed his actions as a legislator, and he could not be counted on as a consistent party man. He acted in favor of the public good as he saw the public good. Because in his thinking a political party had to be based on principle, he favored the paternalistic approach of the older parties and could not accept the newer mass politics of the nineteenth century whether promulgated by Democrats or Whigs. Although he supported the positive liberal state in the economic sphere and approved of the Whig concept of expanding opportunity throughout the society, he would not support all the Whig programs and reforms. Weed was an unabashed politico and was perhaps correct in his assessment of Barnard as unbending and unrealistic. Barnard was not enough of a political opportunist for Weed. However, Weed did not give up on Barnard as a future candidate for the Whigs. Indeed, within a few months Barnard would reenter national politics.

ALBANY FEMALE SEMINARY, No. 67 DIVISION STREET.

15.

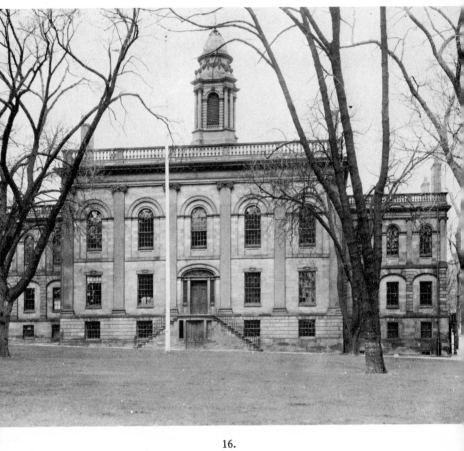

16.

17.

Chapter V

UP THE POLITICAL LADDER:
U.S. CONGRESS

The New York Whig Party wanted Barnard to be its candidate for Congress in 1838 from the district which included the city and county of Albany. He had demonstrated in 1837 that he was a strong vote getter and popular with the electorate, and it was anticipated that his name would add strength to the ticket. Barnard had recurring bouts with bronchitis, and related health problems continued to plague him, so he informed the Whig leaders publicly that he did not desire the nomination. However, in private he indicated that in spite of a concern for his health his position was not inflexible and he would accept the nomination "if accompanied by a unanimous request" of the convention. Barnard received the nomination, and a committee of Whigs was sent to inform him of the wish of the party and to urge him to accept. Under these circumstances Barnard, who continued to view politics from a patrician stance, felt obliged to comply. He found the pressure quite gratifying because he was "not conscious of ever having courted the popular favor by any sacrifice of honor, dignity, or truth . . . ." He had received the nomination though he had not "put expediency in the place of principle."[1]

Most of the Whig campaign effort consisted of attacks on Van Buren and the subtreasury plan. In his speeches to political audiences Barnard preached the Whig creed and promised that as Congressman he would fight the financial program of Van Buren. The congressional district which he would represent continued to be a leading trade, business, and manufacturing center, and Barnard pledged to defend the Clay brand of Whiggery in support of those interests.

Barnard's opponent Albert Gallup was praised by the Democrats as a self-made man reared in the community in contrast
to the more aristocratic Barnard who was a relative newcomer.
Gallup supported Democratic financial policies and opposed a
national bank, which Barnard continued to favor. However, the
onus of the Panic of 1837 continued to be associated with the
Democrats, and the Whigs scored a substantial victory in the
election. Barnard's election in the tenth district was a Whig gain.
He made a strong showing and ran ahead of the Whig gubernatorial
candidate, William H. Seward, in Albany County. The Whigs
secured majorities in both houses of Congress, but the New York
representation was close, numbering twenty-one Whigs and nineteen Democrats. On the state level Whigs elected Seward and
Bradish to the posts of Governor and Lieutenant Governor and
continued to control the Assembly. [2]

Never one to follow blindly party policy, Barnard became
involved in a dispute with his fellow Whigs shortly after the
election over the selection of the candidate for Senator. Weed
supported Nathaniel P. Tallmadge, a Democrat who had split
with Van Buren over the subtreasury and had since identified
himself as a "Conservative" urging the election of Whigs to
office. Weed, ever the practical politician, saw that the Democratic split would benefit the Whigs and desired to reward Tallmadge
with the Senatorship in return for his support of Whig candidates.
Barnard opposed Tallmadge for the Senate because he felt that
the position should be filled by a faithful Whig. He was quoted
in the Albany *Daily Advertiser:* ". . . if the office of Senator
was elected by the people . . . neither he [Weed], nor any other
sane man in the State, would dare to present Mr. Tallmadge,
as a candidate for the suffrages [sic] of the Whigs." Weed
intimated that Barnard desired the Senate seat himself, and Barnard admitted that he had considered it. He expressed a preference
for the Senate over the House but repeated his real desire to
be out of office altogether. Although he continued to resist the
selection of Tallmadge, Barnard never championed his own candidacy. In true patrician rhetoric, he declared that public life
had no charms for him. Despite Barnard's efforts, Tallmadge
continued to be the choice of Weed and other Whig leaders. [3]
The kind of political maneuvering responsible for this selection
was distasteful to Barnard and was among the many differences
he would have with Weed.

In the months before his term began in Congress Barnard continued his legal practice and his work as a trustee of the Albany Female Seminary and wrote a historical account of the life of Stephen Van Rensselaer. As the newly elected Congressman and a Clay partisan, Barnard responded eagerly to the task of playing host to Henry Clay when he visited Albany during the summer.

During the fall of 1839 Barnard made plans to go to Washington for the opening of the Twenty-sixth Congress. It had been ten years since Barnard had been the young Congressman from the Rochester area. He had made social visits to Washington during the interim, and now was returning for the first of three consecutive terms in the House. During his six years of service Barnard's skills as an orator, scholar, and independent thinker were favorably remarked. John Quincy Adams listed him, Thomas Corwin, Nathan Sergeant, and Richard Biddle, each of whom he thought might claim first place, as the outstanding House orators. In assessing Barnard, Adams praised him for the strength of his convictions while noting that he could be obstinate and stubborn. He recorded in his Diary that Barnard's principles were generally the best but "dashed with errors the more dangerous because honestly entertained and rooted in a profound and vigorous mind."[4] It came to be well known during Barnard's years of service that he did not always follow party policy but supported only that legislation which was in accord with his principles. *His* interpretation of the Constitution provided justification for protective tariffs, a national bank, and federally sponsored internal improvements. Thus he was a constant advocate of such measures.

While in Congress Barnard associated socially with many of the leading citizens of Washington. Adams had been President when Barnard had served as Congressman from Rochester, and now the two were colleagues in the House and for a time neighbors in Washington. In addition to Adams, dinner companions and friends included Daniel Webster, Francis Granger, Washington Hunt, Hamilton Fish, Robert Winthrop, and Leverett Saltonstall. His wife and children divided their time between Albany and Washington and spent part of each session with him.[5]

Barnard's three terms spanned the years 1839–1845, when attempts to revise the tariff, establish a national bank, and annex Texas were the paramount issues. Other subjects of importance included efforts to obtain a uniform law on bankruptcy, the land distribution bill, and election of House members by districts.

Of special significance would be the growing rift between John Tyler and the Whig Party.

The first order of business for the Twenty-sixth Congress, which convened in December of 1839, was disputed election returns from New Jersey. The seats from five New Jersey districts were contested by Whig and Democratic claimants. The Whigs held the commission from the Governor of New Jersey, but the Democrats maintained that they should not be seated because of electoral fraud. The dispute was crucial because if the five Whigs could be kept out until the House was organized, the Democrats would be in control. The Whigs, including Barnard, maintained that the claimants with the Governor's commission should be sworn while the Democrats protested such action. Not until the lapse of two weeks was the House organized, when Robert M. T. Hunter from Virginia, a Democrat who was a subtreasury supporter, was elected Speaker as a compromise candidate. Barnard voted reluctantly for Hunter, yielding only on the final ballot when there seemed to be no other way of getting the House organized. When the Committee on Elections ruled that the five Democratic claimants were to be seated, the Democrats were assured control of the House.[6] The exclusion of the Whigs made a profound impression on Barnard; it was evidence of the kind of political dealings which he never could accept. Barnard was appointed to the Judiciary Committee when committees were announced.

Early in the session the House dealt with the issue of abolition petitions. In 1836 the House had passed a gag rule which provided that all such petitions be laid on the table without debate. Subsequent gag rules reaffirmed the principle, but the matter of petitions continued to be a point of contention in the House. In December of 1839 a resolution was debated which stipulated that all these petitions be referred without debate to a select committee. A majority of House members, including Barnard, voted for this resolution; however, it did not pass because the two-thirds vote needed to suspend the rules of the House could not be obtained. Although Barnard was not an antislavery advocate, he, along with many other Whigs, was a consistent defender of the right of petition. Like Adams, he believed it to be a Constitutional guarantee. In March of 1840 Barnard made an effort to circumvent the gag rule. He presented a petition against the admission of Florida into the union until slavery was abolished within her borders and moved its reference to the Committee on Territories. The Speaker ruled that under the standing resolution adopted by the House the petition could not be received. John Quincy Adams then appealed the chair's decision. However, Barnard could see the futility of the attempt and withdrew his petition. While not the fighter for the right of petition that Adams was, Barnard remained a steadfast opponent of the gag rule throughout his Congressional years.[7] He believed in open and honest debate on issues and felt that reason and truth would prevail.

During February of 1840 debate took place on further appropriations for the Cumberland Road. Barnard delivered what Adams called an "excellent speech of about two hours" in which he repeated his earlier support for federal projects for the construction and repair of roads and harbors and for the removal of obstructions from rivers. He insisted that money expended on internal improvements eventually would be reimbursed to the government through the general benefits it would bring to the whole country. Barnard criticized the administration policy which called for suspension of works of this nature because of the lack of funds. It was incomprehensible to him that projects which had not been completed might now be halted. He advocated the use of a temporary loan or an increase in the tariff to pay for such projects. He made a special request for an appropriation for works already begun in the Hudson River but emphasized that his concern was not solely for New York but for the entire nationwide system of improvements. However, Barnard's speech received little attention from the House, which, according to Adams, was thoroughly weary of the subject,[8] and efforts to obtain the appropriation were unsuccessful.

During March the House considered the treasury note bill which called for an issue of twenty to thirty million dollars worth of government paper in the form of promissory notes. Once again Barnard found himself at odds with the membership of the House. He did not oppose government borrowing by a direct loan but did oppose this bill because the treasury notes would be circulated as money. His objection was not to the creation of currency but to the method of doing it. He felt that this bill gave authority to the executive to establish a treasury bank, thereby conferring an extraordinary amount of patronage. However, the bill passed 110 to 66, with Barnard voting with the minority.[9]

In June of 1840 the House considered the subtreasury bill

which had previously passed the Senate. Barnard delivered a
lengthy and admirable address against the bill, but Adams
recorded that he spoke to "stone pillars." Barnard contended
that a subtreasury system put the public money into the hands
of the President, who could then favor certain banks over others.
The result, as in the case of the treasury notes, would be an
Executive bank with extensive patronage. However, Barnard lost
again when the subtreasury bill passed the House 125 to 107
and became law with President Van Buren's signature.[10]

The session adjourned at the end of July with both the subtreasury and treasury note bills, which Barnard had opposed, written
into law, while the internal improvement bill which he favored
had failed. He was disappointed by the outcome of the session
and incensed at the lack of decorum and respect for speakers
which was manifest in the House. On July 17 he and John Quincy
Adams had left the House in disgust as George Dromgoole,
"drunk in the Chair," presided. Barnard was eager to return
home.[11]

Barnard's wife and daughters had accompanied him to
Washington but were often homesick for Albany. His wife complained about the wet climate and the uncomfortably cold houses
in Washington. She shared her husband's distaste for Van Buren,
whom she referred to as *"His Majesty."* She enjoyed the social
life of teas, small parties, dinners, and balls and she was proud
of her Congressman husband. Writing to her sister-in-law she
commented: "he has won laurels, *puffs* and compliments from
every quarter. My head is almost turned, and my *fingers* ache
from cutting out the numerous articles from different papers."
Mrs. Barnard and the daughters had returned to Albany at the
beginning of the summer and Barnard joined them at the end
of the session.[12]

During the remainder of the summer Barnard was frequently
invited to address Whig meetings and rallies. Interest in the
upcoming presidential campaign had increased throughout the
spring and summer. Barnard was an early Clay supporter, while
fellow Whigs Weed and Millard Fillmore supported Winfield
Scott. However, unable to agree on platform and issues, Whigs
eventually came to the support of William H. Harrison and John
Tyler because it looked as if the military hero Harrison might
have the best chance of obtaining a Whig victory.

Barnard was disappointed that Clay was passed over for the nomination, but he did support Harrison, and in the fall of 1840 assumed an active role in the campaign. By then it was evident that the Whigs had accepted the implications of majority rule and mass politics, and they geared their rhetoric accordingly. Because Barnard feared for the country if Van Buren were reelected, he temporarily put aside his patrician stance and accepted the active political campaign designed by the Whigs. He was involved in this campaign to a greater degree than he had ever been before and worked for the party throughout the summer and well into the fall. For a brief time he was the editor of an Albany campaign paper, the *Unionist*. The first issue, appearing on September 19, voiced support for Harrison: "We believe in the ability and power of the people for self government . . . [and] believe that there can be no check upon the office holders but the people. . . ." One paragraph on the first page further summarized the object of the paper:

> We battle for the people's rights. A democratic government must rest solely on the support of the people. No man, how high soever his situation may be, can be a democrat, who does not acknowledge this great cardinal principle. No administration can be democratic, which does not yield implicit obedience to the popular will. This test of democracy is clear and indisputable; no argument can overthrow it—no fallacy evade it. . . .

Whig doctrine was outlined in such vague phrases as support for only one presidential term, the integrity of public servants, and the safety of the public money. The paper, though short-lived, was part of the larger log cabin campaign attempt to popularize the Whig candidate through skirting issues and making a direct appeal to the democratic aspirations of the common people.[13]

Barnard was more useful to the party on the lecture circuit than he was as editor and made major addresses at public meetings in Syracuse and Rochester in support of Harrison. He was renominated for Congress and embarked on a vigorous speaking tour in support of his own candidacy. His theme was familiar—that of the destructive influence which the Van Buren administration was having on the country.[14]

Barnard was certain that the temper of the country was adverse to Van Buren and that he would be defeated. He wrote to a friend late in October that he considered the contest already decided and that New York would record "her condemnation" of the administration. Barnard's prediction was accurate, and

the Whig national victory in November was acclaimed throughout
New York. Barnard scored an impressive victory over his Democratic opponent, James M. French, with 6,351 votes to 5,973.
Barnard ran twenty-two votes behind Harrison in Albany County
but 117 votes ahead of Seward. His reelection returned him to
what would be a Whig Congress, although New York's delegation
would now number nineteen Whigs and twenty-one Democrats.[15]

The second session of the Twenty-sixth Congress, the lame
duck session, met early in December. Almost from the beginning
it was evident that few significant bills would be passed and
that Harrison would be forced to call an extra session in the
summer. However, Barnard introduced a bill for establishing
a uniform system of bankruptcy, which he and many other Whigs
saw as necessary to relieve some of the ill effects of the Panic
of 1837. The bill failed to pass, and the session ended in March
of 1841 with meager results. Barnard was hopeful that much
of Clay's program would be enacted at the extra session.

Barnard's plans for the future were in a state of uncertainty
during the concluding months of the session. In private he let
it be known that he would accept a Senate seat. He believed
that his services could be important to the new administration
and wrote to a friend in Albany ". . . the House is not the place
where I can be most useful." There had been some talk that
Tallmadge might resign, thus creating a vacancy in the Senate.
However, Barnard was very much aware that if a vacancy
occurred, Seward would be a strong contender for the seat. Personally he did not want to see Seward get it nor did he believe
that Whigs in Congress, with the possible exception of Christopher
Morgan, would support Seward. Placing Seward in the Senate,
he declared, would "disgust and ruin our party in New York."
However, Barnard was reluctant to make any efforts on his own
behalf although he wrote to his friend that he believed that Webster
would support his bid for the Senate. Others would have to lay
the groundwork and do the maneuvering. Barnard felt that Weed
would be against him, so he did not communicate his wishes
to him although he did discuss with him other possible appointments from New York as well as the probable composition of
Harrison's cabinet. However, no groundswell of support
developed for Barnard. Tallmadge, in spite of rumors to the
contrary, did not resign, so Barnard remained in the House.[16]

*   *   *

When Harrison took office in March, 1841, Whigs rejoiced and looked forward to the enactment of the Clay program. The extra session was promptly called for the summer. Meanwhile Barnard returned to Albany, where he received the news of President Harrison's death. John Tyler assumed the Presidency—an event which was to cause severe adjustments in the plans of the Whig leaders.

Initially most Whigs expressed support for Tyler and were hopeful that he would stand by Whig principles as outlined by Henry Clay. Caleb Cushing of Massachusetts suggested in a letter to Barnard that the Whigs make a public demonstration of their confidence in Tyler. Cushing called on Whig legislative leaders, including Barnard, to assume a more active role in the organization and operation of the party. Barnard agreed with Cushing and offered to do what he could in Albany. Weed, too, expressed his confidence in Tyler.[17]

The goals of the Whig leaders included legislation for distribution of the proceeds of the sale of public lands among the states, revision of tariff duties, repeal of the subtreasury and establishment of a national bank, and securing a temporary loan to supply the needs of the Treasury. Although the Whigs had a majority in both the Senate and House, there was an uncertain element in the White House, and Whig fears of how Tyler would respond to the proposed legislation increased as the time approached for the extra session. Yet the presidential message carried hopeful signs as Tyler recommended tariff revision, distribution, a suitable fiscal agent, and repeal of the subtreasury.

The special session met during the summer, and with Whigs in control of the House Barnard was selected Chairman of the Judiciary Committee, the committee on which he had been a member in the Twenty-sixth Congress. In this capacity he again worked for reforms which he felt would foster equality of opportunity. His most significant accomplishment involved his efforts to secure the passage of a uniform bankruptcy law. In 1800 Congress had passed such a law; it was repealed three years later, and since then bankruptcy laws had been largely a matter of state legislation. From time to time Congress had considered uniform bankruptcy legislation and sentiment in its favor had increased after the Panic of 1837. It was estimated that there were close to 500,000 persons in the country who needed relief in order to enter business again. In the Twenty-sixth Congress the Senate, responding to numerous petitions and memorials, had passed a bankruptcy bill, but the House failed to concur.[18]

At the beginning of the extra session Tyler sent a message to the House with a memorial signed by three thousand citizens of New York asking for a bankruptcy law. Memorials were also presented from the legislatures of six states where there had been severe debtor distress: Maine, Massachusetts, New York, Louisiana, Mississippi, and Michigan.

Barnard and the Judiciary Committee considered the requests and recommended passage of a bankruptcy law essentially the same as that which had passed the Senate at the previous session. The bill provided that persons who were unable to meet debts were deemed bankrupt if they so declared themselves. However, the intent of the bill was to benefit both the debtor and creditor. The effects of the debtor were taken into custody, but provision was made to prevent debtors from losing all assets. After the law had compelled the debtor to the performance of his contract as far as his means would go, he was released from further legal liability. The effects of the insolvent were held as a common fund for the benefit of all creditors, thereby assuring all some redress and restraining each from pursuing his independent remedy.

When the bill was debated in the House, there were strong arguments for and against it. Some critics were opposed to the voluntary section of the bill, believing that it made it too easy for one to declare bankruptcy. Other opponents feared that the bill as a piece of federal legislation was intended to interfere in the rights of individual states. Still others contested the constitutionality. Supporters argued the need for uniformity among the states and denied that there was any infringement on the rights of states or interference with the Constitution.

In line with his consistent support of business interests, Barnard led the fight in the House to get the bill debated and adopted and delivered two leading speeches in its support. Stressing the widespread distress throughout the country, he pleaded the necessity of such legislation; '' . . . if there be one moral obligation stronger than another resting in Congress at this day, it is to pass a bankrupt law.'' He quickly dismissed both the Constitutional and state sovereignty arguments. There was no doubt in his mind that the federal government did "possess the full power and authority over the subject of bankruptcies." The obligation to establish a national system of bankruptcy was as important as that to establish national courts, or to regulate national trade, or to create a national post office. The bill was no threat to state sovereignty because in the United States citizens were citizens of a nation as well as of a state and as such subject to the laws of both. In trade activities they dealt with each other without regard to state lines, and the proposed law by providing uniformity among the states would foster favorable trading conditions within the country. A federal bankruptcy law, he concluded, should by no means be construed as an attack on the states but as an essential piece of legislation.[19]

However, a motion to lay the bill on the table carried on August 17, 1841, and it seemed that it would suffer the fate of the previous one. Then came a logrolling operation. The bankruptcy bill was not the only piece of legislation under consideration, and its fate was intimately linked with the plans of the Whigs for distribution and tariff revision. In fact, passage of a bankruptcy law was not a major issue in the Whig program. However, no part of the program could be passed on its own merits but only through a bargain. In the case of the bankrupt bill a successful effort was made to link bankruptcy with distribution. Weed, who had come to Washington, led the behind-the-scenes negotiations in which Barnard also participated. Clay Whigs were most desirous of obtaining distribution, and eastern votes were obtained for distribution in return for western votes for bankruptcy. Reconsideration of the bankruptcy bill was moved and carried 109 to 98. Then the bill itself passed by the narrow margin of 110 to 106, Barnard voting with the majority in each case. The law was scheduled to go into effect in February of 1842.[20]

Meanwhile the House passed the distribution bill 116 to 108. This bill provided for distribution of the proceeds of the sale of public lands among the states and contained a provision for preemption. Since part of the opposition to distribution had been based on the fear of increased tariffs to provide the necessary revenue, an amendment was attached to the bill providing that distribution would be suspended if future tariff duties went above twenty per cent. The end result was that by linking bankruptcy to distribution and preemption, passage was secured for both, and Tyler signed both into law.

When a Whig-sponsored treasury loan bill was debated during July, much of the debate again dealt with the broader question of federal power. Many Southern representatives opposed the bill as federal legislation which interfered with the rights of states. Francis Pickens of South Carolina called the bill "oppressive to the South." Barnard defended the bill as the best way of funding the public debt. However, his remarks were directed less at the merits of the bill than at his concern for the extension of federal power. While arguing for nationalistic legislation, he also attempted to ease the fears of Southern Congressmen. He did not believe that the interests of the sections need be antagonistic, and he was worried that Southerners, out of concern for their section, might turn to attacking the Union itself. Making a strong plea for the Union, his voice ringing with emotion, Barnard exclaimed:

> We do not think you can afford to part with it [the Union]; we know we cannot. . . . You will be eternally talking about going . . . but . . . we must not separate . . . if we can help it. . . . We will not let you go while a rag of the Constitution or of our country's glorious flag remains to cover us with.

When the debate concluded, the bill passed. Whigs, including Barnard, were gratified that the needs of the treasury would be met, but the larger question of federal power would come to the fore again.[21]

One of the major goals of the Whig Congress was attained during the summer, when the subtreasury was repealed, an action which Barnard supported. But the repeal left the question of a national bank still unsettled. It was over the bank question that Whig differences with the President came to a head. Clay wanted a centralized bank with unlimited power to establish branch banks, whereas Tyler desired a decentralized system with greater state control. Barnard consistently supported a bank along the lines drawn by Clay. During August and September two separate bank bills passed the House and Senate, only to meet Presidential vetoes.

For most Clay Whigs, including Barnard, the final bank veto marked a turning point in their relations with Tyler. Although Tyler had supported repeal of the subtreasury, bankruptcy, and distribution bills, he had failed to come through in the establishment of a national bank, and this was an essential part of the Clay program. In September the Whigs in Congress met and passed resolutions indicating their displeasure at Tyler's lack of cooperation with the party, particularly voicing their dismay at the bank veto. Barnard was not a member of the committee which drew up the anti-Tyler resolutions, but he agreed with the sentiment. He wrote to his sister that there was great difficulty with the "accidental President . . . and we [the Whig Party] have been on the point . . . of breaking to pieces." The results of the session were a severe disappointment to the Clay Whigs, who had hoped to have Harrison as their puppet while they enacted their program. Instead they had had to deal with a President who had states' rights leanings and who used the veto on legislation which he considered not in accord with his principles. Although Whigs had to admit that some successes had been achieved in the passage of the bankruptcy and distribution laws, the lack of support for a bank seemed a betrayal on the part of the President. Dissatisfaction with Tyler continued to grow, and Whigs looked with anxiety to the future.[22]

The lengthy summer session had been a strain on Barnard, who was described by his wife as "pale and thin." Mrs. Barnard and the girls spent the early part of the summer in Washington with him but returned to Albany before the session ended. Soon after Barnard's return to Albany at the close of the session, he was appointed a delegate to the Whig State Convention at Syracuse, which met early in October. Addressing the Convention, Barnard attacked Tyler's bank veto, saying the bank bill had been ". . . *the* prominent measure of relief promised by the Whigs." Barnard advised Whigs to remain united in spite of this failure and to continue to work for Clay's programs.[23]

Throughout October the Whigs held meetings and rallies at which Barnard was a frequent speaker. Writing to his friend Leverett Saltonstall before the election, Barnard indicated that the Whigs in New York were "united in sentiment and feeling" in spite of the dissatisfaction with Tyler. Although he was pessimistic about the outcome of the pending state elections, he did not despair for the Whig Party. "Whenever the time comes for us to rally as a National party, I think we shall do it."[24]

The second session of the Twenty-seventh Congress assembled in December of 1841. The two major issues were the establishment of a bank and tariff revision. There was evidence of a change in the political climate as Tyler had reorganized his cabinet excluding the Clay Whigs, but in his message to Congress Tyler voiced sympathy with changes in the tariff, thereby giving some encouragement to Whigs.

Before action was taken on either a bank or tariff, however, efforts were made to repeal the recently enacted bankruptcy law before it should go into effect in February of 1842. Support for repeal came from those who had questioned the constitutionality of the bill in the previous session and from others who felt that it provided an easy shelter for debtors. Barnard took a stand against these efforts and presented a number of petitions from his constituents against repeal. Though repeal was approved by the House, it was rejected in the Senate, so the law stood.

With repeal blocked the law went into operation as scheduled. Approximately 34,000 persons took advantage of the law, with debts of $440,934,000 wiped out and $43,697,350 surrendered by debtors. However, the law continued to be unpopular with debtors and creditors alike. Creditors were distressed because large numbers of debtors were discharged from debts and because of the high cost of administration—both of which reduced the amounts paid to creditors. Debtors complained because the law had not preserved all the various protections provided in some of the state laws. Many Whigs who had advocated passage of the law did not see it as permanent policy but only as a temporary measure of relief. Some political realists had pushed for the law to get the votes of an estimated 500,000 bankrupt debtors and now urged its repeal in order to appeal to the 500,000 creditors. In spite of all the opposition Barnard continued his defense because he believed that a uniform and permanent law was necessary for stable business conditions.[25]

The question of repeal came up again at the next session in January of 1843, with Barnard still fighting against it. His efforts were not successful, however, and repeal passed the House by a vote of 140 to 71. The Senate concurred and the bill became law with the President's signature. The law for which Barnard had struggled and which had been in operation only a little over a year was taken off the books.[26]

During discussions over the first repeal attempt in 1842, Congress also considered the tariff and Tyler's recommendations for a bank. Barnard's position on the tariff remained what it had been—one of support for the protective principle. A decade had passed since enactment of the tariff of 1832, a protectionist measure levying high duties of approximately thirty-three per cent. It was followed by the Compromise Tariff of 1833, which provided for a considerable degree of protection for nine years followed by a reduction to a uniform rate of twenty per cent.

As the date of expiration of the Compromise Tariff approached, Barnard had argued in 1841 for a complete revision of the tariff. Pointing out that the Compromise Act was not sacred, he had advocated that duties be raised above its provisions to obtain the necessary revenue and afford protection to domestic industries. On articles like tobacco, which he considered ". . . at once a luxury and a vice . . .", he wanted higher duties in order to obtain all the revenue possible.[27]

In the summer of 1842 Whigs drew up a provisional tariff bill, the purpose of which was to continue the existing tariff until August 1 while Congress undertook a complete tariff revision. Duties were kept at the June 1 level or above twenty per cent but distribution was not suspended. The House passed this bill 116 to 103, with Barnard voting with the majority. Tyler vetoed the bill because of the distribution feature and directed that revenue continue to be collected under the law of 1833. Barnard as well as other Whigs voiced disapproval of the President's veto; however, Congress could not muster sufficient votes to override it.

This left unsettled the question of the validity of the tariff of 1833. Tyler had directed that duties be collected under this act in the absence of new tariff legislation. The President's view was in accord with that of his Secretary of the Treasury, who argued that the Compromise Act was still valid. The House questioned the administration's position, and the matter was referred to Barnard and the Judiciary Committee. The committee concluded that no duties were collectible or had been since June 30 when the Compromise Act had expired. New legislation therefore was necessary before any duties could be collected after that date. The committee supported the concept of a provisional tariff to cover the interim period. No immediate action was taken on the committee proposal, but Congress continued to consider general tariff revision. Barnard repeated his support for an increased tariff, believing that the Compromise Act did not represent fixed policy. He denied the contention that duties were a tax on consumers for the benefit of domestic producers. In his view, prices were not permanently raised by protective duties. He expanded his argument to include a discussion of states' rights by emphasizing that duties operated the same throughout the country and were not more detrimental to the South than the North. The net effect of a protective tariff was beneficial to all.[28]

The House passed a tariff bill late in July by the narrow margin of four votes, with Barnard voting in favor. The bill also passed the Senate, but Tyler again used the veto because, although the duties remained above twenty per cent, distribution was not eliminated. When the provision for distribution was removed, a tariff bill passed both houses and was signed by Tyler late in August of 1842.

At this session of Congress bankruptcy legislation and tariff revision were not the only occasions on which the relative strength of federal power over state was debated. The question came up again in the matter of electing House members. As a result of the 1840 census it was necessary for the House to be reapportioned. While considering reapportionment, Congress debated a proposal which would provide for the election of all House members from single districts. The bill provided that one representative would be elected from each district and the number of districts in a state would be equal to the number of representatives to which it was entitled. Walter T. Colquitt of Georgia led the opposition to the bill, insisting that the states should retain control of elections. Barnard delivered a lengthy address in favor of the bill. The Constitution, he noted, provided that states make the general regulations on elections but there was a reserved authority "over the whole subject to Congress. . . ." The federal government had the "*ultimate* power" because a lack of uniformity in the manner of conducting elections among the several states demanded the "interposition" of the federal government. To Southerners who argued that this bill was an order from the federal government and that care should be taken to "order and command sovereign States . . . lest . . . this Government and the States [be brought] into conflict . . .", Barnard answered that it did not constitute an order but simply a law which Congress had the right to pass. He looked with disfavor on those who saw the federal government as the "creature of the States" and considered members of Congress mere representatives of sovereign states or a "congress of ambassadors" from "sovereign powers." Barnard also saw the political implications in the issue. Those states which elected by general ticket usually elected members of the same party, while a state like New York, which used the district system, elected a large delegation nearly balanced politically. Such representatives split on most questions, thereby decreasing the effect of their votes when compared to the unified vote of a state electing by general ticket.[29]

Barnard's forceful arguments received the praise of the *National Intelligencer* and the Albany *Evening Journal,* and the bill passed by a narrow margin. However, the tariff was generally considered the most significant accomplishment of the session which ended in September.

In the fall of 1842 Barnard was again nominated for Congress. The Democrats chose James M. French to oppose Barnard as in the previous election and predicted that due to the difficulties within the Whig Party not one of the three Whig incumbents running for office in New York would be reelected. Barnard made a number of speeches in support of his candidacy and emphasized in particular his support of the tariff of 1842. He also expressed his growing disenchantment with Tyler, charging him with deserting the party that had brought him into power. He lamented that Clay had not received the Whig nod in 1840. When the results were in, Barnard was the only New York Whig reelected to Congress, and the *Argus* termed him "the solitary representative of departed Whiggery." In his victory over French, Barnard again ran ahead of the Whig candidate for Governor, Luther Bradish, in Albany County. Barnard proved once more that he was popular in aristocratic and conservative Albany. However, the dissension in the Whig ranks was revealed in New York's representation in the Twenty-eighth Congress. Of the thirty-four representatives elected, only ten were Whigs, whereas in the two previous elections representatives had been almost evenly divided between the two parties.[30]

Shortly after the election the Twenty-seventh Congress met for its third session. At this time Tyler determined to push his own plan for a banking system, the exchequer. Barnard refused to support the administration, remaining committed to a Clay national bank. Most of the other Whigs also opposed the President's proposal, and the exchequer met a resounding defeat in the House in January of 1843. In February Barnard presented a substitute plan to operate until a national bank could be established. He proposed authorizing the Secretary of the Treasury to borrow a sum from specie-paying banks not to exceed $15,000,000. However, Barnard's plan, like the President's, was rejected.[31]

Near the end of the session Weed again visited Washington and while there was invited to Barnard's "mess" for dinner. The two men had known each other now almost twenty years and were cordial though not intimate friends due to real differences between them. Other guests were Barnard's colleagues in Congress John Greig and Henry Van Rensselaer of New York and Jared Ingersoll of Pennsylvania. Weed called the group "a very select and refined circle, all being gentlemen of high social positions." Dessert was served on the veranda, and as the guests moved from the dining room, Weed recognized someone he had once known, a porter named Brady. He stopped to talk with him, greeting him cordially and reminiscing about a time when Weed had had to borrow his coat in order to be properly attired for dinner. Recording the incident later, Weed wrote amusingly that his "fastidious friend Mr. Barnard attempted to interrupt" their conversation from a "sense of horror" that a friend whom he had invited to dinner would not only talk amicably with a servant but voluntarily confess that he had worn a porter's coat to a Washington dinner.[32]

When the session was over in March, the Whig Congress had met for 450 days and passed over 400 bills. However, Barnard was not pleased with the results. He outlined his views in a letter to his constituents published in the Albany *Evening Journal* on March 17, 1843. He could not conceal his disappointment that once the Whigs were in control, they had not been effective in enacting the desired legislation. Worst of all they had not furnished the country with a national currency, and they had not done enough for internal improvements. The tariff, although a positive gain, was secured only by sacrificing distribution.[33] One positive achievement which Barnard applauded was the passage of the Remedial Justice Bill. As Chairman of the Judiciary Committee he had borne the major responsibility for getting the bill through the House after it had passed the Senate. The law provided for the removal, before trial, of certain cases of international importance from state courts to the federal courts. The purpose was to give jurisdiction to the courts of the United States over all questions arising out of relations between the United States and foreign nations. Webster had advocated such a law and praised Barnard's efforts in securing it.[34]

In the months between sessions Barnard resumed his law practice, political activity, and lecturing. In August he was pleased to play host to John Quincy Adams when the old gentleman stopped on a return trip from Buffalo, Rochester, and Utica. After being cheered at stops along the way, he arrived in Albany on August 2. A large crowd assembled in the park in front of the Capitol to greet him, and Barnard delivered a welcoming speech on behalf of the people of Albany. Replying to Barnard's warm remarks, Adams spoke to the audience for half an hour, emphasizing his fight in Congress for the right of petition. At the conclusion of his remarks Adams greeted and shook hands with over five hundred Albany citizens and then retired to Barnard's home, where he was entertained at dinner. After dinner Barnard gave Adams a tour of Albany and the surrounding area. The next morning Adams concluded his brief visit and departed by rail for Boston.[35]

Soon after Adams' visit Barnard had recurring health problems and as the time approached for the fall elections, he limited his political role to an occasional address.

In December of 1843 the Twenty-eighth Congress assembled. Since the Whigs no longer controlled the House, Barnard lost his chairmanship of the Judiciary Committee and was appointed to the Ways and Means Committee.

Before the House took up the regular business of the session it had to deal with an alleged violation of the recently enacted District Election Law. Congressmen from New Hampshire, Georgia, Missouri, and Mississippi had been elected by general ticket in defiance of the law. Since the result was of benefit to the Democrats, the Whig members of the House signed a protest against seating the members from these states. Barnard was selected to present the protest to the House, and his name headed a list of fifty signers, including such colleagues as John Quincy Adams, Hamilton Fish, Robert Winthrop, Washington Hunt, and Jared Ingersoll. The Democratically controlled House was reluctant to recognize Barnard for the purpose of reading the protest. For over a week Barnard made repeated attempts to present the protest and have it written into the House records. Barnard succeeded in getting the protest recorded in the *Journal* on December 5 only to have it expunged from the record six days later. In the meantime, however, news of the protest spread to the newspapers, and the resulting publicity helped the disgruntled Whigs to plead their case. Late in December the dispute was referred to the Committee on Elections, which reported back to the House in January. The committee voiced the opinion that the District Election Law was not binding on House members and that those elected by general ticket were entitled to their seats. The committee contended that the recently enacted law was an attempt to compel states to conform to certain rules established by Congress beyond its authority. A conflict "of sovereignty between the Federal Government and four of the independent States of this Union" was involved, and in this case federal power had to yield to that of the states.[36]

Such an argument called forth a strong dissent from Barnard as well as from the minority members on the Committee on Elections. Debate on the report occupied one entire week during February. Thirty members had spoken before Barnard rose to address the House in opposition to the majority report. In a stirring defense of the law passed by the previous Congress, Barnard, arguing on Constitutional grounds, voiced his "abhorrence" at the "dangerous doctrine" which had been expressed in the debate—the idea that "it is within the Constitutional competency of the House of Representatives to pronounce a law of Congress unconstitutional and void." Under the Constitutional system of checks and balances the legislature had no power to annul a statute. For the House, therefore, to pronounce a statute void was in the "spirit of insubordination and lawlessness." Furthermore, he contended that the law presented no threat to states' rights: "State rights were carefully considered and respected, both in the system and in the mode of establishing it [election by districts]." However, for the House to claim the right of judicial condemnation was a new kind of nullification; ". . . nullification here puts on a new phase. Once it was grave, solemn, sincere, earnest—acting from deep though mistaken convictions." Here, Barnard concluded, it was "wanton" and "cruel." His rhetoric was in vain, however, and the disputed members were seated.[37] Once again as in the disputed New Jersey election, Barnard was incensed at the political maneuvering and lack of principle in the House.

The outcome of two other issues at the session likewise resulted in disappointment to Barnard. Along with other Whigs from the North, Barnard continued, but in vain, to oppose the gag rule. In addition, he still pushed for appropriations for internal improvements and on January 17 had delivered a lengthy speech on the subject. Commenting in his Diary on Barnard's remarks, Adams shed some extra light on his colleague's temperament. While praising his argument as one of "irresistible force," Adams noted that it contained "a stern and peremptory tone and manner, which irritates even those whom it convinces." He continued: "There is a tone of acid in Barnard's oratory which curdles his eloquence." Near the end of the session Congress did pass a bill, supported by Barnard and other New York Whigs, which applied to Eastern harbors and included an appropriation of $50,000 for the Hudson River.[38] It was vetoed by Tyler.

By late May Barnard's criticism of Tyler had reached the point where he discussed with Adams the possibility of instigating impeachment proceedings. Adams convinced Barnard that such a move would be impractical, but when the session ended in June most Whigs were, like Barnard, discouraged and the party was disorganized.[39] Whigs held rallies to try to strengthen their party and, with the enthusiastic support of Barnard, turned once again to Henry Clay at the national convention.

As Barnard reviewed the session, it was evident that not only the lack of positive action by Congress and Tyler's resistance bothered him, but also the whole trend of expanded democracy. He could not bring himself to attribute the ills in the country to the Whig Party, so he placed much of the blame on the Democrats. In a series of letters to his constituents prepared for the Albany *Evening Journal* he expressed the belief that

> . . . [the] popular mind of the country had become . . . corrupted and debased in the . . . vices of that new school of politics of which he [Jackson] became the chief . . . there is something dangerous to law and order, and to true constitutional freedom, prevailing at the bottom in the policy and practices of the modern Democratic Party.

The Whig Party, on the other hand, received his praise. It had the support of the "best and wisest men of the land"—by whom Barnard meant men of "cultivation" and "character."[40]

* * *

Barnard was inactive in party affairs for the rest of the summer and in September of 1844 announced that he did not want to be renominated for Congress. The reasons given in public statements included his failing health and the need to devote more time and attention to his private affairs, including study and writing. He was quoted in the Albany *Evening Journal* as saying that in the past six years he had done "literally" nothing for himself. Other reasons were more subtle. Barnard never became reconciled to the political maneuvering in the House, and the lack of decorum there was a constant source of irritation to him. He described the House as a place where "order seldom reigns, courtesy never," and where "many will not listen" to fellow speakers. He did not like to speak to "unwilling auditors" or to speak under the limitation of time. The growing trend toward ungentlemanly behavior manifested in crude manners, brawls, and drunkenness was not something that Barnard accepted easily. The political realities of the 1844 election also entered into his decision. Not only was Barnard concerned about the fate of the New York Whig candidates, but he felt certain that the Whigs would not control the Twenty-ninth Congress. In a Congress controlled by the opposition all his efforts would be futile. He wrote to his good friend Hamilton Fish, who had urged him to run, "What good could I do in such a Congress?" A more realistic difficulty was that Barnard anticipated that he would be defeated in 1844, and he did not want to suffer a loss. He had differed with Weed and the majority of the Whig party in the antirent dispute; and again, as in the Anti-Masonic episode sixteen years earlier, by siding with the interests of wealth and property, he had placed himself against the popular will. In view of all these factors Barnard preferred the face-saving course of asking not to be nominated.[41]

Clay was defeated in November and his defeat saddened Barnard, who wrote to Fish, ". . . I grieve and lament . . . as if it [the United States] were conquered by a horde of barbarians." The Albany district went to the Democrats, as he had feared.[42] Following the election Barnard visited friends, continued his historical writing, and then prepared to return to Congress for the lame duck session.

When Congress convened in December of 1844, Barnard resumed his place as a member of the Ways and Means Committee. He continued to vote in support of the right of petition and was pleased to be a member of the Congress which repealed the gag rule. However, his continued efforts to secure appropriations for internal improvements, especially for clearing obstructions from the Hudson, were in vain.[43]

Overshadowing all else at this session was the question of the annexation of Texas. In April of 1844 an annexation treaty had been negotiated but failed to pass the Senate. However, Tyler was determined to get Texas, and in June had placed the correspondence relating to Texas before the House and asked for annexation by an act of Congress. Since the time for adjournment was near, no action was taken. When James Polk, who was known to favor annexation, was elected President, Tyler apparently regarded it as a mandate for annexation, and the question thus came again before Congress in December of 1844.[44]

In mid-December the Committee on Foreign Affairs reported out a joint resolution for the annexation of Texas. Debate went on into January of 1845, with most Whigs as well as some Northern Democrats voicing sentiments against immediate annexation. Some Whigs opposed any annexation of territory; others opposed annexing areas that were likely to contribute to the slavery controversy.

Barnard had been adverse to annexation when it had been discussed at the previous session and now was one of several opposition speakers. He argued that annexation was for the purpose of "enlarging the territorial limits of slavery" and increasing the political power of the slave interest. He felt that the possession of Texas was not necessary to secure the institution of slavery. On the contrary, the best security for slavery was to "let it rest just where it stands, on the compromises of the Constitution." Slavery, he continued, would last as long as the "States in which it exists [were] willing to let it last." The North, Barnard intimated, would stand forever by the compromises of the Constitution if only the South would allow the Constitution and Union to stand. He further believed annexation would "add nothing to the national wealth, the national prosperity, the national security, the national respectability, or the national honor." Not only did Barnard disapprove annexing territory which might intensify the slavery question, but he opposed any and all annexation. He was dismayed at the idea that areas with people little accustomed to republican forms and with institutions and laws no more in accord with those of the United States than those of "Russia or China" might be admitted to the Union. However, the main thrust of his argument and the one which he returned to again and again was that the true object of annexation was ". . . *to enlarge the area of slavery*. . . ." He concluded that the government was not created to be the "abetter and promoter of slavery. . . . No, No, No, a thousand times, No. . . . Men of the South, let this institution of slavery . . . for God's sake, let it rest on the basis where the Constitution has placed it." He predicted that the admission of Texas would prove an element of overwhelming ruin to the Republic.[45]

Several Whigs, including Barnard's colleagues John Quincy Adams, Robert Winthrop, and Washington Hunt, also were vehement in opposition to annexation. The New York Whigs voted against the joint resolution, but it carried and Texas was annexed.

The annexation of Texas was the last in a long series of disappointments to Barnard, whose six years in Congress were over in March of 1845. He regretted leaving the many friends he had made in Washington but was relieved at departing from what for him had been a constant battlefield in which he was often on the losing side. For the most part Barnard had voted with Northern Whigs on economic policy and in opposing the annexation of Texas. He had fought hard for a national bank, an increased tariff, the uniform bankruptcy law, and election of Congressmen by districts.[46] Yet in only one area, that of the tariff, had success been obtained, and this had been at the cost of sacrificing distribution. He had found himself in a difficult position time and time again as, on the one hand, he had supported economic and political nationalism while, on the other, he had attempted to reassure the South that centralization of power and legislation for tariffs or internal improvements did not constitute a threat to slavery. His pronouncements that the Constitutional provisions were sufficient safeguards for slavery did not reassure Southerners, who continued to fear Northern encroachments. Barnard's disenchantment with Congress was complicated by the fact that he was at odds with many New York Whigs because of their different positions on reform, slavery, and property rights. These issues would cause the dissolution of the party and end Barnard's career as an elected political servant. To wrestle with these problems Barnard returned to Albany and spent the next five years in legal work, writing, lecturing, and political activity within the party. His main focus would be an attempt to bring the Whig party in line with his views.

18.

Chapter VI

ANTI-ABOLITION WHIG

By 1850 the Whig Party was in the throes of dissolution. Signs of the strain which had existed from its beginnings became more apparent in the late 1840's. Much of the problem stemmed from the nature of the party, composed as it was of a dissimilar group of men rarely able to unite on issues with the exception of their bold denunciations of Jacksonian democracy. True, Whigs tended to be nationalistic in outlook, seeing a natural harmony of interest among the groups in American society, and they tended to favor positive governmental action at the state and federal levels for the benefit of the society. In general, they supported universal manhood suffrage, the necessity for a sound financial structure, and a government-regulated medium of exchange. Yet areas of disagreement within the national party and various state parties were more numerous than areas of agreement. Northern and Southern wings of the party frequently disagreed over the tariff, a national bank, and the right of petition. The greatest difficulty for the party, however, became the formulation of a response to the slavery question. The antislavery sentiment of the North flowed mainly into the Whig Party, but on the national level the party attempted to avoid an antislavery stand in order not to alienate Southern Whigs. The national party, as well as the party in states like New York, had distinct liberal and conservative wings contending for control of policy and patronage. The conservative group generally was composed of merchants, traders, industrialists, and lawyers who believed in tradition and stability. Most of them were men of some means who looked askance at the leveling tendencies and reform ideas associated with Jacksonian democracy. The more liberal wing of the party received much of its support from farmers. The leaders of this wing were more sympathetic toward reform and did not hesitate to court immigrant and antirent voters. However, the areas of agreement, when coupled with splits within the Democratic Party, were sufficient to make possible an occasional success for the Whigs as a national party. Similar differences operated within the Democratic Party as well and were evidence of the widespread strain which social change was causing throughout the country.

The liberal and conservative wings of the New York party were in frequent battle. Dissension arose from a struggle over party leadership, from a contest between Cotton and Conscience Whigs, and finally from a fundamental difference in attitude about the nature of the party. Control of the New York Whig Party was in the hands of an oligarchy of party leaders. Thurlow Weed, of the liberal wing, reigned as dictator of the New York Whigs. William H. Seward and Horace Greeley were aligned with Weed. Barnard was a member of the conservative wing. He was never the primary political leader of the group, but provided much of its philosophical underpinning and was an adviser to the conservative leaders in their challenges to Weed. At one time or another the assault on Weed was led by Millard Fillmore, Francis Granger, and Luther Bradish; Barnard supported these efforts to wrest control from Weed and the liberals.

The conservative creed, as preached by Barnard, was rooted in tradition and resistance to change. Weed, by contrast, saw political implications in widespread social change and over the years shifted his positions. Support of reform proposals conciliated the people at large, and popularized the Whig cause and party. Seward, even more than Weed, worked for changes within the established order. The difference in attitude toward the necessity for change and the rate of change was certain to lead to problems when the party was confronted with issues involving immigrants, property rights, and slavery.[1]

Barnard and Weed, both products of western New York, were from very different backgrounds. Barnard was born to wealth and position; Weed was a self-made man. In the 1820's, when both lived in Rochester, they had been on friendly terms.

However, they were on opposite sides in the Anti-Masonic dispute, and Weed developed doubts about Barnard as a suitable representative of the people at that time and again after his first term in the New York State Assembly. Yet with the exception of the Anti-Masonic period, he never withheld support from Barnard in his campaigns for the Assembly or the House of Representatives. In the thirties and forties Barnard received the endorsement and support of the Albany *Evening Journal*. Particular praise was given to his positions on the tariff and internal improvements and to his scholarly orations. Yet Weed frequently was critical of Barnard's patrician attitude and lack of understanding of the masses of the people.

Part of Barnard's difficulty was that he could not accept Weed's leadership and rejected the implications of the school of practical politics—of which Weed was a master—with its appeals for mass support. Barnard's refusal to accept Weed's political practices was a major factor in the personal animosity toward both Weed and Seward which Barnard developed over the years. He saw himself as a man of principle and viewed Weed as a politician and demagogue who would not hesitate to court the favor of the voters in an attempt to win elections. One illustration of this was the dispute between the two men over the selection of Nathaniel P. Tallmadge as the Whig candidate for Senator in 1838. Barnard would not support the Democrat-turned-Conservative Tallmadge under any circumstances because Tallmadge had not declared himself a Whig. Weed favored Tallmadge because it was a politically astute thing to do. However, at this point there was enough good will on both sides to make an attempt to smooth over differences. Writing to Weed, Barnard said that he never doubted that Weed's "heart was anywhere but in the right place." Barnard found his own problem to be that "in politics or out of politics" his opinions and acts were "always honest, though they may be mistaken." In December, 1839, Weed and Barnard clashed again when Weed published information about Barnard's vote for Speaker of the House. Barnard voted for a subtreasury man although he had written privately that he would not cast such a vote. When Weed disclosed the contradiction, Barnard scolded him severely for using information which had been written to him in private. Barnard was never willing to admit that he was not wholly a man of principle, and he preferred to keep undisclosed incidents in his own political career that tended to reveal that he, too, operated on the basis of political expediency. Further discord developed when Barnard desired to be the Whig choice for United States Senator from New York. He was handicapped not only because he would not openly push his own candidacy but also because he could not secure Weed's support.[2] Relations between the two men continued to cool, and by the late forties Barnard and Weed were cooperating on little else but the cause of internal improvements. Barnard labeled Weed a "demagogue," and as Weed led the Whigs more and more in the direction of antislavery, Barnard became more severe in his criticism.

The relationship between Barnard and Seward took a similar turn. They had fought together for educational reform in the late thirties and early forties, but thereafter bitter feelings developed between them. Seward lamented that Barnard had denied the party the use of his "great abilities" by wasting "such powers in a futile effort . . . to build a party upon no foundation, but . . . conservation of property . . . [instead of] on the foundation of national justice and the conservation of Human liberty." He felt that Barnard was unrealistic and impractical when it came to politics.[3] Because Barnard was never a political or social intimate of either man, there was less and less incentive to smooth over differences, and by 1849 there seemed little hope for any reconciliation. Personal differences, when coupled with underlying ideological differences as demonstrated in attitudes on property rights, slavery, and the directions the party should take, became significant contributing factors in the eventual party split.

When the antirent controversy in the early 1840's caused New York Whigs to examine their views on property rights, Barnard and other conservatives found themselves at odds with the more liberal leadership. Barnard defended the right of contract and the landlord position and had little sympathy for the tenants. Weed and Seward were critical of the aristocratic land tenure system, sympathized with tenant demands, and were anxious for antirent support for Whig candidates. Weed was convinced that Barnard lacked understanding of the situation, and he attacked Barnard's article on the antirent movement which appeared in the *American Whig Review* in December, 1845. Barnard, according to Weed, had obtained his facts from books, legal documents, and the landlords but had not made an examination of tenant grievances. For his part, Barnard attacked Weed and also Horace Greeley for editorial efforts which he alleged promoted the antirent cause.[4]

Barnard wrote often to his good friend Hamilton Fish expressing his disappointment at the favorable attitude many Whigs had taken toward the antirenters. When the Whigs were victorious in the 1846 elections in New York, Barnard cautioned that the victory was no cause for rejoicing because much of the success was due to the antirent controversy and to splits within the Democratic Party rather than to steadfast attachment to Whig principles. Barnard praised Fish, who had lost his bid for Lieutenant Governor, for not courting the antirent vote, writing that it was better to have lost than to have sacrificed principles. Early in 1847, writing again to Fish, he penned a bitter indictment of the Whig Governor, John Young, for leniency in proclaiming a general amnesty to those who had been convicted of resisting the authorities during the dispute. Barnard argued that the offenses committed by the antirenters were "smacking of treason." The worst part of the episode, however, was that from that time on the Whig Party in New York would be called the "sponsor for antirentism."[5] The political implications of antirentism were particularly distasteful to Barnard, who deplored the coddling of antirenters to gain votes, but antirentism was not the only problem for the Whig Party. A larger one, that of slavery, was coming to the fore.

Closely connected with the slavery question was the Whig response to the Mexican War. Barnard agreed with Weed and Seward and with most Whigs in opposing the annexation of Texas and the war. In fact, in many ways he seemed closer to Whig liberals on this point than to party conservatives. Many conservatives were mild in their opposition in order not to anger Southern Whigs. By contrast, Barnard's denunciations were vivid and bitter. After his retirement from Congress in 1845, Barnard resumed his law practice and as the chief political contributor to the *American Whig Review* wrote a series of articles dealing with the war.

His first article, published in the summer of 1846, was a vitriolic attack on the Democratic administration for waging a completely unjustifiable war. It was a war of ambition with a view toward "national aggrandizement," a "war of the President's own seeking," the object of which was the acquisition of more territory to enlarge the area of slavery. Coupled with his distaste for the war as such was a feeling repeated again and again in subsequent articles that the war would extend the area of slavery. Here Barnard's denunciations would appear to place him in the antislavery camp with Weed and Seward. However, Barnard's position was based not so much on hatred of the institution and concern for human rights as it was on the fact that the war and annexation of territory would renew debate, discussion, and agitation in the halls of Congress, the newspapers, the pulpits, the lecture platforms, and, in fact, any place where people gathered. Barnard wanted silence on all issues related to slavery because a reopening of the question, he believed, would endanger the Union.

In other articles Barnard defended Whig war critics and voiced his disdain of the Democratic attempt to stifle criticism of the war. He felt particularly incensed at what he considered Polk's provocation of the war. However, like most Whigs, once war was an accomplished fact Barnard urged that the administration be supported in the "necessary prosecution of the war."[6]

Yet, fearing that the results of the war would tear the Union apart, Barnard called for an early peace. Mexico would make peace, he was convinced, if the administration gave up its demand for territorial conquest. In his distaste for the war Barnard displayed pacifist tendencies which he would show again prior to the outbreak of the Civil War.[7]

In his writings Barnard showed that he differed with some of his Whig colleagues on the broader aspects of expansion. Some Whigs opposed the annexation of territory which might be opened to slavery but did not oppose all annexation. Barnard expressed views akin to the no-territory position of Daniel Webster. He did not want any remote areas brought into the Union for any reason: "We want our own Republic and Union, with a homogeneous people, men of the same general race, blood, education and habits, forming a consolidated nation. . . ." Bringing "strange" people into the Union would be disastrous because they would not be accustomed to Republican forms. Far worse, the annexation of territory would destroy the constitutional balance of slave and free states. Moreover, Barnard feared giving political power to the "new, strange, distant, foreign States . . . with only a handful of population and that of the worst kind."[8]

At the same time Barnard drew further away from the broadened party approach of Weed and Seward. He wrote to Fillmore, who was elected Comptroller of New York in November, 1847, that Weed was running the party into the ground. He urged Fillmore to wrest control of the New York party from Weed in order to keep it "true to its cardinal principles."[9] Barnard's resistance to Weed's leadership grew as he felt that his own grasp on political power was threatened. In New York politics he had seen a constant shift of power from patricians like himself to the politicians who sought mass support. He could not accept the fact that Weed from humble beginnings pulled the political reins in New York while aristocratic, well-educated gentlemen like himself increasingly had little influence in state politics. Now he feared in addition a transfer in the political nerve center of the nation from the East to the West. This would be intolerable to the narrow and provincial elitist who appears to have desired that the western boundary of the United States be drawn at the Mississippi.

In the winter of 1848 the peace treaty was concluded with Mexico. The territory acquired as a result of the war led the country into another sectional crisis and the Whig Party into an internal crisis of its own. In the presidential campaign of 1848 both Democrats and Whigs tried to avoid the slavery question and sought noncontroversial candidates. Barnard preferred Clay or Webster and was not enthusiastic when the Whigs chose Zachary Taylor. In a private letter to Fish he wrote that he would be the last man to propose a "mere" military man for the presidency. However, he saw a current for such a move which could not be resisted. He continued: "It may be our destiny to have another military chieftain for President . . . so long as wars last I am inclined to think that this is a destiny from which an elective Republic cannot well escape." Eventually he did support Taylor, as he had Harrison eight years earlier, and used his pen to further the Whig cause.[10]

In the fall of 1848 Barnard endorsed Taylor in an article for the *American Whig Review,* an article which pleased Weed. Much of it was devoted to praising the Whig stand not "to extend the area of slavery." Barnard called on "free soilers" to vote the Whig ticket because Whigs recognized that it was the duty of Congress to keep slavery out of the territories:

> Let the great national party of the Whigs have the sway in the country, and the North will have nothing to fear from the encroachments of slavery . . . it is a common sentiment with Whigs that

slavery is a great evil, political and moral; they have never done, and never will do, anything to extend and perpetuate it.

However, in the article Barnard's own ambivalence toward slavery was reflected. While courting "free soilers," he also called on Whigs of the North to stand by the compromises of the Constitution. In a plea for national unity he tried to assure Southern Whigs that they could still find a home in the Whig Party.[11] However, as Barnard came to realize, his had become an untenable position. Whigs could not please "free soilers" and at the same time expect to hold the ranks of Southern Whigs.

Taylor won a narrow victory in November, and the conservative New Yorker Millard Fillmore was elected Vice President. In New York Hamilton Fish was successful in his bid to become Governor. Once the Whigs were in office, problems within their ranks over patronage and slavery became even more apparent. Immediately there ensued a struggle over the division of the spoils.

Throughout the late forties Weed and Seward, motivated both by a sense of moral commitment and by the prospect of attracting antislavery votes to the Whig party, had become steadfast in support of an antislavery stance. During the years 1846-1847, the Albany *Evening Journal* had carried on an antislavery campaign calling for free labor and free soil. Although admitting that the compromises of the Constitution which dealt with slavery should be adhered to, Weed argued that compromise did not mean repeated concessions to the South. The North must demand that free soil once acquired remain free. Weed and Seward urged Taylor to use the appointment power to strengthen the liberal wing of the party in order to move the party in an antislavery direction.

Within a few months after his endorsement of Taylor, and as Seward and Weed moved ever closer to an avowed antislavery position, Barnard went in the direction of militant anti-antislavery, again motivated in part by his refusal to accept the popular politics of the Weed wing. By January, 1849, his views were no longer ambivalent, and in private and public statements he indicated that it would be disastrous for the Whig Party to adopt the free soil doctrines of Seward and Weed. His most violent attack on the liberal wing of the party was contained in his pamphlet *Whig or Abolition? That's the Question.* With Whigs in control in New York as a result of the 1848 election, Weed determined to make Seward United States Senator. The purpose of Barnard's diatribe was to galvanize Whig opposition to Seward as the Whig candidate. He accused Seward of trying to transform the Whig Party into an abolition party, thereby endangering its national appeal. Barnard had never been enthusiastic about the Wilmot Proviso and was now incensed because be believed that even the Proviso was not strong enough for Seward, since it left slavery alone where it legally existed. Barnard charged Seward with asking for complete and universal emancipation. He saw Seward as moving far beyond the Whig doctrine of free territory and predicted that, with Seward as leader, the Whigs could not be a national party, because if he succeeded in his purpose, the Union would be dissolved.[12]

In spite of Barnard's forceful argument, conservatives were not able to block Seward, who was nominated for Senator in February of 1849. Barnard's name was one of those considered by the Whigs at the time, but he was not a serious contender.[13]

However, conservatives were not completely disheartened, because they were hopeful that Fillmore would persuade Taylor to include substantial numbers of them in the division of the spoils. Barnard was desirous of a diplomatic post for himself and met with Fillmore in Washington in March of 1849 to tell him that he would accept a mission in Europe if one were offered. Unlike his reticent posture when asked to be a candidate for Congress from 1838 to 1842, Barnard now used every means at his disposal to push his case. After asking Fillmore's aid, in a written statement to Secretary of State John M. Clayton he outlined numerous reasons why he should receive a diplomatic post. He summarized his long career of public service, the fact that he had given his time willingly and for the most part with inadequate compensation, that he had been a faithful member of the Whig Party and had the support of many leading Whigs for such an appointment. In addition, he believed such a move would aid in uniting the Whig Party in New York by demonstrating that conservatives were not being ignored. Barnard also mentioned his intellectual qualifications and noted that his failing health would be improved by a stay in Europe. He admitted that it was the first time in his life that he had ever made known "a personal desire to receive any place or position whatever, whether from the people or the government."[14]

Clayton and Taylor also received numerous letters from Albany citizens requesting Barnard's appointment. As early as March, 1849, five Albany Whigs recommended Barnard's appointment to a diplomatic post. Fellow New York conservatives Washington Hunt and John A. Collier wrote to Taylor and Clayton detailing Barnard's eminent qualifications. Hunt repeated Barnard's contention that such a move would have a beneficial effect on the party.[15]

It was becoming increasingly apparent to conservatives that they needed help from the national administration if they were to have any say in the New York party. In the fall, they lost another test of strength when nominations were made for state offices. Barnard's name was presented as a candidate for Secretary of State, but he lost by a two to one vote to Christopher Morgan, a Seward supporter.[16]

While continuing to criticize the direction in which the party was tending under the leadership of Weed and Seward, Barnard called on conservative Whigs, nevertheless, to remain Whig and not to stay away from the polls in the fall elections. He advised them to work with him in the meantime to change the direction of the party back to what he felt was its true base—a national party united under the leadership of an eminent conservative like Daniel Webster. In the November elections, however, Whigs lost half of the state offices and the Assembly. Writing to President Taylor, Fish blamed the lack of success on the fact that many Whigs had refrained from voting.[17]

During this time Barnard continued his fight for an appointment abroad. The claim was pushed hardest by his good friend Fish, who was on friendly terms with both wings of the party and tried to act as a mediator between them. Fish asked Taylor to appoint Barnard to one of the principal foreign courts, preferably Berlin, suggesting that the appointment would be expedient because it would placate conservative Whigs, and the Whigs of New York could offer Taylor substantial support only if they were not hopelessly divided.[18]

Barnard desired an early decision from the President because his name was one being advanced as a candidate for the presidency of Columbia College. When Taylor did not respond to the requests of either Fillmore, Fish, or local New York citizens, Fish contacted him once more. Again he urged the diplomatic post, pointing out its importance "to the future strength of the Whig party in New York." Fish wrote that because Sewardites were favored over conservatives for appointments, conservatives felt that they were being kept from all positions of influence and honor. He concluded on the threatening note that the result might well be that conservatives would continue to refrain from voting for Whig candidates as they had in the recent election.[19]

After prodding Taylor, Fish sought out Seward at the same time in an attempt to obtain his support for Barnard's nomination. Writing to Seward he admitted, " . . . you do not like my friend Barnard *as much as I do* . . .", but he asked Seward as a personal favor to him to use his influence to secure an appointment and repeated the arguments he had expressed to Taylor. Seward's answer to Fish was a polite but firm no. Although Seward had a great deal of respect for Barnard's intellectual qualifications, he expressed his disappointment that Barnard had not used his outstanding abilities for the good of the Whig Party. Seward believed that rewards should go to the party faithful, and he felt that Barnard had not only not been one of the trusted followers, but he had balked the party leadership at every turn.[20]

Barnard was incensed that the requests of Fillmore and Fish were apparently being ignored by President Taylor. In mid-December of 1849 he wrote a detailed analysis of conditions within the New York Whig Party to Fillmore. The party, he said, was composed of two "not very harmonious elements—the Radical, and the Conservative." Barnard noted that the "prevailing sentiment" of the party was conservative but the leaders were radicals. They controlled the press, conventions, and the patronage, but their tactics were offensive to him as well as to other conservatives. Unless their leadership was checked, Barnard predicted an end to the Constitution, the Union, law and order, and the "structure of civil society." He lashed out at radicals for bringing the party into association with "Anti-Rentism," "Fourierism," and other combinations which struck at "property and social organization." Barnard remarked that the Whigs in New York were losing the backing of 30,000 conservatives who would refrain from voting rather than support an abolition party. The Whigs would lose this large class of citizens —"the men of property, the men of education, the thinking, virtuous and religious men of the community . . . ", he continued smugly. The party would never be respectable nor strong without them. He called on Fillmore to see that conservatives received a share of the plums and urged him to attempt to change the direction of the party through a judicious use of patronage. He was sure that his appointment to a diplomatic post would demonstrate the good faith of the administration to the conservatives. While Barnard's letter revealed much about the Whig difficulties in New York, it indicated even more about his own pique at being ignored by the party leaders. Barnard did not want to admit that conservatives were a distinct minority in the party. True, in a close election their failure to support Whigs might result in a victory for the opposition, but they were never as large a group as Barnard wished.[21]

Fillmore did continue to support Barnard's claim for a diplomatic post, but he had little or no influence with Taylor. The President took his advice in the matter of appointments from Weed and Seward, not from the Vice President. Fish then went to work on Weed and a month later convinced him that Barnard's appointment should be pushed. As a personal favor to Fish, Weed set the wheels in motion by asking Secretary of State Clayton that Barnard be granted a post. Weed and Seward later visited Taylor on Barnard's behalf. As the result of such intervention Barnard was tendered the post of chargé d'affaires either at The Hague or Vienna, neither of which was a full mission. To the surprise of Weed, Seward, and especially Fish, Barnard refused. Writing angrily to Fillmore, he argued that New York was entitled to a full mission. He would accept the appointment to Vienna only if it were raised to that level. He continued, " . . . it has been deemed well enough to send me into exile . . . they [Weed, Seward, and Taylor] . . . believed that I could *be had* for a chargéship."[22] Once again Barnard refused to recognize the realities of the newer politics. He had unrealistically thought that his appointment, based solely on his qualifications, was almost a foregone conclusion. He would not come to grips with the fact that conservative influence was decreasing in both state and national politics and that conservatives were not going to receive all the spoils that they desired.

Fish was embarrassed that after all his efforts Barnard had refused the offer. He wrote to Seward to thank him for supporting Barnard's case and in turn apologized for his friend's rejection. He concluded that the difficulty arose from the fact that although Barnard was a man of great abilities, he was a desperately bad politician.[23]

In addition to confrontation over the division of the spoils, the New York Whigs came to blows over the various Compromise measures which were devised for the Mexican cession. In the winter of 1850 opposition to the Compromise was voiced in the New York legislature, and strongly free soil antislavery resolutions were endorsed to be sent to Washington. Barnard opposed the resolutions because they expressed the "ultra" views of Seward. He believed that such resolutions played into the hands of agitators and abolitionists who deliberately exaggerated the differences between the North and South. What was needed at this critical time was firm adherence to the "Constitution and the Union of this great Republic." Barnard worked behind the scenes to draw up more moderate resolutions, which were offered in the Assembly by Colonel James Monroe of New York City. Their thrust was that slavery, if let alone, would not go into the territories because nature would exclude it. Therefore, there was no need for antislavery resolutions or legislation. The Assembly did not accept these or other more moderate resolutions but instead acted favorably on the antislavery resolutions as had the Senate. These were forwarded to Washington, where the main battle over the Compromise was being waged in the Senate. Barnard reported in a confidential letter to Fillmore that the antislavery resolutions had been "forced" through the legislature even though the real sentiment of the state was "utterly opposed to them." The Whig party should not be misled by such actions but should continue its effort to stand for the Union and oppose the "ultraists" and "fanatics" of the North and South.[24] Barnard could not concede that perhaps his own assessment of the political climate in New York was inaccurate and that the state had substantial numbers of citizens with strong antislavery feelings.

During March all eyes were on Washington. On the seventh, Webster defended the Compromise in the Senate and pushed for his territorial plan. Legislation was not needed to exclude slavery since by soil and climate the territories were unsuited for it. Seward, by contrast, opposed the Compromise measures and asked for adherence to a "higher law" and regard for the moral issues involved. He called on the federal government to circumscribe the limits of slavery and to favor its ultimate extinction. President Taylor did not support the Compromise and advocated the immediate admission of California and New Mexico as free states without first requiring that they become territories. Weed and Seward supported Taylor's position; most conservative Whigs favored some form of compromise although not all supported the Compromise in its entirety. Barnard continued to favor Webster's position that legislation was not necessary to prohibit slavery.[25]

While debates on the Compromise continued, Barnard did not give up his fight for a foreign post. In spite of the fact that he had embarrassed his friend Fish and lost his initial bid, he did not consider the case closed. He continued to urge Fillmore to explain to the President what he considered to be the desperate situation among New York Whigs. He wrote to Fillmore that the state had not been treated "with common decency." Did not New York with three million citizens have one man whom the administration could appoint? Barnard could not contain his anger at being slighted: " . . . my blood boils when I see this state treated, and held up before the country, as too poor in character and talent to be entrusted with any share in the higher business of government. . . . " And then haughtily he wrote that New York had men of talent and it was not their fault that "the times, and the sway of the meanest systems of party politicians, have long held them in comparative retirement." However, Barnard was careful not to blame Fillmore for his lack of success. He placed that blame on Taylor for not distributing the patronage as he should. He then asked Fillmore to go with Seward to the President and urge a full mission. Barnard did not seem to realize that he was asking the impossible of Seward, who had already done all he would.[26]

Barnard's efforts were in vain so long as Taylor was in the White House, because Taylor continued to respond to the wishes of Weed and Seward. In July of 1850 an abrupt change occurred with the sudden death of the President. With Fillmore at the helm there would be adjustments in patronage as well as a new attitude in regard to the Compromise.

Fillmore had expressed antislavery sentiments during his political career in New York, but observers now were uncertain about his response to the Compromise. Barnard had visited with him in Washington during the debates over the Compromise measures and had the distinct impression that he favored the Compromise and would vote for it if his deciding vote became necessary.

Later he had informed Fillmore that there was substantial support in Albany for the Compromise. Much to the disappointment of Weed and Seward, Fillmore, as President, believing that it was necessary for the sake of the Union, did come out for the Compromise. With the President's support assured, the way was paved for success of the Compromise. Through the efforts of Stephen A. Douglas, the various parts of Clay's Compromise became law. Barnard was pleased with the result and concluded that the heart of the people was with Webster and Clay because of the broad antisectional views they maintained.[27] However, not all New York Whigs were happy about the passage. Seward, Weed, and Fish were opposed, in particular, to the Fugitive Slave Law and felt that it would not receive the support of the major portion of the party.

Immediately after Fillmore became President, Barnard wrote to him to offer his service and counsel. He suggested that Webster be made Secretary of State because he stood on national ground and had the "confidence of the South." He encouraged Fillmore to be President in his own right and not to follow Weed's suggestions that he simply carry out Taylor's policies. He urged him to treat the liberals in the party with consideration and kindness and tolerate their "peculiar opinions," but there should be no mistake about who should lead the party.

> I do not want to see their peculiar and ultranotions incorporated into the Whig creed and made to supercede that creed . . . nor do I want to see the Whig party—a national party—converted for their uses into an abolition or free soil, or sectional party.[28]

At the same time Barnard wrote to Webster expressing the hope that he would become Fillmore's chief adviser. He believed that Webster enjoyed the confidence of both the Northern and Southern politicians and with his counsel the Fillmore administration would be "eminently national, constitutional, and conservative." It would have the support of the Whig party and the confidence of the country.[29]

On July 12, 1850, Barnard again wrote to Fillmore advising him to use the patronage at his disposal to bring the party around to a conservative mold. He made several specific suggestions for nominations of conservatives in place of the names put forth by Taylor. He did not push his own case with Fillmore at this time but wanted Fillmore to leave no doubt in the minds of

Weed and Seward as to who was now in control and how patronage
would be distributed in New York.[30]

Weed was incensed that Fillmore might listen to Barnard, and
considering the past difficulties between Barnard and Weed it
was not surprising that Weed attempted to counter Barnard's
advice. He stingingly attacked Barnard in the Albany *Evening
Journal* for standing aloof from the masses. He lashed out at
him for doing little but "writing prosy Essays against 'isms'
and making dull speeches against 'progress.'" If Barnard's advice
were followed, the Whig Party would never be anything but
a minority faction. He called Barnard one of the "Drones of
party" who was fond of coining phrases about conservatism and
urging compromise.[31]

Fish, however, occupied a middle position and suggested to
Fillmore as he had to Taylor that appointments be used to unite
the party in New York, with each wing receiving its share. Fish
again suggested Barnard's name for a diplomatic post. At Barnard's urging Fish also wrote to Webster presenting Barnard's
name.[32]

Within a month, Barnard had his appointment to the coveted
post at Berlin. Since it was a full mission, he was elated. He
thanked Fish for his assistance and remarked that he was amused
that while most newspapers applauded the appointment, Weed
kept silent. He was pleased, he continued, at the opportunity
to go abroad in the service of his country. What he did not
admit openly, but what was evident from his statements, was
that he felt that he deserved the political plum of a diplomatic
post.

Writing to Fillmore to thank him for his appointment, Barnard
brushed aside all his own efforts for over a year to obtain the
post. Although he had humbled himself in pursuing the position,
even to the point of embarrassing his friend Fish, he still wanted
to preserve the image of having been sought. He wrote that
he was sure that Fillmore's selection of him for the Berlin mission
had been based on his qualifications and not on considerations
"connected with mere party views." Yet Barnard was the one
who had pushed his claim over and over again on the basis
of rewarding deserving conservatives.[33]

Early in September Barnard visited Washington, obtained
instructions from the State Department, and at a friendly meeting
with President Fillmore discussed the crisis through which the

country had recently passed. Both were relieved that the Compromise measures had been approved. Barnard recorded in his Diary after leaving the President that the country had been saved from "imminent danger" and that "Disunion and Faction" had been crushed.[34]

While Barnard rejoiced at his own success in securing an appointment and in his belief that the future of his country was secure, the passage of the Compromise measures brought to a head the divisions within the New York Whig Party over slavery. The real eruption came at the end of September at the Whig convention in Syracuse. Barnard, busy with preparations to go abroad, was not one of the Albany delegates but he took an interest in the proceedings and counseled conservative Whigs what course of action to take. He wanted the convention to adopt resolutions which would "show itself to be Whig, and national . . ." and to approve the Compromise measures. He was hopeful that the conservatives would control the convention and bring the "factionists" around to their point of view.[35]

The conservatives were in a minority at the convention, yet one of their men, Francis Granger, was selected chairman largely due to Weed's efforts to preserve harmony. The storm broke out when the resolutions were debated. The convention rejected conservative resolutions praising the Compromise and adopted instead those which did not endorse the Compromise but praised Seward's antislavery stand in the Senate. As a result, the conservatives, led by Granger, walked out of the convention hall. The Silver Grays, so called from Granger's graying hair, had bolted. Barnard's sympathies were clearly with the Silver Grays, and unrealistically he predicted in a private letter to Fillmore that the walkout would strengthen the party because the liberals would "now fall off from . . . [their leaders] like leaves from October trees" since the leaders had no patronage or anything else to offer. He urged Fillmore to stand by the conservatives and build a true Whig party around them. However, he met with leading conservatives Granger, Hugh Maxwell, and Hiram Ketchum and advised them to urge the Silver Grays to join the regular Whigs in support of Washington Hunt, the Whig candidate for Governor, who was a moderate and not an avowed follower of Seward.[36]

The surface unity in the New York Whig Party was only a thin veneer over the deep divisions which existed—divisions which would soon become apparent not only in the national party but in the entire country as well. Barnard wanted to believe, as did many others, that a solution had been found for the slavery question. He wanted no discussion of the moral issue involved and felt that if agitators would keep silent, the problem would subside. When he had originally requested a diplomatic mission, Barnard had mentioned as his motives improvement of health, utilization of his eminent qualifications, and encouraging party unity. From his correspondence it is also evident that an underlying factor was his gradual realization that the divisions within the party over slavery were significant and that there was little chance that the New York Whig Party would be recast in the conservative mold. In order to escape the dilemma of belonging to a state party whose leadership and direction he could not accept and of being a Whig who would not be listened to by local party leaders, he was seeking refuge in a foreign mission.

During September and into early October Barnard kept in touch with friends in the Whig Party while making his travel plans. Yet it is significant that much more of his attention was directed toward his European tour than toward the problems among the New York Whigs. He obtained letters of introduction from Edward Everett and submitted requests to Fillmore and to Webster that he be allowed the use of a naval vessel in the Mediterranean so that he might visit various ports in the region for his health. He left personal affairs in Albany in the hands of his brother-in-law, Richard DeWitt, and put his house up for rent. The family left for New York City early in October and sailed for Europe on the *Zurich* on the sixteenth of the month.[37]

19.

20.

Chapter VII

GENTLEMAN ABROAD

Twenty years had passed since Barnard had traveled to Europe. He had gone then as a grieving young man. Now he was returning with his family as a mature gentleman proud to be of service to his country. He was eager to revisit many of the European cities he had enjoyed and to reestablish ties among the intellectual and social elite. For the first few days the ship encountered rain and fog, but the remaining days of the voyage were "balmy and delicious." Barnard apparently could not get his mind off party politics, for enroute to Europe he wrote to Fish expressing his continuing concern for the Whig Party. Optimistically he predicted, however, that the Whigs would unite and elect Washington Hunt Governor. He expressed the hope that Fish would be selected U.S. Senator from New York.

The Barnards reached France on November 4, 1850, and settled down in Paris for two weeks of sightseeing before going on to Berlin by rail, with stops to visit Aix-la-Chapelle, Brussels, and Cologne. They arrived in Berlin, which would be home for the next three years, on December 3.

Soon after their arrival the Barnards rented a large apartment within a mile of the Tiergarten near the center of Berlin. They found Berlin a charming city, and Barnard especially enjoyed the many fine buildings and museums.[1]

On December 10 Barnard presented his credentials to the King of Prussia, Frederick William IV. He wrote with pride to his brother that he made his appearance in a "court dress consisting of a coat embroidered in gold and underclothes to match, with sword and chapeau.'' For the rest of the month the Barnards attended social and diplomatic functions at which they met the members of the diplomatic corps. Early in December, Barnard was introduced to Baron von Humboldt, the trusted adviser to the King, and the two men remained on friendly terms throughout Barnard's tour of duty. At a reception given later in the month Barnard met the famous historian Leopold von Ranke. Although Barnard thought himself a scholar and enjoyed that reputation at home, he did not pursue scholarly activities while in Berlin, and his relationship with Von Ranke was limited to occasional social meetings.

For their first Christmas the Barnards attended services at the English Chapel, which served as their place of worship throughout their stay in Berlin. Writing to his friend the Reverend Horatio Potter back home, Barnard remarked that he was attempting to have the church services ''Americanized'' by requesting a prayer for the President of the United States. His efforts were unsuccessful and the services remained ''. . . strongly English—so we all pray for the Queen.''[2]

At the end of the first month Barnard reported to Fillmore that he had received a very cordial reception from the royal family, which he felt indicated a feeling of ''high regard'' for the United States. He praised Fillmore's recent message to Congress, particularly the firm support which had been voiced for the Compromise measures. Barnard took heart from the fact that the Whig candidate Hunt had been elected Governor in New York, in spite of the party divisions, and continued to hope that the slavery issue could be compromised.[3]

Attending social functions continued to be a main activity of the Barnards while in Berlin. During the winter of 1851 there were frequent receptions given by Prussian royalty and members of the diplomatic corps. Barnard objected to the fact that many of these functions were held on Sundays, but he attended most of them. However, Mrs. Barnard and the daughters went to few of the Sunday events, ''not having overcome their scruples about the propriety of doings on Sunday. . . .''

Early in February the King and Queen held a reception for the diplomatic corps to which the ladies went attired in trains and the gentlemen in court dress. Barnard described the Queen's train as made of velvet, trimmed in ermine, and borne by six pages. At this reception the older Barnard daughter Cora, now in her early twenties, was presented to the King and Queen. During the remainder of the month there were numerous balls, receptions, and concerts. Barnard's letters were full of comments about these social events, indicating that he found real pleasure in this aspect of diplomatic life. The social season was repeated in much the same manner during the winter of 1852.[4]

The Barnards entertained German and other foreign diplomats formally at the Legation. More informal gatherings were held for Americans who were visiting Berlin and American students attending the university in the city. Barnard enjoyed entertaining as well as being entertained and indulged some of his more extravagant tastes while in Berlin, ordering that various varieties of Rhine wine, claret, and champagne be sent to the Legation for himself and his guests.[5]

During his years abroad Barnard depended on his good friend Hamilton Fish to attend to many personal matters at home. They wrote long newsy letters to each other and exchanged gifts. Once Barnard asked Fish to send some "decent black tea." Fish obliged with thirty pounds of tea, and also at various times he sent molasses, buckwheat, English biscuits, candy, and American crackers. He wrote that he feared that Barnard would consider him a "bore" because he wrote such long letters. He often inquired about Barnard's health, which showed some improvement during the tour abroad. Fish looked in on Barnard's Albany house, which had been rented to Governor Hunt, and advised Barnard that there had been cigar smoking in the library contrary to his stipulation of rental. Barnard enjoyed Fish's long letters, sent gifts to the Fish children, and corresponded with Mrs. Fish, too. On one occasion he teased her about the fact that she had found Senator Charles Sumner "charming." He wrote that he knew other ladies who found him so "in spite of his politics." He added: "It is an old trick of his . . . to make himself agreeable to ladies."[6]

Throughout his stay in Berlin Barnard was concerned about his personal finances. As Minister his salary was $9,000 per year, with an additional sum provided initially for travel expenses and household goods. He also was entitled to a contingent expense account for the Legation to purchase small items such as stationery, stamps, and newspapers. He did not find the amounts sufficient and wrote to Secretary of State Webster that his expenses for the first year exceeded his salary by $2,500. He estimated that he might receive $1,000 from the resale of household goods when he was ready to return but this would do little to alleviate his plight now. Even with a small family, no "expensive habits," and only a "meager show of hospitality," he would have to draw a considerable sum from his private sources. He concluded: "Some of the governments have shown what they think of the importance of the missions they maintain at Berlin by their salaries." By way of example he cited England, which paid its minister approximately $12,000.[7]

During their stay in Berlin the Barnards particularly enjoyed visits of friends from New York. One such visit took place in the summer of 1851, when their neighbors from Albany, the John V. L. Pruyns, stopped in Berlin for two weeks. The Barnards delighted in showing them the sights and entertained them at the Legation almost daily.[8]

Another of the pleasures afforded by a diplomatic post was the opportunity it gave for travel. Barnard's health always seemed to improve when he got away from his official duties. He did not feel that the months out of Berlin conflicted with his work as Minister, but he always assured the State Department in Washington that he would hasten back to his post if needed there. Shortly after the visit of the Pruyns, the Barnards toured Switzerland and parts of Germany. They visited Nuremberg, Ulm, Zurich, Geneva, Baden, Heidelberg, and Frankfort and then, by steamer, arrived in Bonn early in September. After a tour on the Rhine they traveled across Germany by rail and returned to Berlin on September 30.

Barnard's desire for extensive vacations was one of the causes of the strained relations which developed between him and the Secretary of the Legation, Theodore Fay. There were difficulties between the two men almost from the day of Barnard's arrival. Fay had been appointed interim chargé before Barnard arrived. However, with a Minister at the Legation, Fay was demoted to the rank of secretary with a consequent reduction in salary. The two men saw each other socially in Berlin, but Fay frequently refused dinner invitations to the Barnards. When Barnard went on European jaunts, more work was thrown on Fay, who continued to be paid as a secretary. Shortly after Barnard returned from the trip to Switzerland, Fay informed him that he would like to go to Italy for the winter for his health. Barnard was not receptive to the idea and recorded in his Diary that Fay's absence would "throw labor on me which I am ill able to bear." Fay did not make the trip.[9]

The Barnards embarked on another extensive tour in 1852. They left Berlin in March and traveled to Vienna. From there they continued to Rome and Naples, and late in May visited Munich. They returned to Berlin early in June. On June 10 Fay left for a vacation, and once again Barnard expressed his disapproval. The entry in his Diary read: "It is one thing for a Secretary of a Legation to be without a Minister, and another for a Minister to be without a Secretary." In the fall of that year the Barnards left again and visited Holland and Belgium before spending six weeks in Paris.[10]

After Barnard was established as Minister in Berlin, Fish wrote to ask him if he would prefer to be transferred to London in case the Minister there decided to return home. Barnard replied that he would not ask for a change in position, but if Fish wanted to speak to the President, it was acceptable to him. He hinted to Fish that he would actually prefer Paris if that post should become vacant because London would ruin him financially. The mission to London was not offered to Barnard, who later wrote to Fillmore that he would have accepted had it been but that he was quite content in Berlin. Later he confided to a friend in Albany that he was relieved not to have been transferred to London because it would have cost him $10,000 above his salary.[11]

While abroad Barnard corresponded with his family in the United States and took an interest in their well-being. He wrote to his brother Timothy that he would not cease to be concerned for his family simply because he was in a high diplomatic station. He described the political and social scene to his brother and complained about the numerous parties on Sunday. He worried about his sister Eliza after the death of her husband and sent her money from time to time.

Barnard's brother-in-law, Richard DeWitt, handled financial and business affairs in Albany for him throughout his three-year absence. Since it was necessary for Barnard to draw on his private funds to supplement his salary, it was not possible for DeWitt to invest as much of his savings as Barnard had hoped. Barnard was appalled to learn from DeWitt that taxes were eating up substantial sums of his money and asked: "Does anybody else pay as much? Or am I really the richest man in Albany!"[12]

There were no outstanding problems between the United States and Prussia during Barnard's tour of duty, and his duties as Minister were largely routine. The German Confederation, created at the Congress of Vienna in 1815, consisted of thirty-six states, plus city states, with Prussia and Austria the two dominant members. As Minister to Berlin Barnard had responsibility to the component states of the Confederation, with the exception of the Habsburg Empire. The consuls throughout the German states also came under his jurisdiction, and since there was not a full minister in Vienna, occasionally Barnard was called on to contact the Austrian government. However, most of his work consisted of protecting the rights of American citizens and reporting on conditions in Europe to the Secretary of State. Barnard was conscientious about his position when he was in Berlin and at times attempted to make more of it than was demanded. He wrote to Fish that the difficulty of the job was increased by the fact that he did not know German and had to read German documents and newspapers through interpreters. He complained that everything written in German was lengthy and obscure and so it was difficult to get a precise idea of its meaning.[13]

Barnard did not learn German while abroad and insisted on his right to use English in his communications with the Prussian government. He wrote to both Fillmore and Webster that the right of American ministers abroad to use the language of their country in official correspondence was "a thing to be firmly insisted on and maintained." The Prussian Prime Minister, Baron Manteuffel, refused to accept this point of view and asked that French, the language of diplomacy, be used; however, he would accept English if a French translation were provided. Barnard reluctantly accepted this compromise but replied to Webster that he insisted on the "principle that he be allowed to use English. . . . Each nation has the right to use its own language, in treating or communicating with others."[14]

When Barnard arrived in Europe in 1850, the political scene was similar to that when he had visited twenty years earlier. Europe had undergone a series of revolutions in 1848, and the effects were still being felt. Writing to his friend John C. Spencer in Albany, Barnard said that his first impression was that "German politics . . . [were] a puzzle to all mankind." Some politicians wanted to bring Europe back to the conditions of 1815 by installing legitimacy everywhere, eliminating constitutions, and making governments absolute. Barnard predicted, however, that if absolutism prevailed there would be an "upheaval of the masses" within twenty years. When he had visited Europe previously, he had advanced constitutional monarchy as the best choice for European governments. His observations as Minister strengthened that belief. However, he felt that conditions in Europe were not properly understood in the United States because people in his country applauded revolution in Europe. Barnard believed that widespread revolution would not only fail to establish democratic principles but would end by entrenching absolutism. He was as skeptical of revolution as a force for change as he had been twenty years before. The "truth is," he wrote in a letter to Fish, "revolution, with its present character . . . is not only powerless to promote free or liberal institutions in Europe, but hangs on the cause as a millstone and a curse."[15]

When news of the cordial reception accorded the Hungarian revolutionary Louis Kossuth in the United States reached Barnard, he wrote in his Diary disapprovingly: "His demonstrations & speeches, his appeals to the people against the Govt. and even to party, are intolerable. Yet the Senate proceeds to make a public demonstration towards him!" Barnard thought his observations on postrevolutionary European affairs might be useful to Webster and wrote to him that the response to Kossuth caused great dissatisfaction and some unfriendly feelings toward the United States in Berlin. As Minister, he promised to "meet the unfriendliness" in the best way he could and to attempt to correct the wrong opinions in regard to the character of the American government and American people. To the foreign diplomats in Berlin, he emphasized that the United States pursued a policy of neutrality and nonintervention in relation to Europe.[16]

Kossuth's American reception caused Barnard the embarrassment at diplomatic functions of being slighted by the Austrian Minister, Baron Prokesch. The Minister of the Netherlands talked to the Austrian at Barnard's request. Prokesch then explained to Barnard that personally he had no ill feelings but that circumstances compelled him to be reserved.[17]

Writing to Webster in February of 1852, Barnard said that

the reception afforded Kossuth proved that Americans were misin-
formed about European politics. Popular orators in the United
States gave the impression that there was a simple struggle going
on in Europe between absolutism and democracy, and they
advocated the overthrow of all monarchies. Barnard viewed the
democratic element in European society as ''a power capable
of doing a great deal of mischief and of causing rivers of blood
to flow'' but incapable of bringing about liberal reforms. He
asserted that before 1848 there had been a tendency toward liberal
reform, with the governments themselves often taking the
initiative. However, after the revolutionary disturbances, repres-
sion increased. The revolutionary parties, he asserted, wanted
more radical changes than the governments were willing to accept.
Barnard continued to believe that constitutional monarchy offered
the best promise for European countries but predicted that such
a governmental form would be established only if the revolutionary parties set reasonable goals.[18]

Barnard noted in a dispatch to Webster that the leaders of
the revolutionary party were distrusted and looked on with
''horror.'' The King had been able to increase his power because
most of the Prussian people felt that it was only through him
that they were secure against rebellion. Barnard declared: ''It
is the violence and manners of the ultrarevolutionary party in
Europe which makes the governments strong.'' In spite of the
fact that many desired a republic, they would settle for less because
they wanted ''law and order'' even more.[19]

Barnard did not find the entire European picture gloomy and
expressed a more favorable attitude toward Louis Napoleon. He
called Napoleon III ''a very clever man'' and felt that his building
of the Second Empire would make France strong and assure
peace in Europe.[20]

During Barnard's tenure as Minister, Prussia and Austria com-
peted for control of the smaller German states. Barnard believed
that Prussia would emerge as the stronger power but that ''ir-
reconcilable differences'' between Prussia and Austria meant that
no plan for uniting Germany was likely to develop in the near
future. In February of 1853 Prussia and Austria signed a commercial treaty that might have been the foundation for a greater
degree of détente. However, the improvement did not materialize.

Barnard's most time-consuming task as Minister was not reporting on conditions in Europe but easing the difficulties experienced by American citizens who traveled in Prussia for business or pleasure. For missionaries there was a particular problem. Unlike the United States, where religious freedom prevailed and church and state were separate, Prussia had an established church and a government intolerant of sectarian influences. In February of 1851 American Methodist missionaries were banished from the Duchy of Brunswick. Barnard interceded with the Prussian authorities on their behalf. The authorities rejected his appeal on the grounds that Prussia was able to provide for the religious wants of her own people and that missionary activities disturbed the peace.[21]

Barnard took a much bolder step when he intervened on behalf of the Baptists. The American Missionary Union engaged Prussian Baptists as missionaries within their own country. However, the Prussian authorities objected to the "irregular, noisy, and tumultuous" activities associated with the rites of baptism and refused to permit these missionaries to carry on their religious practices. Barnard could do nothing officially because those involved were Prussian subjects, but he wrote to the King as a private citizen asking for religious toleration and fair treatment. He pointed out that the missionaries were not associated with the Anabaptist sect but were "highly conservative" loyal subjects who had no intention of disrupting society. King Frederick William granted relief to some of the ministers who had been fined and suggested that the Baptists form a church organization under control of the state, which then would protect their religious activities.[22]

Barnard had to cope with other problems which developed from alleged infringement of the rights of American citizens visiting Prussia. Some German-Americans returning to their original country deliberately ignored the repressive censorship laws and restrictions on freedom of the press; other American citizens were not aware of the Prussian laws. A United States citizen, the Reverend Charles Brace, was arrested on a charge of being a revolutionary and of carrying incendiary pamphlets. Brace had met Barnard while in Berlin as part of his European tour. Barnard vouched for the traveler as a scholar and clergyman and gave his personal assurance that Brace was not involved in revolutionary activities. The joint efforts of Barnard and of the American chargé in the area, Charles McCurdy, effected Brace's release.[23]

Many Americans were detained in Prussia because the authorities found irregularities in their passports. Prussia would accept only passports issued by the State Department and validated at a Prussian consulate. A Mr. Henry de Sandt appealed for Barnard's help when he was not allowed to continue his travels because of an allegedly invalid passport. Sandt, who was not actually a United States citizen although he had stated his intention of becoming one, had obtained his passport from the Mayor of St. Louis instead of the State Department. Because the passport was invalid and Sandt was not a citizen, Barnard would go no further than to advise him to tell the Prussian authorities the truth. Barnard wrote Webster requesting more vigilant supervision of passport issuance to prevent similar incidents. He made the same request to Edward Everett when he became Secretary of State following Webster's death. Everett assured Barnard that the Department would do what it could to prevent Americans from embarking on travels with invalid passports.[24]

By far the most common problem with which Barnard had to deal was that of former Prussian subjects returning from the United States to their homeland for business or pleasure. Some of these persons had become naturalized United States citizens, while others had simply stated their intent to become citizens. Prussia required military service of its young men and certificates of emigration granting permission to leave the country. Many who returned to Prussia briefly without having complied with these requirements when they left were arrested, fined, or seized for military service. With neither the United States nor Prussia recognizing the right of expatriation, Barnard's task of defense was difficult. It was further complicated by the fact that Prussia feared revolutionary activities and sometimes seized persons suspected of spreading revolutionary ideas on the pretext that they had emigrated without a certificate. Barnard determined to become the defender of any naturalized American citizens who were apprehended. He tended to view the matter as one calling for personal diplomacy on his part. He would contact the appropriate Prussian representative of the German state involved and ask for assistance in having the fine rescinded or the detained traveler released. Barnard, in addition, asked Manteuffel (in his capacity as Foreign Minister) to relax the rigid application of Prussian law in such cases and allow naturalized American citizens to return to Prussia without harassment. Barnard had some success with his personal diplomacy and was able to secure release or reduced fines in many cases. However, the official policy of the Prussian government was not changed.[25]

Barnard was incensed when he learned that his efforts on behalf of these citizens were not fairly reported in the press in the United States. The New York *Tribune* of July 14, 1852, carried an article which suggested that the rights of American citizens in Germany were not protected. Barnard wrote to Fish and asked his assistance in giving the facts to the public. He outlined for him several cases in which he had intervened successfully and indicated that the previous ministers in Berlin had not concerned themselves with such matters. He asked Fish to insert an article in the Albany *Evening Journal* to the effect that "The American minister at Berlin is performing his proper duty to his country, and to his countrymen, including naturalized as well as native citizens." Barnard admitted difficulties from German fear of democratic propaganda from the United States and from the practice of keeping careful watch on all those returning to Germany. He asserted, however, that some who asked for help were not bona fide American citizens.

Fish secured a vindication of Barnard in the *National Intelligencer,* but Barnard was not satisfied with the response of Weed in the Albany *Evening Journal*. Weed informed his readers that international law was wholly on the side of the United States. Barnard felt that such a statement was misleading because Prussian law did not permit emigration without the consent of the sovereign. Yet, in spite of this, Barnard had made repeated efforts to secure more lenient treatment for naturalized American citizens returning to Prussia for short stays.[26]

Barnard failed to obtain State Department support of his actions on behalf of former Prussians returning to their homeland. Replying to him in January of 1853, Secretary of State Everett drew a distinction between native-born and naturalized citizens. Until a foreign-born individual was naturalized, he was subject to the laws of his native land. Furthermore, it was the opinion of the President that if one violated the Prussian law by emigrating without a certificate or without having performed military service and then returned, the United States could not protect him.[27]

Barnard replied to Everett that he would follow official policy, but he continued to put his own interpretation on the official opinion and to carry on his personal diplomacy. Conrad Schmidt, an American citizen born in Hanover, was arrested because he had not served in the military. Barnard contacted the Prussian authorities, stated the policy of the State Department, but at the same time attempted to persuade them that the law should be relaxed. Writing to Manteuffel, he again expressed the official policy but asked for leniency. Barnard's intervention secured the release of Schmidt.[28]

Barnard enjoyed this personal diplomacy and continued to pursue it for the rest of his months abroad. He wrote to one of the American consuls: "I never fail to make what effort I can for the relief of our naturalized citizens, who are seized in this country for soldiers." He craved recognition at home for performing above and beyond his regular duties, and his intervention on behalf of religious toleration and the rights of American citizens was an attempt to secure it.[29]

At the time Barnard asked Secretary Everett for his official opinion, an extradition treaty between the United States and Prussia was before the United States Senate. The treaty, proclaimed in June, 1853, provided for extraditing those charged with the crimes of murder, arson, robbery, forgery, and embezzlement. Article III provided that neither of the contracting parties would be bound to deliver up its own citizens. A naturalization treaty between the United States and the North German Confederation was not concluded until 1868.[30]

Barnard's duties abroad left him time to keep up with events at home, and he was informed about politics in the United States through the regular receipt of newspapers, visits from friends, and his extensive correspondence with Fish. As early as the winter of 1851 Barnard was concerned about who might be the next Whig candidate for President. Although Fillmore and Webster were the most prominent of the Whigs, he did not believe either of them had a chance of attaining the Presidency. His desire continued to be to "see a sound and thorough going Union man elected to the Presidency."[31]

In February of 1851 Fish was a leading contender for one of the Senate seats from New York, and Barnard, of course, was eager that he receive the party nomination. However, he confided in a letter to his friend John C. Spencer in Albany that if Fish lost his bid, it would be partially his own fault for attempting to appease both wings of the party. Barnard thought that Fish would do better to side once and for all with the conservatives and build a base of support around them. Although he realized that Weed still controlled the party in New York, he continued to oppose his leadership. He wrote to Spencer: "Can I be mistaken in saying, that the alliance of Seward and Weed cannot fail to be fatal to any candidate for the Presidency, be he who he may?" It would be a "fatal error," he continued, if Fillmore were to pursue a policy "calculated to restore the Seward clique. . . ."

The party division due to contests for party leadership and differences over slavery did create a stumbling block to Fish's success. Fish wrote to Barnard during the winter of 1851 while he was being considered for the Senatorship that for some Whigs he seemed to lean too much to Seward and for others not enough.[32]

Barnard was distressed that Fish had not become the undisputed leader of the party in New York. With Fish as the leader, Barnard felt that the Whig Party would not be sectional. He could not bear the thought of Fish being associated with the Weed-Seward wing and warned Fish to be wary of Weed's efforts on his behalf. Writing of Weed and his associates he poured forth his venom:

> What a pitiful occupation seems that of the demagogue in the United States—the Abolitionist, the Anti-Renter, the Socialist! Pigmies, pigmies, all, and mishapen [sic] and deformed at that!

Barnard felt that Weed wanted to use Fish in an effort to consolidate the party around Seward. He predicted that Seward could "never be more than the head or leader of a faction; he [could] never lead a great national party." Barnard urged Fish again and again to assume the responsibility for uniting the New York Whigs. He believed that Fish had great popularity and prestige which could be used to heal party divisions. His lengthy letter was full of praise for Fish for being liberal and conservative at the same time. Fish was neither an "ultra" liberal nor an "ultra" conservative. Barnard preferred the middle road but had trouble defining what it should be. He concluded rather ambiguously: "There is no difficulty in being conservative, and at the same time progressive. Such in truth is the real doctrine of the Whig party, rightly understood." He counseled Fish that he could not unite the two sections of the party by standing between them. Large numbers of Whigs who "repudiated and abhorred" the leadership of Weed and Seward would mistrust Fish if he associated with them. With Fish at the head, not associated with Weed, however, the "ultraists" on both sides would yield.[33]

In March Fish was elected to the Senate, and Barnard was elated. However, he continued to lament the fact that party divisions remained, and again he called on Fish to become the undisputed leader of the party in New York. He suggested that "a broad platform of principles, at once conservative and liberal, and national will do it" [unite the party].[34]

In an exchange of letters after Fish had been selected Senator, Barnard voiced optimism about the future of the New York Whig Party, but Fish was less optimistic, lamenting that agitation over the Fugitive Slave Law had created "jealousies and animosities" among Whigs, and he feared that there was little hope for permanent harmony. "The prospect is gloomy . . .", he concluded.[35]

That personal feuds continued to be a barrier to party harmony was shown by an incident when Weed visited Europe during the winter of 1851–52. Barnard, happening to be in Rome at the same time as Weed, left his calling card at Weed's hotel. Weed in turn left his card, but neither made a serious attempt to see the other. On the day Weed was to leave the city, Barnard was at Weed's hotel visiting a friend from Albany and met Weed by accident. Barnard opened the conversation with, "I was afraid you would leave Rome without my seeing you." Weed replied that he had intended to do so. Unwilling to face the realities of practical politics and ignoring the inconveniences he had caused Weed over his appointment as Minister, Barnard found it difficult to understand Weed's attitude. Barnard later wrote to Fish that he could not believe that Weed would bring political animosities abroad with him.[36]

The incident was only one of many indicators which showed that Whig ranks were far from united. Conservatives had hoped that Fillmore would provide the leadership to unite the party nationally, as well as within New York, but Fillmore had been able to do neither. Whig attentions were now directed to the presidential contest in the fall of 1852. Webster, Scott, and Fillmore were the main contenders for the nomination. Scott was acceptable to Seward, while conservatives supported either Fillmore or Webster. Prior to the Whig convention Weed attempted to cast doubt on Fillmore's candidacy by printing a statement, which he attributed to Barnard, to the effect that had Fillmore had the opportunity while Vice President, he would have voted against the Compromise measures. Fillmore issued a denial and was distressed because such a stand on his part would be inconsistent with his support of the Compromise after he became President. He contacted Fish, who in turn wrote Barnard in an attempt to clear up the matter. Barnard had talked with Fillmore about the Compromise measures while they were under consideration and had reported the conversation to Fish, who in turn had talked to Weed. However, Barnard was certain that he had disclosed no information on how Fillmore would vote, because Fillmore at the time of the conversation had not made up his mind. Fish conveyed Barnard's account to Weed, who, in November of 1852, announced in the *Evening Journal* that his earlier information had been incorrect. Although Barnard felt he was vindicated, and Fillmore said he entertained no ill feelings toward him, the incident showed how easily misunderstandings developed between the two wings of the party.[37]

Discussing the incident in a letter to Fish, Weed shed some additional light on the continuing feud between the patrician and the dictator. He wrote:

> I do not dislike Mr. Barnard although we differ so widely in political sentiment and sympathy. My difficulty is that he puts *me* so low down in his scale of political morality. . . .

Weed admitted that Barnard was perhaps right in his assessment of him as a politician because he often found it necessary to do many things to elect good men to office, ''. . . even as good men as he [Barnard] is.'' However, he was distressed that Barnard could not appreciate the realities of running for and staying in office.[38]

It was evident that Fillmore commanded no position of leadership among Whigs, since General Winfield Scott received the nomination at the convention. Barnard wrote a letter of consolation to Webster and reported that he would support Scott reluctantly. However, writing to fellow conservative Abbott Lawrence, he stated that he did not believe Scott could be elected.[39]

The Democrat Franklin Pierce was victorious in November, and the result of the election coupled with the death of Clay

during the summer and of Webster in the fall seemed to some
to symbolize the end of the Whig Party. Fish shared his disappointment with Barnard, writing: "None of us appreciated the extent
to which the Whig party was disorganized—perhaps I might say
demoralized." But in January of 1853 Barnard wrote to Fish:
"My hopes for the Whig party—I mean for a National and Conservative party—always rise with its defeat. . . . I have still an
abiding confidence in the conservative feeling and principles of
the American people." However, by May Barnard was no longer
as optimistic. In a letter to Fish he said he felt a "grieving
disrelish for party politics; and especially for such party politics
as exist with us, where it is difficult to know who is who and
what is what." Although disenchanted, he did not feel any less
attachment to principles or any "less repugnance to shallow
demagogues and dishonest politicians" and repeated that there
was something in the name Whig which "still stirs my sympathies
and my affections." However, he would withhold his support
from a party tied to "isms" and a party which did not have
"enough of sound constitutional and political principle."[40]

The Democratic victory in November of 1852 had personal
as well as political significance for Barnard. With the opposition
party in control, his tour of duty would soon be over. Shortly
after the election he asked Fish to find out the wishes of the
administration about "replacing Whig diplomats in general, and
myself in particular." He planned to resign his post but hoped
that he would be allowed a reasonable time to depart. He preferred
to remain until the fall of 1853 and would have no objection
to staying until the spring of 1854, especially since his health
had shown considerable improvement.

In February of 1853 Barnard wrote a cordial letter to President-
elect Pierce congratulating him and indicating his desire to leave
his post in the fall. In March he wrote a letter addressed to
the Secretary of State making the same request.[41]

Fish contacted Secretary of State William L. Marcy to see
what plans the administration entertained for foreign diplomats
and learned that the fall of 1853 would be an acceptable date
for Barnard's departure.[42]

Fish so informed Barnard, but Barnard received no official
word from the administration, much to his displeasure. He wrote

to Fish that he would continue to take care of the necessary business of the Legation, of course, but he would not confine himself "rigidly" to his post. He made plans to go to London and Paris where "the ladies need[ed] to make some purchases" before returning home. He concluded:

> . . . this business of dividing the "spoils of victory" among the harmonious elements of the Democratic party is a mighty labor, and until the herd of hungry cattle are stalled, nothing else will be thought of.[43]

As Barnard's tour of duty wound down, his thoughts were more and more on returning home. Throughout May and June he sent detailed instructions to his brother-in-law for remodeling his house in Albany. He asked to have the three sofas and eighteen chairs in the two parlors reupholstered and new curtains made for the parlors and dining room. In addition, he wanted a balcony along the front of the house, a skylight for the roof, a wine room and storage room on the third floor, and the chandeliers connected for gas. After outlining these extensive plans, he added that he did not want *"too much expense."* DeWitt took care of most of the arrangements with the exception of selecting the new carpet, which was left to Mrs. Fish. (Not all the work was completed when the family returned, but before winter they were settled comfortably in their home.)

Early in June Barnard at Berlin received notice from Washington of the appointment of his successor, Peter Vroom. He was incensed because at the same time he was informed that he could vacate his post whenever it was convenient and leave the Legation in the hands of the American consul in Berlin until Vroom arrived. There was no American consul in Berlin, and Barnard wrote to DeWitt: ". . . the Administration has gone on, blundering."[44]

Barnard informed Marcy that he planned to leave in September and hoped that his successor would arrive by that time.[45] As planned, the family traveled to London and Paris and then sailed for home. They made plans to stay with the Fish family when they arrived in New York City, and Barnard wrote dryly to Fish that he hoped that they would arrive on time and that he would tell the ship captain "what the Senator expects his vessel to do—so he must look out!" The Barnards reached New York at the end of October and after a ten days' visit returned to Albany. The three years abroad had been gratifying. Barnard's health had improved; he had enjoyed the aristocratic manner in which he had lived and the extensive travel. He also felt that he had served his country well, especially in his efforts in support of religious toleration within Prussia and in his attempts to safeguard the rights of American citizens. [46]

21.

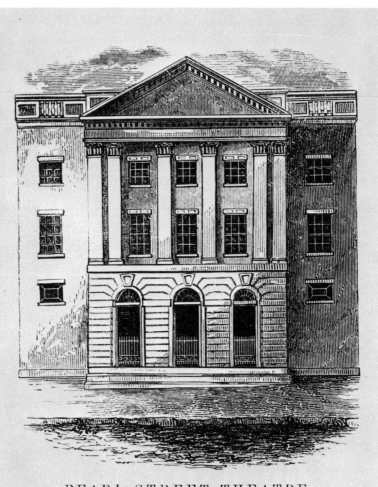

PEARL STREET THEATRE.
1825.

22.

Chapter VIII

THE DANGER OF DISUNION

The years remaining to him following his return from Berlin Barnard spent in Albany. Poor health forced him into semiretirement, but occasionally he represented wealthy clients in the Albany area, and he prepared two legal arguments which were published in pamphlet form. He continued to be involved in civic and political affairs, but most of the time he lived the life of a gentleman of leisure enjoying fine food and wines and good friends. He played billiards and whist for recreation and went for drives in the country. Much of his time was spent in reading and writing as it had been throughout his life. He showed a dry sense of humor in his later years, and the Albany *Evening Journal* quoted him as saying about a proposition to outlaw alcoholic beverages that: "The use of pleasant beverages will cease universally, just when there shall be no more savory viands, and all men shall live on dried peas and acorns."[1]

Political associates remained important to Barnard, and he wrote frequently to his old friend Fish, as well as to Robert Winthrop and Millard Fillmore. In addition, he corresponded with many nonpolitical friends in the Albany area and throughout the East. He continued to be concerned about his brothers and sisters as well. He remained a devoted father and husband, and on his twenty-fifth wedding anniversary he wrote his wife a tender and affectionate letter running to six pages. He felt especially blessed that so much good fortune had come to them and that they would now enjoy their last years together. He asked his wife to forgive his faults, praised her fine qualities, and repeated his belief that each person should live for a purpose. He revealed his own dissatisfaction at not having achieved widespread acceptance of his political views but concluded with his certainty that the principles by which he had lived were ones to command her respect and love.[2]

Barnard continued to enjoy a reputation as a lecturer, and during the last six years of his life received over a dozen invitations to address literary and educational societies. Most of these requests he declined for health reasons, but he did make at least one speech. Shortly after returning from Europe, in an address entitled *Political Aspects and Prospects in Europe,* Barnard reaffirmed the ideas that he had formed while abroad. He told his Albany audience that the revolutionary parties in Europe hindered the progress of liberal reform because their demands for immediate changes were excessive. He believed that absolutism in Europe should be controlled through constitutional means and that republican institutions would come to Europe if changes were made slowly and gradually, ''not by a word and a blow. . . .''[3]

After his address on Europe, Barnard did not accept invitations to speak, even rejecting a request from the New York Bar Association to prepare a discourse on the life of his friend, the New York jurist John C. Spencer.

Ill health continued to plague him, and his correspondence until the end of his life reveals an obsession with his physical condition. He wrote to a friend that his health had been ''dreadful'' for the first six months of 1855 and that his ''three keepers'' [Mrs. Barnard and the daughters] watched him carefully. However, he added: ''. . . no jailers were ever more humane!'' In the fall of that year he informed his brother that it was ''not probable that I shall set my foot outside my door . . . till next May. Fortunately, I bear imprisonment well.'' Three years later he confided to his brother that he was ''utterly unable'' to write or to engage in any useful activity.[4]

Perhaps the concern with his health accounted for the fact that Barnard engaged in an extensive correspondence with friends, including personal letters which often did not touch on politics. He showed particular concern for those who lost loved ones and wrote to a recent widow: ''Who knows better than I do, what it is to have the heart cleft in twain in the early season of its brightest summer day?'' He continued, ''. . . who knows better that such a wound is long in healing—that such a wound never heals!'' He counseled her that time was a great "soother" and that the best way to handle the problem was to depend on her friends and her church. In a final paragraph of the letter he elaborated on his own personal philosophy—a philosophy which had changed little since he was a young man. He continued to believe that Providence largely determined man's destiny but that all men should ". . . do no wrong to any [and] . . . lead honest and devout lives in simplicity.'' He praised those who kept their minds active because such activity enabled them to better understand God's plan.[5]

In other letters to friends Barnard revealed that beneath a severe and cultivated exterior there had developed a man of warmth and feeling. Now in his late fifties Barnard particularly enjoyed visits and letters from women friends and wrote on one occasion that he sometimes received a "double benefit from ladies [sic] letters. . . . I fancy as I hold them that I can feel a warmth in them that is not expressed & can read unwritten, mystic lines between the written ones.'' To a friend who had visited him in sickness, he wrote that she had made the "fleeting days" so "precious" that when she visited him again, he would "think that spring has come in the midst of winter.'' Writing to another friend, Mrs. Thayer, he asked her to see that her husband forgave "any impertinent interest I take.''[6]

In spite of his poor health Barnard took a lively interest in politics, particularly the fate of the Whig Party. He was prevented from assuming a leadership role, but he tried to influence party affairs through his extensive correspondence. In order to write comfortably Barnard had designed a special library chair. It had a writing table attached to the side and could be used as either a chair or lounge. It was placed in his library in front of the window through which he could see the river. He wrote as long as he could and then "slept from sheer exhaustion about half the time.''[7]

When Barnard had returned to New York in the winter of 1853-1854, the New York Whig Party was disorganized and continued to be rent by divisions. The split in 1850 had a lasting effect, and the party had lost the New York governorship in 1852. In the same year the conservative wing suffered an additional blow when Fillmore failed to receive the Whig nomination for President. In 1853 the party rallied briefly and won several state offices, but its success was due more to splits within the Democratic Party than to strengths within the Whig. Although both wings supported internal improvements, they could agree on little else. Conservatives and the Weed wing continued to differ over slavery and the general direction for the party. To complicate matters the party had to formulate a position in response to the Kansas-Nebraska bill, which came before Congress in 1854. The intent of the bill was to erase the Missouri Compromise line prohibiting slavery in the Louisiana territory and establish in its place the principle of popular sovereignty. Northern Whigs had been steadfast supporters of the Missouri Compromise, and Whigs throughout New York now voiced disapproval of the Kansas-Nebraska bill.

Barnard had supported the Missouri Compromise but was not able to participate in party debates on the Kansas-Nebraska bill. In March of 1854 on a visit to Washington he had contracted a severe case of bronchitis. It was thought for a time that he would not survive, but he was able to return to Albany, where his health remained precarious throughout the spring. He then spent the entire summer trying to build up his strength. He wrote to Fish that he had not lost interest in politics in spite of the fact that he was not able to take an active part.[8]

In the meantime New York Whigs divided in their responses to the Kansas-Nebraska Act after its passage. While both wings of the party condemned the act, the conservative opposition was of a much milder variety. The difference became apparent at the Whig state convention which met in September of 1854. Myron Clark, an antislavery and temperance man, was nominated for Governor and the convention resolutions indicated a determination to oppose any further extension of slavery. The resolutions were too strongly antislavery for the conservatives, who objected in particular to the hostility at the Fugitive Slave Law. However, the conservatives had little impact on the convention proceedings. Barnard, who did not attend the convention, approved neither the Clark nomination nor the resolutions.[9]

Francis Granger, the conservative Whig who had led the bolters out of the party in 1850, now wanted to bring the conservatives or old-line Whigs together once again. The situation he faced was that although conservatives opposed the Nebraska act, they did not support the antislavery stance of the Whig Party in New York. They also rejected any fusion of the Whigs and another party for the purpose of forming a sectional party. In other words, they would oppose any attempt to unite the Whigs with the newly formed Republican Party. Barnard was contacted to see if he would participate in an effort to reestablish a conservative coalition. He declined to become actively involved for reasons of health, but indicated that he would support such an effort. Writing to Granger, he said: "I belong to no party that is not national in its politics."[10]

Granger's attempt to reconstruct the Whig party on a Silver Gray basis was derided by the Albany *Evening Journal,* which called it an attempt to form a "select" party for the benefit of "some respectable old gentlemen."[11]

The conservative effort amounted to little and had no significant impact on the election. Clark won the Governor's chair for the Weed wing of the party; his narrow victory was due largely to splits within the Democratic Party, but it also revealed how little influence the conservatives retained. Barnard was unhappy about the result and wrote to Mrs. Fish that he did "not recognize him [Clark] as the chief and representative of any Whig party to which I ever did, or ever can belong."[12] He was reluctant to face the fact that conservatives had no chance of controlling the New York Whig Party and that their influence was steadily declining.

After the 1854 elections, parties were in a confused state not only in New York but throughout the country—a condition which continued well into 1855 and beyond. The Whigs had been under strain since the Compromise of 1850. Conscience and Cotton Whigs formed an uneasy alliance, with each trying to pull the party in its direction. Some Whigs who were strongly antislavery joined the Republican Party when it came into being in 1854. Some found temporary refuge in the American Party—a party built largely on opposition to the foreign born.

Barnard, like most Whigs, was perplexed about the condition of the parties. He would not support the Whig party as it was organized in New York and wrote to Fish in December, 1854:

I am an individual Whig, but where is my party? . . . What calls itself the Whig party now in this State, with Clark at its head,

is just no Whig party at all. It has not one element of nationality
in its whole composition; and it is the mere broken remnant of
a party at that.

Barnard deplored the state of things because he felt "as much
necessity for a national and conservative Whig party now as
ever before." However, he concluded sadly: "The Whig party
is nowhere; and there . . . it is likely to stay."[13] For the next
five years his main effort was directed toward reconstructing
the Whig party along national lines in accord with the ideas
of Webster and Clay. Since he wanted the Whigs to back off
from their identification with abolition, most of his written statements on directions for the Whig party centered on slavery, and
he showed little concern for issues like the tariff or internal
improvements. He was and would remain until his death a full-
blown Cotton Whig.

As the outlook for a satisfactory political resolution to the
slavery question worsened, Barnard became more depressed and
noted to Fish in the summer of 1855 that the conditions in the
country were ominous. He feared that the nation might be headed
toward disunion. He placed the blame on the demagogues and
fanatics in the North who were stirring up antislavery sentiment.
A truly national Whig Party could avert such a crisis—a crisis
which he attributed to a shift in Northern thinking. Many Northerners now felt that it was not enough to forbid slavery in the
territories, but that attention should also be given to its eradication
in the South. He accused the abolitionists who had left the Whigs
to join the Republican Party of attempting to sway other Northerners in a sectional direction. He predicted, "A Presidential
election conducted by sectional parties, with nothing but slave
issues between them . . . would be the last election ever held
in the Union."[14]

While despairing for the Whigs and entertaining still the hope
of a national party, there was, however, a slight shift in Barnard's
thinking at this time. He indicated that until a Whig party was
reconstructed along national lines, he would support other movements which would fight against sectionalism. While for the
next five years he never lost hope for a reunification of the
Whigs, at the same time he supported both Know-Nothing and
Democratic candidates in an attempt to defeat Republicans
because he regarded the Republican as the most sectional and
least national of the parties.

Barnard charged the Republicans with attempting to array the North against the South by putting the "negro question" above all others. When Barnard had called on men to recognize slaves as human beings in Congress in 1828, there was no love for slavery in his remarks. By 1855, however, he no longer viewed slavery as an evil institution; now he praised its benevolent aspects. In a revealing letter to Fish he wrote that there were model plantations in South Carolina and Georgia where "slavery shows to advantage." Although he approved of the institution, he did not sanction the actions of Southern filibusters in attempting to annex more territory in order to increase the area of slavery. He advised that the best course was to sidestep the Negro question altogether and reestablish a party along national lines. Nothing could "resist the march & power of a conservative & national party." He feared, however, that men were not taking the threats of disunion seriously. "Disunion stalks abroad in the midday sun, and on all sides men take off their hats & salute it with respect as it passes along in the public streets!"[15]

In the fall of 1855 Weed was successful in uniting his wing of the Whig Party with the Republican Party in New York. Since the Weed wing represented the largest number of Whigs, the absorption of it into the Republican ranks dealt a death blow to the New York Whig Party as a political entity. Conservatives were once again faced with a decision. Those who did not join the Republicans had to determine whether to support the Know-Nothings or attempt to reorganize the Whig Party without its antislavery element. James Brooks, publisher of the New York *Express* and a conservative Whig, along with the conservative Amos Hadley turned to Barnard for advice. Still longing for a national party, he suggested that a reorganization of the Whig Party be attempted.[16]

In a letter to Brooks, which was circulated among Whigs, Barnard advised conservatives that under no circumstances should they support the Republican Party because it appealed to fanaticism and was hostile to half the Union. What he termed the national Whig position could be used as a basis for reorganization since it looked to compromise but at the same time went far enough in the direction of antislavery. He reminded his readers that Northern Whigs had defended the Missouri Compromise and had never been willing to see slavery carried to territories already free or to see any territory conquered or annexed for the purpose of widening the area of slavery. He felt that the Republicans had moved far beyond what he considered sound Whig doctrine in regard to slavery in declaring that all territory was to be free. He interpreted Republican doctrine to hold that slavery could not exist anywhere except "maybe" in the southern states. The Republicans, he warned, were embarked on a holy crusade. Barnard favored an equitable division of territory and did not want the South shut out of its share. The party which would have his support would be a national party which maintained federal authority over the entire nation with a regard to harmony of interests. Ignoring Whig differences over the years and looking back to a bygone era, he declared that Whigs of old desired a united country with its people one in language, in heart, and in habits, manners, and customs. Whigs "stood by old landmarks when nothing was to be gained by change, and they adopted change when that promised to lead to improvement & . . . true progress." For any question arising out of slavery the Constitution should be the guide because there was nothing that could not be settled by constitutional means. What was needed to counter the Republican Party was a national party embracing men of national sentiments from the Democratic and Know-Nothing parties as well as the Whig; ". . . a party national in all things will not fail," he concluded.[17]

In October of 1855 under the prodding of R. Anthon West, editor of the New York *Commercial Advertiser,* and James Brooks, a group of approximately ninety old-line or conservative Whigs met in New York City. Though Barnard was not one of the Albany delegates, the address and resolutions criticizing the Republicans reflected his thinking. Those attending indicated, as Barnard had earlier, that a reorganization of the Whig Party should be attempted.[18]

Weed, through the pages of the Albany *Evening Journal,* opposed any efforts to resurrect the Whig Party. Barnard was labeled "a somewhat frosty politician," an "old fogey," and a "fossil." His letter to James Brooks in which he had outlined reasons for not voting with the Republicans was subjected to a severe attack. Since all men professed love for the Union and Constitution, Barnard's attachment to the Union and repeated statements to that effect were called irrelevant issues.

On November 1 the *Evening Journal* carried a scathing indictment of Barnard's position. The article, signed "Senex," began with a personal attack on Barnard: "You do not pretend that you have ever been wrong yourself—in opinion or action." The writer pointed out that it was inconsistent for Barnard to argue on the one hand that Whigs had never wanted to see slavery carried to territory already free or to see territory annexed to increase the area of slavery, and on the other to assail the Republican platform for the principle that "all territory of the United States is to be declared free territory by Congress." The Whigs who had left the party to join the Republicans were the strongest opponents of slavery, and the writer sensed that what angered Barnard most was that antislavery had become the most prominent plank of the Republican Party. Barnard was assailed for refusing to admit that there was strong antislavery sentiment throughout the state. He was accused of shifting his own views from a position mildly antislavery to a pro-Southern stance. Now he had the nerve to call the proslavery South national and the North sectional.[19]

The attack did not cause Barnard to back off from his views, and late in October he and Washington Hunt, Luther Bradish, and Francis Granger met in Albany and agreed to make an all-out effort to defeat Republican candidates. The Albany *Evening Journal* termed Barnard and his political friends "a drag and a hindrance upon desirable progress."[20]

As election day approached in November of 1855, however, no reunited Whig party had been formed, and the left-over Whigs had failed to nominate a ticket. Although Barnard continued to oppose fusion with either the Know-Nothings or the Republicans, he advised the remnants of the Whig Party to vote for Know-Nothing candidates, at the same time cautioning them not to become part of the American Party organization. When the votes were counted, the Know-Nothings had secured a plurality of votes in New York, receiving, no doubt, those of many Whigs.[21]

Barnard began now to look forward to the 1856 presidential election. He and James A. Hamilton, the eldest son of Alexander Hamilton and a leading conservative, undertook a lengthy correspondence mapping election strategy. Barnard thought that a Whig national convention was out of the question. Looking back to the older paternalistic and elitist party structure, he wanted a score of leading Whigs to decide on a candidate and present his name to the public. Because of his continued poor health Barnard could not assume an active role in such an effort, but he agreed to contact many of the leading conservatives through correspondence in an effort to gain their support.

While wanting desperately to see the Whigs regroup, Barnard knew that the task would be difficult if not impossible. Therefore, be believed the remnants of the party should take as their primary goal the defeat of all Republican candidates. In a letter to his brother he indicated that "National Whigs" who had always held "American sentiments in just & Constitutional moderation" should support a candidate who would also be acceptable to the American Party. He suggested John Bell as a possible Presidential nominee with Robert Winthrop or Hamilton Fish for Vice President, or a slate with Fillmore for President and Bell or John J. Crittenden as Vice President. Discussing possible nominees in a letter to Fish, he wrote: "This is my opinion—old fogey as I am."[22]

Upon reflection, Barnard decided that Fillmore would be the best choice since he would have greater national appeal. He then directed all his efforts to gaining support for Fillmore. He wanted no platform or discussion of the slavery issue: "The Constitution is a Platform broad enough."[23]

In his attempt to revitalize the party, Barnard corresponded with Whigs outside of New York. Men whom he felt should be part of the effort included Fish in Washington, Rufus Choate, Robert Winthrop, and Edward Everett of Massachusetts, Edward Bates of Missouri, John P. Kennedy of Maryland, R. W. Thompson of Indiana, John Bell of Tennessee, and John J. Crittenden of Kentucky. Within New York, fellow conservatives R. Anthon West, Luther Bradish, Francis Granger, James A. Hamilton, Washington Hunt, Samuel Ruggles, and George Law were active along with Barnard in searching for direction for the party.[24]

Early in December, Hamilton urged a group of old school Whigs to meet in January of 1856 in New York for the purpose of naming a candidate. Barnard supported this idea although he indicated that he would not be able to attend. Not all conservative Whigs agreed, however. West wrote to Fish that it "would never do for a private meeting of even such [prominent] Whigs to make a Presidential nomination because the rank and file would resent it." However, he did not oppose a meeting to discuss future plans and to decide on the propriety of calling a convention. In addition, he suggested that Barnard publish an article stating reasons why Whigs should not unite with Know-Nothings.[25]

Barnard followed West's suggestion and prepared an address. He attempted to dilute the Americanism of the Know-Nothings by saying that the Whigs were older "Americans" than the "Americans." He asserted that Whigs had always cautioned against the too ready admission of foreigners to all the political privileges of American citizenship; therefore, it would be logical for the Know-Nothings to merge with the Whigs. Although he would not have the Whigs unite with the Know-Nothings, a merger the other way around would be acceptable. Above all, the Whigs must not emphasize slavery when they reorganized. The founding fathers, he argued, had differed widely in their opinions about slavery, but this did not prevent them from writing a Constitution and forming a government. Now the Constitution should be taken as a guide for all questions arising out of the slavery controversy.[26]

The preparation of the address sapped Barnard's frail health, and once again he was forced to remain behind the scenes in the effort to reestablish the party. He continued to protest against attempts to merge the Whigs who had not gone with the Republicans with the Know-Nothings but approved the idea of the American Party endorsing the Whig candidate. This should not prove difficult as "the great body of genuine Whigs have a strong odor of Americanism about them."[27]

Fish observed the efforts to reorganize the Whig Party, nationally and in New York, from his Senate post in Washington. Like Barnard, he felt that the ranks of the Whigs had dwindled significantly, so he did not recommend calling a national convention. However, he did not agree with Barnard that a few Whigs make a nomination. In line with West, he feared such action would be open to the "charge of dictation." Unlike Barnard, Fish wanted not even so much as a tenuous association with the Know-Nothings because of their "objectionable creed." He informed Barnard that under no circumstances would he support former President Fillmore.[28]

In spite of the opposition from his close friend Fish, Barnard continued his efforts to get the remaining Whigs to name Fillmore. He tried to convince Fish that the Whigs had to compromise with the Know-Nothings in order to survive. He felt that the party would retain its own identity, to an extent, by nominating Fillmore before the Know-Nothings did. He told Fish that the Whigs should endeavor to bring Americans into a reconstituted

Whig Party by avowing "such Americanism as the Constitution itself teaches." Barnard then made the same suggestion—that Whigs should support Fillmore as Whigs—to Hamilton, Granger, and West.[29]

While the correspondence among the Whigs continued, plans went ahead for a meeting in New York. In January a handful of the more prominent conservatives, not including Barnard, met to discuss directions. West, Hamilton, and Ruggles were armed with letters from Whigs in and around New York who could not attend. Based on this correspondence and the consensus of those attending the meeting, it was agreed that a national convention would not be desirable. But Hamilton was instructed to issue a call for another meeting in New York to discuss further courses of action. Those attending the meeting determined that a circular should be composed and sent to Whigs throughout the Union recommending that Whigs remain independent of other parties.[30]

In a letter to Fish after the meeting West discussed the fact that conservatives were unable to settle on a leader. The letter also shed light on the reasons why conservatives remained a distinct minority within the Whig Party. Because they refused to accept the newer politics, they found themselves powerless, and in their frustration they were able to develop neither strong leadership nor an effective organization. It was not because of his poor health alone that Barnard did not want to become the undisputed leader of the conservatives but also because, on his own admission, he had "no skill in political management." West would not support Barnard for the same reasons that he would not support Hamilton. He felt that both men were too far removed from the people. West wrote to Fish that Hamilton was "too much like your friend Mr. Barnard who clearly sees what is ethically pure, right and good and honestly acts up to it, but scarcely makes allowance for the popular dimness of vision and obliquity of purpose which must be taken into account." In addition to the leadership problem, West was concerned that the dwindling numbers of conservative Whigs were not enough upon which to build a new party. In a perceptive statement he commented to Fish: "Are we deceiving ourselves in supposing that we have a respectable nucleus for an organization?"[31]

While the remnants of the Whigs were still searching for direction, Fillmore received the nomination of the American Party in February. Barnard was distressed that the Whigs had not acted decisively on his suggestion to name Fillmore first, but he felt that many conservatives would now support him. Barnard seemed to be blind to reality when he wrote to Fish after the nomination that the Whigs should not be disheartened but should meet and prepare an address. He was pleased when West and Hamilton indicated that they would support Fillmore, but he tried once again, unsuccessfully, to enlist the support of Fish.[32]

While urging the remnants of the Whig Party to support Fillmore, Barnard continued to plead for a national party of conservatives which should divert attention from the issues raised by slavery. His position was strengthened when Charles Sumner was assaulted in the Senate chambers by Preston Brooks. Barnard, who had defended the right of free speech and petition while in Congress, felt that the attack was an "outrage" but that Sumner's speech was uncalled for and "unworthy" of a gentleman and Senator. He deplored such events as serving to increase the agitation over slavery.[33]

During the summer Barnard was well enough to visit New York and Boston and in both places talked to "several leading Whigs." He was discouraged to learn that many would not vote for Fillmore because they felt he had no chance of success.[34] In the meantime, the Democrats adopted a platform which endorsed popular sovereignty and selected James Buchanan as their nominee, while the Republicans denounced the Kansas-Nebraska Act and chose John C. Fremont.

Still believing that Fillmore had wide national appeal in spite of some indications to the contrary, Barnard now undertook a major effort in support of his election. For publication in newspapers and in pamphlet form, he prepared a letter to Hamilton which he hoped would clarify the issues and gain voter support for Fillmore, especially from doubting conservatives. He reported to Fillmore that more than half of the South would support him because Southerners realized that "fanatical slavery men" in connection with unscrupulous Democrats in the North had carried things too far.[35]

In the lengthy letter, which was widely distributed during the summer, Barnard attempted to bring together many of the views he had expressed previously to his friends in private correspondence. The theme was familiar—Fillmore should be elected as the only means of assuring the safety of the Union. He praised the Compromise measures of 1850 as "measures of complete pacification" and decried the Kansas-Nebraska Act because it had upset an "arrangement for slavery" which "had existed for an entire generation without one loud complaint from any quarter." Refusing to admit that issues raised by slavery required constant attention and new responses, he launched into an attack on the Democrats. They had brought Texas into the Union in order to extend slave territory. The Kansas-Nebraska Act, he charged, was a Democratic measure which had been unnecessary as slavery would not go into Kansas because of the soil and climate. His letter continued: "Southern men, who care nothing for Democracy, wanted to extend the area of slavery. Northern Democrats, who care less than nothing for Slavery, wanted to perpetuate their hold on place and power." The Democrats, he asserted, were a sectional party whose object was to extend slavery; hence no true conservative could support such a party.

He opposed the Republicans even more vehemently than the Democrats. The Republican Party stood on "no national ground" but was a Northern party waging a war of "implacable hate against the entire South." He accused the Republicans of harboring a "deadly hostility to slave-holding." He defended slavery and the right of the Southern states to maintain it. Slavery, he asserted, was protected by the Constitution, and the Republican Party by opposing slavery was repudiating the Constitution. Barnard predicted that the election of the Republican ticket would mean a triumph of free states over slave states and the result would be disunion. The only wise choice, therefore, was a vote for Fillmore "as the only sure means of silencing sectional agitation, restoring harmony, and giving the country once more rest under the Constitution and the Union." He hoped that the remnants of the Whig Party strengthened with an "army of conservatives from other political organizations" could thus control the election.[36]

Barnard sent copies of his pamphlet to twenty-five friends, including Fish, who remained unconvinced. Fellow conservative Luther Bradish supported the views, and along with Barnard expressed the hope that Whigs would make a substantial showing in the election in support of Fillmore.[37]

In August of 1856 a group of the remaining New York Whigs, including Barnard's friends Granger, Hamilton, Hunt, and West, met in Albany and endorsed Fillmore. This demonstration of support by the 800 old-line Whigs who attended the meeting pleased Barnard, who was unable to attend. He was hopeful that the response shown at the meeting was indicative of wide support for Fillmore, because he believed that a Fillmore victory could be used as a basis for a revitalized Whig coalition. However, in September Barnard received a sharp political blow when both Fish and Hamilton voiced their determination to vote for Fremont. Fish decided that the resolutions of the Republican Party were in accord with the Declaration of Independence and the Constitution, and he supported Republican resistance to the spread of slavery to the territories. Hamilton agreed with Fish partly because he felt that Fillmore had no chance of winning. The ensuing correspondence between Fish and Hamilton was published in pamphlet form—a move which decidedly decreased the effect of Barnard's previously published pamphlet. When Barnard wrote to Fish expressing regret over his decision, he told his old friend that he had feared it for some time. Writing to Hamilton, Barnard expressed anger and hurt and noted that Hamilton's decision to vote for Fremont made him "really ill."[38]

Still there were some conservatives in addition to Barnard who supported Fillmore, and a Fillmore meeting was held at Union Square in New York, September 12. Again Barnard did not attend. The same month a Whig national convention in Baltimore, national in name only, voiced support for Fillmore. However, the *Tribune* stated the case with accuracy: "There is no such thing alive as a National Whig Party."[39]

The slow death of the Whig Party began in 1850 with differences over the Compromise. It was hastened by the Kansas-Nebraska Act. The party existed only as a shadow in 1856, and even the old Whigs no longer held out much hope that they could ever again constitute a significant political force. It was with a heavy heart that Barnard witnessed the end of the Whig Party when the election results were recorded in November. The victory was with the Democrats, but the Republicans had scored an impressive triumph for a new party. Fillmore made a poor showing, obtaining only 874,000 popular and eight electoral votes.[40] The wide national appeal which Barnard had predicted had not materialized.

For almost a year after the election Barnard was politically inactive. He invited Fillmore to dinner when the former President visited Albany, continued to correspond with Fish, and enjoyed a visit from Edward Everett in March of 1857, but these associations were based on long friendships. Barnard went to Newport for the summer, where his health improved momentarily. However, when he returned to Albany in the fall, he was ill again. He participated in the political scene only as an observer and wrote to Fish, who had gone abroad after concluding his term in the Senate, "I am still 'fossil' enough to call myself a Whig." Unrealistically, he hoped yet to see the Whigs rally.[41]

Barnard still longed for a national conservative party on the model of the old Whig Party, but now he was not very optimistic. Writing to Washington Hunt, he said sadly but with some spirit still, ". . . the times are out of joint" and "you and I and some others may have to set them right. . . ."[42]

The times were difficult. A depression that struck the country in 1857 resulted in lower agricultural prices and widespread distress. At the same time the controversy over slavery was heightened by the war in Kansas, the Lecompton Constitution, and the Dred Scott decision. Barnard blamed the Democrats for the conditions in the country and was particularly critical of Buchanan for supporting the proslavery forces in Kansas and thus keeping alive Northern agitation just as it might have subsided. Barnard also expressed regret over Buchanan's failure to put an end to the filibustering efforts of certain Southerners. He wrote to Fish in the winter of 1858 expressing again the need for a Union party: ". . . a very large majority of the slave-holding population do and will adhere to uphold the Union. When things come to the worse, they will be found on the side of a Union party."

By May a major shift had occurred in Barnard's thinking and he was no longer as critical of the Democrats. He called on conservatives to support Democrats rather than Republicans, whom he continued to label "a mere party of fanaticism." However, he was worried because the number of disunionists in the South and in Congress was growing. He charged that many Southerners wanted to create "a great confederacy where slave labor [was] to be the leading feature not only in their political economy, but in the frame of their social system. . . ." He could never condone such a policy because it would exacerbate tensions and hasten the end of the Union. Neither did he approve of the Dred Scott decision. He felt that the court had exceeded its power and that the result would only be more agitation.[43]

Barnard again returned to Newport for the summer of 1858. He regretted that he could not be active in political affairs but accepted the fact reluctantly that his period of usefulness was probably over. Sadly, he wrote to Fish: "I have only two seasons; the winter in which I hybernate [sic], & the summer in which I vegetate." His days were spent resting, visiting, dining with friends, and going for rides. In spite of their political differences, the friendship between Barnard and Fish remained close. They continued to correspond with each other about political as well as personal matters. Barnard wrote to Fish in August that he saw little prospect for a rebirth of a national party in the near future and now definitely preferred the Democratic Party because it had "some odor of nationality about it."[44]

That fall Barnard received still another blow when the conservative New York *Commercial Advertiser* came out for the Republican Party. He now stood almost alone as first Fish, then Hamilton, and now West joined the Republican camp. These defections coupled with Seward's "irrepressible conflict" speech were almost too much for him to bear. "What a country! What a prospect!" he wrote to Washington Hunt.[45] His depression deepened when New York went Republican in the midterm elections.

In January of 1859 Hiram Ketchum initiated another attempt to unite conservatives. He wanted to reestablish a national party based on the principles of Clay and Webster. Again Barnard did not participate in the New York meeting, but he approved the effort, though he expected little to come from it. He now hoped and predicted that the Democratic Party would score a victory in 1860.[46]

Nevertheless, Hiram Ketchum as well as the conservative J. Phillips Phoenix continued to seek Barnard's opinion about the course conservatives should pursue. Replying to them in February of 1859 he wrote: "I am still a Whig." While he would like to see the party revived, he would take no part in such efforts. If it were impossible to weld the remnants of the Whig Party into a viable force, he advised that they should take as their prime duty that of seeing that Republicans were defeated.[47] Although Barnard repeatedly called himself a man of principle and a steadfast Whig, he had moved from a position of flirting with Know-Nothings to that of actively advocating a Democratic victory. His hatred of Weed and Seward and the Republicans was so deep that he would now join forces with his former opponents, the Democrats, in an attempt to assure a Republican defeat. Barnard never admitted that there were inconsistencies in his position because he felt that he remained true to Whig principles while the party had changed.

Throughout the summer of 1859 Barnard took no part in party affairs, but visited Newport, Lebanon, and Saratoga Springs for reasons of health.

In the fall he returned briefly to legal activity. He had been inactive at the bar since 1857, when he had prepared an argument defending property rights in the Trinity Church case. In the winter of 1859-1860 he prepared an elaborate argument for the Albany Bridge case, working each day as long as his strength permitted. Writing to Fish he commented: "I would give all my old clothes & part of the new if I could go to Washington to present the argument." Since the 1840's there had been support for the construction of a bridge at Albany across the Hudson, but the proposal was fought by the owners of ferry boats and of boats in the coasting trade and by some local citizens. In 1856, after the New York legislature had authorized construction of the bridge, a suit in opposition was initiated by some boat owners who had secured permits from Congress to operate in the coasting trade, which extended to internal rivers. Barnard argued in support of the state's power to construct the bridge just as it had power to construct roads and canals. The first part of his argument was in accord with his lifelong support of state as well as national internal improvements. However, in the second part of the argument, in which he dealt with the relationship between federal and state power, there was a decided change. During his years in Congress, he had supported national internal improvements, tariffs, and a bank and had championed the supremacy of federal power while allowing states control over their domestic institutions. Now he called for curtailing national power and for a limitation of the interstate commerce power of the federal government. States, he argued, were sovereign over their waters. Barnard used the second argument because he now feared that any extension of federal power would set a dangerous precedent for an attack on slavery.[48] He had come to believe that the Union could be saved only by deemphasizing its nationality and upholding the power of the states.

The shift in emphasis reflected in the Albany Bridge case

did not mean, however, that Barnard would not support legitimate Union meetings, because he still believed in the principles of balance and compromise. During the winter of 1859-1860, after the raid at Harper's Ferry, meetings were called in many Northern cities, including New York, Boston, and Albany to voice support for the Union. When such a meeting was called in Albany, he was sympathetic although he indicated that he could not attend. He wrote pathetically to Fish: "I am a prisoner & recluse for so much of my time." However, on request, he did agree to prepare the resolutions. Although he favored Democratic candidates, in his draft he cast some of the blame for the crisis in the country on the Democratic Party. Since the Albany meeting was composed largely of Democrats, the unfavorable references were deleted before presentation. Barnard then refused to allow the watered-down resolutions to be presented in his name. He felt that the public had a right to know all relevant information and did not approve of using Union meetings as facades for the Democratic Party. However, he continued to favor Democratic candidates over Republicans.

Writing to Fish about the incident involving the resolutions, Barnard looked to the future of his country with great misgivings, and noted that it would be an easy thing to dissolve the Union. There existed a feeling in the South that the government, due to the intermeddling of the North, had "failed to offer . . . security for property, person & life." If this feeling were intensified, the South would "rush upon dissolution." Angrily, he continued: "There is madness at the North. . . . A great & *dominant* party . . . teaches: 'It is the natural duty of the slave to kill his master, & all who restrain him of his freedom. . . .' "[49]

In February Barnard's health was again precarious, and he declined to address a Union meeting in Albany. However, in his letter of refusal, he outlined his reasons for believing that the Democratic Party was less dangerous to the country than the Republican. He regretted that passions were running high in both the North and South but advised that the country would be safer "under the rule of the Democratic party" because the Democrats retained national characteristics and national prestige. He favored the movement to bring national Union men together in council if saving the Union was their primary purpose.[50]

However, when the Democrats met in convention in April, they could agree neither on a candidate nor a platform. The Southern Democrats wanted the party to sanction federal protection of slavery in the territories, whereas the Northern Democrats stood by popular sovereignty. The convention subsequently adjourned and convened again in June in Baltimore, at which time the Southerners walked out. The remaining Democrats nominated Stephen A. Douglas, and the Southern Democrats later nominated John C. Breckinridge. At the Republican convention in May, Abraham Lincoln received the nomination on a platform which opposed the expansion of slavery while supporting a high tariff and internal improvements. Conservatives who could support none of the above candidates combined to form the Constitutional Union Party and nominated John Bell and Edward Everett. Their platform was simply the Constitution and the Union. The Albany *Evening Journal* termed the party an "effort to galvanize the venerable bones of the Whig party."[51]

Although Barnard had been calling for support of Democratic candidates, he had professed nationalism and looked to the Constitution and the Union for solutions to problems in the country throughout his political career. Now he backed off from support of Democrats and advocated the Constitutional Union ticket. He continued to heap scorn upon the Republicans and was quoted in the New York *Times* in July as saying:

> If there are any old Whigs who can find reasons for desiring the success of the sectional party calling itself "Republican" which they could not find four years ago, I am not one of them. My objections to that party are stronger every hour it exists.[52]

To elaborate upon his position Barnard prepared during the summer of 1860 what was to be his last political tract. The pamphlet was published and circulated throughout the country under the titles: *The Dangers of Disunion, Truths for the Voters,* and *Truths for the Times.* It had one theme: all efforts must be made to assure the defeat of the Republican Party because disunion would follow its success.

Few of the ideas were new, and once again, as he had in his published letter to James Hamilton recommending the election of Fillmore, Barnard outlined thoughts he had held over the past six years. His remarks clearly demonstrated his evolution from mild antislavery to that of antiabolition. He now charged the

Republicans not only with wanting to abolish slavery but criticized them for believing in the ". . . natural and equal right of the African race in this country, to be free, and to be admitted to . . . citizenship." He deplored the Republican attempt to view the Declaration of Independence as a "kind of original bill of rights securing personal and political freedom to every human being within the United States." Barnard did not look to the Declaration for answers to slavery but only to the Constitution. The Constitution, he argued, recognized and protected slavery. Viewing slaves as property, he wrote that slaves "were no more citizens . . . than if they had been still in Africa." He would not recognize "the African race . . . as citizens or as having any rights of equality or liberty in the country. . . ." He called Seward and Lincoln the "most ultra abolitionists; they are identical with . . . Garrison, Phillips and Cheever. . . ." Their only object was to marshal Northern states against Southern. "The temper of its [the Republican Party's] loyalty to the Union is exhibited in the torrents of vituperation and abuse which it pours out on the South. . . ." The Republican antislavery administration would be "purely" Northern and sectional. "Confusion, bloodshed and anarchy are the least that can be expected. . . ."

Barnard conceded there were large numbers of disunionists in the South waiting for an opportunity to secede. The election of a Republican president would provide the excuse. Voters could prevent disunion by supporting Bell and Everett and "the Constitution, the Union, and the enforcement of the Law."[53]

The Albany *Evening Journal,* which supported the Republican Party, attacked the pamphlet, but it received laudatory praise in the *Argus,* the Democratic paper. The *Argus* was pleased at the verbal blow at the Republicans, and Barnard was now hailed for his efforts to prevent disunion and assure peace.[54]

Shortly before the election Barnard wrote to Fish of his fears of the outcome in spite of all his efforts on behalf of the Union. He called it a "trembling age" and confessed that the effort to defeat Lincoln might fail.

Barnard supported the Bell-Everett effort in New York; it was spearheaded by his friend Washington Hunt, aided by fellow conservatives James Brooks, William Duer, and Hiram Ketchum. In an attempt to defeat Lincoln, the Bell-Everett men met with the Democratic leaders and agreed to split the electoral votes in New York. There would be eighteen Douglas electors, ten for Bell, and seven for Breckinridge. However, the fusion ticket failed, and Lincoln carried New York with 362,646 votes to 312,510 for the fusion ticket headed by Douglas. Thus Lincoln received the state's thirty-five electoral votes.[55]

During the months following the election, Barnard's health worsened, and in January of 1861 he wrote one of his last letters to Fish. He felt that "wreck and ruin" were "close upon us," and he advised Fish to use his influence within the Republican Party to save the Union. Still hoping for compromise, he urged that a line separating slave and free territory be drawn on the analogy of the Missouri Compromise; as a possible solution, he suggested that two "monster states" be created in the territories—one Northern and one Southern. He desired that the North "treat the Slave States as having equal rights with the Free states in the Union, in all that concerns their domestic affairs. . . ." He believed that if Fish and other conservatives within the Republican ranks were to take "a bold stand in favor of equitable division of the territories," bloodshed could be prevented. Fearing war but desperately hoping it could be avoided, he added that under the Constitution the government had the power "to *suppress* insurrection," but when states banded together and revolted against the government, refusing to render it obedience, it was not a case "to be treated as insurrection." He concluded: "Almost any sacrifice should be made to avoid a collision of arms."[56]

For the next few months Barnard watched events with deep apprehension. Early in April his condition began to decline rapidly, and sadly he witnessed the beginning of the war which would tear the country apart. Death came at the age of sixty-four on the morning of April 24th at his home in Albany.[57] It was ironic that on the day of his death the newspaper headlines and almost all the articles were devoted to coverage of the war—a war which Barnard feared but predicted. His death received scant notice among the war news, and few remembered his warning.

23.

24.

Chapter IX

A MAN OF PRINCIPLE

Two months after Barnard's death, his friend Edward Everett, who had known him since 1827, delivered a eulogy before the Massachusetts Historical Society. Barnard had been elected an honorary member of the society after writing his discourse on the life of Stephen Van Rensselaer. Everett's stirring eulogy praised Barnard as a statesman, jurist, accomplished scholar, and enlightened patriot. Yet with his death the memory of this reserved, respectable gentlemen faded from the minds of most of his countrymen. Influenced by the classical education of his youth, his legal training, and his stern and orthodox Christian upbringing, Barnard's ideas had been shaped in an earlier period and had proved unrealistic and impractical in an age of increasing social tension. As the years passed, Barnard became more conservative in response to the quickening pace of social change.

Barnard's conservatism was grounded in a belief in determinism, and a faith in progress through slow evolutionary change. Since there was an overall plan for the universe, few changes were needed and reform efforts were, therefore, useless. This outlook governed his idea of the good society. He supported the positive liberal state for the purposes of fostering economic and educational opportunity. However, unlike many Whigs, he never made peace with the general reform sentiment. He opposed the Anti-Masonic and antirent movements, and he fought bitterly against the antislavery stand of the Whig and Republican parties. This strain of personal conservatism which he advocated with his pen, his voice, and through a lifetime of political activity was at variance with the dominant ethos of the age. Yet he grappled with the issues of prison reform, temperance, sectarian religion, race, women's rights, and dissent in a time of war. If his solutions were not widely accepted, at least he addressed many of the problems society faced. He articulated his ideas in such a way that they had meaning to patrician gentlemen like himself, helping them to realize that they were not alone in rejecting what they felt to be the radical trend toward reform associated with the Age of Jackson.[1]

If Barnard was consistent in his personal conservatism, he showed less consistency in his stand on slavery and the appropriate division between federal and state power. He was a steadfast nationalist during his years in Congress, pushing for extended federal power in all areas except slavery. But somehow he seemed to sense, as early as his first term in Congress, that his nationalism would cause him problems, and he took pains again and again to reassure the South that centralization of power and legislation for a tariff, a bank, and internal improvements meant no threat to slavery. Yet he must have known that the threat was there. If federal power could impose a tariff or build a road, why could it not restrict slavery extension or even attack the institution itself? As slavery became the central issue in the country in the late forties, Barnard shifted his position. Although he had never been an abolitionist, in the late 1820's he had called on men to recognize slaves as human beings. But from 1849 to the end of his life Barnard made the move from a position which had respect for the rights of humanity of the slave to one whose concern was for the rights of property in slaves. As it became apparent that the balance of slave and free states might be upset, he asked for federal protection for slavery. He had moved from mild antislavery to antiabolition and from a nationalistic stance to favoring the upholding of state power.

Barnard's vehement response to slavery was based not only on his personal conservatism but also on his belief that discussion of the issue and unfavorable action in regard to it would mean the end of the Union. The slave issue was a decisive factor in his estrangement from both the Whig and Republican parties. He might have accepted the Republican planks on the tariff and internal improvements, but Republicanism to him became synonymous with the radical antislavery position of Seward. He refused to follow the majority of the Whigs into the Republican Party and essentially remained a Whig long after that party had faded into oblivion. With many in the North, he entertained feelings of Negrophobia and could not support the sectional party which he felt would be sympathetic to Negro rights. Finally, he fell back on a plea for adherence to the Union and Constitution—an idea which no one rejected but a plea which offered no solution.

A second factor which alienated Barnard from the majority of Whigs was his belief in the necessity for an elitist governing class. He refused to accommodate himself to the political realities of the nineteenth century and rejected both the Democratic and Whig acceptance of mass politics. He clung to the older idea of paternalistic and patrician politics. In Barnard's view gentlemen did not seek office but stood for election. The elite with a stake in society should make the decisions for that society. The more he saw this class ignored in political affairs, the more he tried to convince the society around him that such leadership was essential. It was the conservative class who was best equipped to determine what changes, if any, should be made in the organization of society. His patrician view caused his growing frustration with the leadership of Weed, as Weed worked to rid the Whig Party of its aristocratic image. Barnard's hatred of the Republicans and his flirtations with the Democrats in his last years owed much to his personal animosity toward Weed and Seward and the politics of the common man which they advocated. His constant battle with the party leaders and his pressure to try to remake the party in his own image contributed to the dissension within the Whig Party, and, along with the slavery issue, hastened the day when the party would cease to exist as a political entity. The Whig coalition in New York, always precarious, could never entirely rid itself of the prodding of its conservative element. Although the conservatives were a minority and did not control the party, their efforts, spearheaded by Barnard and his colleagues, contributed to the aura of conservatism which, in the eyes of many, was associated with the Whigs. Had Barnard been able to accommodate himself to the newer politics, he might have aided in bridging the gap between the liberal and conservative wings. Instead his continuous pressure on Weed and his unbending determination to have the Whigs be the party of the elite fanned the fires of dissent and contributed to the death of the party he professed to love. It was ironic that the more successful Weed was in welding together a viable coalition, the more critical Barnard became of him. He did not want Weed to succeed because if he did, there might never again be a party of national conservatism devoted to compromise in which there was a prominent place for respectable aristocratic gentlemen like himself.

Barnard's dilemma was that of a conservative caught up in sweeping social change. He straddled the old and the new of the age of egalitarianism. Although Barnard was alienated from the mainstream of thought and action, his ideas had a tempering effect and caused more careful consideration of the predominant reform ideas than there might otherwise have been. Moreover, he appreciated the severe strains which operated throughout the society and correctly predicted the war which followed. Neither the conservatism which he embraced nor the patrician in politics which he represented died with him. Each has remained a significant part of American thought and life.

25.

NOTES

The following abbreviations are used in the Notes and Bibliography:

BHS   Buffalo Historical Society
LC   Library of Congress
MaHS   Massachusetts Historical Society
NYHS   New York Historical Society
NYPL   New York Public Library
NYSHA   New York State Historical Association
NYSL   New York State Library
PaHS   Historical Society of Pennsylvania

References may be abbreviated in the Notes; for full citations consult the Bibliography.

CHAPTER I

1. Barnard to Ebenezer Barnard, August 20, 1826, Barnard Family Papers, LC; Barnard to John M. Clayton, June 5, 1849, Clayton Papers, LC.

2. "Barnard Family Geneology," Barnard Family Papers, LC; Barnard to Samuel R. Betty, August 19, 1844, Barnard Papers, NYSL. Contemporary accounts of Barnard's life include: "Life and Public Services of the Honorable Daniel Dewey Barnard, LLD," *American Whig Review,* VII (May, 1848), 521–532; Everett, *Orations and Speeches,* IV, 339–344; Everett, *Eulogy of Barnard.* The other children were Harriet (1787), Timothy Jr. (1789), Eliza (1804), and E. Henry (1808).

3. Barnard to Ebenezer Barnard, March 7, 1814, Barnard Family Papers, LC; Chester and Williams, *Courts and Lawyers of New York,* III, 1239; Peck, *History of Rochester and Monroe County,* I, 403–404; W. H. McIntosh, *History of Monroe County,* 260–264.

4. *General Catalog of the Officers, Graduates and Non-graduates of Williams College,* 56; Barnard to Betty, August 19, 1844, Barnard Papers, NYSL.

5. Peck, *History of the City of Rochester,* I, 114, II, 27, 368–369; McKelvey, *Rochester, the Water-Power City,* 72–74; Stanton, *Random Recollections,* 35. Records of business and legal activity may be found in the Barnard Family Papers, LC.

6. Barnard to Ebenezer Barnard, July 22, 1819, Barnard Family Papers, LC.

7. Albany *Evening Journal,* April 24, 1861; McAdam, *History of the Bench and Bar of New York,* I, 255; Albany *Argus,* April 27, 1826; Munsell, *Collections on the History of Albany,* II, 83; Barnard to Thurlow Weed, February 17, 1825, Weed Papers, University of Rochester; Harriet A. Weed, *Life of Thurlow Weed,* I, 207–208.

8. Barnard to Ebenezer Barnard, August 20, 1826, to E. Henry Barnard, March 8, 1829, both, Barnard Family Papers, LC; Livingston, *The Livingstons of Livingston Manor,* 230; Rochester *Telegraph,* July 26, 1825; "Livingston Family Geneology," in the possession of Dr. James Livingston of Scotia, N.Y.

9. Rochester *Daily Advertiser,* October 25, November 3, 10, 11, 15, 1826; Albany *Argus,* November 13, 14, December 6, 1826, March 30, 1827; Barnard to Ebenezer Barnard, August 20, 1826, Barnard Family Papers, LC. The vote according to the *Argus* was:

	Barnard	Pomeroy
Monroe	2701	2259
Livingston	1598	1668
	4299	3927

10. Charles Francis Adams, *Memoirs of John Quincy Adams,* X, 321, 371–372; Everett, *Eulogy; Register of Debates,* 20th Congress, 1st sess. (March 28, 1828), 2047.

11. *Register of Debates* (January 4, February 7, 1828), 899, 1468–1478; *American Whig Review,* 522.

12. There are numerous accounts of the tariff. See, for example: Hammond, *History of Political Parties in the State of New York,* II, 256–257; Taussig, *The Tariff History of the United States,* 82–92; Dangerfield, *The Awakening of American Nationalism,* 267–287; Garraty, *Silas Wright,* 50–74. Barnard's role was not a major one but can be examined in the *Register of Debates,* 20th Congress, 1st sess. (March 4, 17, 28, April 9, 10, 11, 1828), 1727–1749, 1924–1935, 2038, 2268–2273, 2289, 2307. Accounts can also be found in the *Niles Weekly Register* and Albany *Argus* for the same period.

13. *Niles Weekly Register,* March 27, April 26, 28, 1828; *Register of Debates* (April 16, 21, 22, May 15, 1828), 2313, 2381, 2385, 2696.

14. *Register of Debates* (February 9, 19, March 3, 1829), 322–339, 360, 386–391.

15. Barnard to E. Henry Barnard, March 8, 1829, Barnard Family Papers, LC; Barnard to Valentine Nutter, January 18, 1828, February

9, 1829, Barnard Papers, NYHS. Over twenty years later Barnard still wrote of his grief at Sarah's death; see, Barnard to Rev. Kip, December 20, 1852, Barnard Papers, NYSL.

16. Barnard to Valentine Nutter, May 25, 1829, February 22, 1830, Barnard Papers, NYHS; Barnard to Luther Bradish, April 4, 1828, Bradish Papers, NYHS.

17. The most complete account of the Anti-Masonic movement is found in McCarthy, "The Anti-Masonic Party." Other works which deal with the incident include: D. Alexander, *A Political History of the State of New York;* Van Deusen, *Thurlow Weed;* Weed (ed.), *Autobiography,* I; Cross, *The Burned-Over District.*

18. *Trial of James Lackey,* 1–24; Barnard to Edwin Croswell, June 10, 1830, reprinted in Rochester *Republican,* June 22, 1830; *Anti-Masonic Enquirer,* October 28, 1828; Weed, *Autobiography,* I, 232–233, 274–276, 283–284; *American Whig Review,* 523–524; Albany *Evening Journal,* July 9, 1830.

19. Rochester *Daily Advertiser,* June 30, 1828; Weed, *Autobiography,* I, 242, 253–256, 300–301, 360; Van Deusen, *Weed,* 45–47; McCarthy, "Anti-Masonic Party," 373–375; Albany *Argus,* July 4, 28, October 10, 11, 1827; *Anti-Masonic Enquirer,* February 19, June 17, July 29, August 12, September 2, 1828. Weed would move to Albany in 1830 and have Anti-Masonic backing for establishing the Albany *Evening Journal.*

20. Rochester *Daily Advertiser,* July 18, 1828; *American Whig Review,* 523–525; Edward Everett to Barnard, July 20, 1828, Peltz Collection (a private collection of Barnard papers in possession of Mrs. John DeWitt Peltz of New York City, hereafter cited as Peltz Collection); Weed, *Autobiography,* I, 302; *Anti-Masonic Enquirer,* August 12, September 30, 1828; Albany *Argus,* October 25, 1828.

21. *Anti-Masonic Enquirer,* October 28, 1828.

22. *Great Republican Meeting in Rochester,* pamphlet (Rochester: 1827?); McKelvey, *Rochester,* 159.

23. Albany *Argus,* November 10, 13, 15, 17, 18, 24, 27, 1828; Rochester *Daily Advertiser,* November 24, 1828; *Anti-Masonic Enquirer,* November 18, 1828. Results were:

	Monroe County	Livingston County
Jackson candidate Gardiner	2989	1215
Anti-Masonic T. Childs	4229	2292
Adams man D. Barnard	678	449

CHAPTER II

1. Rochester *Republican,* March 9, July 5, 13, 1830; Barnard to Valentine Nutter, February 22, 1830, Barnard Papers, NYHS; Albany *Argus,* October 14, November 4, 8, 11, 15, 1830; *Anti-Masonic Enquirer,* October 19, 26, November 16, 1830; Francis Granger to Barnard, November 6, 1830, Peltz Collection; Barnard to Luther

Bradish, November 9, 1830, Bradish Papers, NYHS. The other National Republicans were John Patterson and Emanuel Case.

2. Barnard to Jared Sparks, November 5, 1830, Sparks Papers, MaHS; Barnard to Sparks, January 20, 1831, Sparks Papers, Harvard University Library; Sparks to Barnard, November 19, 1830, Peltz Collection. One of the letters of introduction was to General Lafayette.

3. Albany *Evening Journal,* December 3, 1830; Rochester *Republican,* December 14, 1830.

4. Letters I–XLII, December 20, 1830–May 23, 1831, reprinted in Rochester *Republican,* March, 1831–October, 1831. The following account of his European trip is based largely on these letters.

5. Barnard to Sparks, January 20, 1831, Sparks Papers, Harvard University Library.

6. Rochester *Republican,* July 11, 1831.

7. Albany *Evening Journal,* June 3, 4, July 29, 1831; C. Van Cortland to Barnard, February 24, 1832, Peltz Collection.

8. *National Republican,* February 21, 1832.

9. Albany *Evening Journal,* July 28, 31, 1832; Barnard, *Speech, 1832.*

10. Albany *Evening Journal,* October 23, 26, 1832; *National Republican,* November 5, 1832.

11. Albany *Evening Journal,* November 15, 21, 1832. Monroe County supported Anti-Masonic candidates and Jackson lost there.

12. Seward, *Autobiography of William H. Seward,* 220; "Barnard Family Geneology," Barnard Family Papers, LC.

13. Reynolds, *Hudson-Mohawk Genealogical and Family Memoirs;* Scrapbook, Peltz Collection; Worth, *Random Recollections of Albany,* 46; Will of Dudley Walsh, Surrogate Court, Albany County.

14. Albany *Evening Journal,* February 3, 1834; Munsell, *Collections on the History of Albany,* II, 83.

15. Munsell, *Annals of Albany,* X, 398; Weise, *History of Albany,* 472; *Gazetteer of the State of New York* (1860), 159–167; *New York Annual Register* (1833), 46; Rowley, "The Irish Aristocracy of Albany," 275–304.

16. Savell, *The Governor's Mansion in Albany,* 10; Barnard to Richard DeWitt, March 24, 1853, Barnard Papers, NYSL. Neighbors would include Hamilton Fish who would live at 15 Elk, 1849–1851, and William L. Marcy at 2 Elk, 1833–1839.

17. "Barnard Family Geneology," Barnard Family Papers, LC; Scrapbook, Peltz Collection; Barnard (misc. letters) to E. Henry Barnard, Timothy Barnard and Eliza Voorhees, *passim,* in Barnard Family Papers, LC. In letters to his family Barnard gives a personal account of some of his nonpolitical activities. See also Lewis G. Clark to Barnard, March 9, 1834, Peltz Collection.

18. Albany *Evening Journal,* October 15, 21, November 7, 1833.

19. *Ibid.,* March 19, 29, 1834.

20. *Ibid.,* April 25, 1834.

21. There are many accounts dealing with the Whig Party, although

a new comprehensive study is badly needed. See Flick, *History of the State of New York*, VI, 69; D. Alexander, *A Political History of the State of New York*. I, 398–401; Van Deusen, *William Henry Seward*, 21–25; Van Deusen, "Some Aspects of Whig Thought and Theory," 305–322; Carroll, *Origins of the Whig Party*, 32–48, 52, 56–57, 71, 115, 118; Benson, *The Concept of Jacksonian Democracy*, 62, 105, 131; McCormick, *The Second American Party System*, 108–123, 170, 341. Van Deusen, *Thurlow Weed;* Weed to Charles Whittlesey, August 8, 1834, Weed Papers, Union College.

22. Albany *Evening Journal*, April 20, 1834.

23. Albany *Argus*, October 15, 17, 20, 22, November 3, 4, 1834; Albany *Evening Journal*, October 16, 21, 1834.

24. Albany *Evening Journal*, October 16, 30, 1834.

25. Albany *Argus*, December 4, 1830, October 13, 22, November 7, 13, 15, 17, December 5, 1834; Albany *Evening Journal*, November 7, 1834. The *Evening Journal* pointed out alleged fraud in the Nov. 7 issue, stating that at the Watervliet poll there had been an excess of twelve ballots compared with the poll list; ". . . *it so happened"* that the inspectors threw out eleven votes for Barnard. Barnard did better in the city of Albany than in the outlying rural areas. He carried the 1st, 2nd, and 3rd wards and ran close to Lansing in the 4th and 5th. The *Argus* of Nov. 13 gave the election totals as Lansing, 4944, and Barnard, 4851. The *Argus* of Nov. 15 gave Lansing 4944 and Barnard 4521. The Albany *Evening Journal* of November 17 gave the same total of 4521.

26. Albany *Evening Journal*, September 12, December 3, 9, 1835, February 4, 1836. *Proceedings of a State Convention of Delegates Friendly to the Election of William H. Harrison;* Albany *Evening Journal*, April 9, 1836.

27. Albany *Evening Journal*, May 13, June 9, September 26, 1836; Weed to Granger, March 16, 1836, Weed Papers, Union College.

CHAPTER III

1. Barnard, *An Address delivered 1831*, 5, 12, 16, 18, 22, 31.

2. Barnard, *An Address delivered 1834*, 7–9, 13, 17, 25; *Lecture delivered, December, 1835*, 19, 22.

3. Barnard, *A Discourse Pronounced, July 25, 1837*, 7, 11, 14, 16, 17–21, 27, 42. Barnard also received the Doctor of Laws from Hobart and from Brown in 1853.

4. Barnard, *A Discourse pronounced, August 1, 1838*, 5, 11, 17–19; *An Address delivered, July 18, 1837*, 31, 36, 42; Ekirch, *The Idea of Progress in America*, 219–220.

5. *Address (July 18, 1837)*, 42–45; Barnard to John M. Clayton, June 5, 1849, Clayton Papers, LC.

6. Barnard, "Commerce" (July, 1839), 3–20. Barnard's address before the Mercantile Library Association was reprinted in *Hunt's Merchants' Magazine*.

7. Barnard, *An Address, July 18, 1839*, 6–12, 27, 32–35, 55.

8. Barnard, *Discourse, April 15, 1839*, 1, 7, 17, 30, 37, 56–58. Barnard was made an honorary member of the Massachusetts Historical Society after the preparation of this discourse, which also included the historical account of the Colony of Rensselaerswyck.

9. Barnard, *A Plea, July 1, 1845*, 6–10, 14, 16, 17, 19, 22.

10. Barnard, *Man and the State, Aug. 19, 1846*, 5–6, 10, 15, 17, 20, 25, 39, 40, 44, 50–51; Albany *Evening Journal,* August 22, 1846.

11. Barnard, *The Social System, Aug. 2, 1848*, 5, 7, 17, 18, 27, 29.

12. Barnard, *Anniversary Address, 20th of October, 1843*, 5–6, 9 10, 12, 16; New York *Tribune,* October 21, 1843; *National Intelligencer,* October 25, 1843.

13. Barnard, *James Madison, Feb. 28, 1837*, 7, 10, 14, 19, 36, 39; *An Oration on the Fourth of July, 1835*, 6–50; Albany *Evening Journal,* July 6, 1835, February 28, 1837.

14. Barnard, *Annual Address, 1836*, 120–125, 127–129, 142; Albany *Evening Journal,* April 21, June 11, 1836.

15. Albany *Evening Journal,* January 7, June 13, August 2, 1836; July 27, 28, 1837, August 9, 1838.

16. Albany *Evening Journal,* September 3, 5, 1835. See also, Grimsted, ''Rioting in Its Jacksonian Setting,'' 361–397.

17. Barnard, *Letter to Hamilton,* (1856); Barnard, *Whig or Abolition?* (1849); Barnard, *The Dangers of Disunion* (1860); Grimsted, ''Rioting in Jacksonian Setting,'' 361–397. Barnard never participated in an antiabolition mob but in many other respects he fits the description of those in Richards' *Gentlemen of Property.*

18. Barnard, *Whig or Abolition?*

19. Barnard, *Speeches and Reports* (1838), 44, 48.

20. Barnard, *Social System,* 18.

21. Albany *Evening Journal,* March 2, 28, 29, 1838.

22. *Ibid.,* May 28, 30, June 14, July 6, 10, 24, 1855, March 28, 1856; Krout, ''Maine Law in New York Politics.''

23. For the background and development of the antirent struggle in New York see, Ellis, *A History of New York State,* 160–161; Parker, *Landmarks of Albany County,* I, 114–116; Ellis, *Landlords and Farmers in the Hudson Mohawk Region*, 288–291, 312; Christman, *Tin Horns and Calico,* 13–15.

24. Barnard to James F. Cooper, September 26, 1841, Misc. Barnard Papers, NYSHA; Barnard, ''The 'Anti-Rent' Movement'' (December, 1845), 577–598; Barnard to Hamilton Fish, October 7, 1845, Fish Papers, LC.

25. Albany *Evening Journal,* April 30, May 12, November 24, 1838; Munsell, *Collections on the History of Albany,* II, 220–225.

26. Albany *Evening Journal,* January 3, 1834, July 24, August 9, 1838. Munsell, *Annals of Albany,* IX, 274–79.

27. Hooper, *A History of Saint Peter's Church,* 272–273, 296–297, 307, 316, 326–329; Weise, *The History of the City of Albany,* 368; Munsell, *Collections,* I, 448, 458.

CHAPTER IV

1. Albany *Evening Journal*, October 4, 5, 26, 28, 1837; Albany *Argus*, October 5, 1837.

2. Albany *Evening Journal,* October 26, 28, November 1, 1837.

3. *Ibid.*, November 9, 14, 17, 22, 1837; Albany *Argus,* November 9, 10, 11, 15, 21, 1837. The following totals are from the *Evening Journal* of November 17. The *Argus* report of November 21 differed by a few votes.

Whig		Democrat	
D. Barnard	5338	Edward Livingston	4589
P. Settle	5208	Hezekiah Sharp	4700
E. Raynsford	5274	L. Van Deusen	4726

4. New York State Assembly *Journal* (January 2, 6, 1838), 8–12, 142; Albany *Evening Journal,* January 2, 6, April 12, 1838.

5. Albany *Evening Journal,* January 4, 5, February 8, 1838; Assembly *Journal* (January 9, 1838), 158–159, 163–169; Barnard, "Speech on the bill to repeal the law prohibiting the circulation of small bank notes," in Barnard, *Speeches and Reports, 1838,* 1–48; D. Alexander, *A Political History of the State of New York,* II, 17.

6. Assembly *Journal* (January 10, February 28, 1838), 172, 449; Albany *Evening Journal,* January 10, February 15, 22, 28, April 19, 1838.

7. Barnard, "Speech . . . the Sub-Treasury Scheme," in *Speeches and Reports,* 83–85, 88–89, 90, 95, 100, 105; Albany *Evening Journal,* February 14, 16, 27, 1838.

8. Assembly *Journal* (January 9, March 10, 29, 1838), 158–163, 540, 762, 777; Barnard "Speech on small bill law," and "Speech on Banking . . ." in *Speeches and Reports*, 42, 144–222; Albany *Evening Journal,* February 15, 19, 20, 22, 23, 28, March 29, April 2, 1838; Lanier, *A Century of Banking in New York;* Benson, *The Concept of Jacksonian Democracy,* 98–102; Hammond, "Free Banks and Corporations," 184–209.

9. Albany *Evening Journal,* April 2, 3, 4, 5, 9, 10, 17, 18, 19, 1838; Assembly *Journal* (April 3, 4, 5, 18, 1838), 837–841, 846, 855, 863, 877, 1103, 1123, 1135; Lanier, *A Century of Banking,* 206, notes that the provision for issues against real estate was repealed in 1863.

10. New York State Assembly *Document* No. 55 (January 23, 1838); Assembly *Journal* (January 23, 1838), 231; Pratt, *Religion, Politics and Diversity,* 158–194.

11. Barnard, "Report on the Subject of Religious Exercises, and the Use of the Bible, in Schools," in *Speeches and Reports,* 49–64; Assembly *Journal* (January 23, 1838), 231–33; Albany *Evening Journal,* January 27, 1838.

12. Barnard, "Report on Public Instruction," in *Speeches and Reports*, 121–134; Assembly *Document* No. 236 (March 7, 1838);

Albany *Evening Journal,* March 7, 23, 1838; Graves, *History of the State Education Department,* 10, 28, 36.

13. Assembly *Journal* (March 7, 16, April 13, 14, 16, 1838), 505, 1006, 1025, 1029, 1034, 1058; Albany *Evening Journal,* March 23, April 13, 16, 17, 19, 1838; Graves, *History,* 28–32; *Gazetteer of the State of New York* (1860), 135; Hough, *University of the State of New York,* 79, 92, 547.

14. Barnard to William H. Seward (n.d.) 1839, American Diplomats Collection, PaHS; Edward Everett to Barnard, May 1, 1839, Peltz Collection; Esmond, *Public Education in New York State,* 14, 15; Graves, *History,* 28, 32–33.

15. Barnard, "Remarks in Assembly of New York touching the economical policy of an extended system of internal improvements," in *Speeches and Reports,* 139–141; Assembly *Journal* (March 13, 24, 1838), 566–723; Shaw, *Erie Water West,* 307–312.

16. Assembly *Journal* (April 9, 18, 1838), 923, 1138; Albany *Evening Journal,* April 9, 19, 1838.

17. Barnard, "Speech on small bill law," 44, 48; Assembly *Document* No. 359 (April 17, 1838); Albany *Evening Journal,* March 2, 17, 28, 39, 1838.

18. Albany *Evening Journal,* April 19, July 9, 1838.

CHAPTER V

1. Cora Barnard to Eliza Voorhees (n.d., 1837); Barnard to Harriet Barnard, October 8, 1838, both Barnard Family Papers, LC; Barnard to John Walsh (Strictly Private and Confidential), October 6, 1838, Peltz Collection; Albany *Evening Journal,* October 8, 1838; Albany *Daily Advertiser,* December 20, 1838.

2. Albany *Daily Advertiser,* November 6, 7, 1838; Albany *Argus,* October 5, 10, November 5, 1838; Albany *Evening Journal,* August 21, September 13, 14, October 8, 31, November 8, 9, 14, 15, 1838, February 1, June 20, 1839.

3. Albany *Daily Advertiser,* November 13, December 13, 20, 31, 1838; Albany *Argus,* December 20, 1838; Albany *Evening Journal,* December 17, 1838, February 1, 2, 1839, January 14, 1840; Weed, *Life of Thurlow Weed,* I, 460.

4. Adams, *Memoirs of John Quincy Adams,* X, 320.

5. Barnard to Robert C. Winthrop, May 30, 1842, Winthrop Papers, MaHS; Catharine Walsh Barnard to Harriet Barnard, December 7, 1841; Robert C. Winthrop to Barnard, November 10, 1845; Daniel Webster to Barnard, December 5, 1841, last three, Peltz Collection; Tuckerman, *The Diary of Philip Hone,* II, 120; Adams, *Memoirs,* X, 321, 371–372; Albany *Evening Journal,* May 27, 1842; Dolly Madison to Mary Cutts, February 3, 1842, to Catharine Barnard (poem), March 19, 1842, both, Peltz Collection. Dolly Madison was fond of Mrs. Barnard during the years in Washington and gave her a chair from the White House. It is now in the possession of Mrs. John DeWitt Peltz of New York City.

6. *See, Congressional Globe*, 26th Congress, 1st sess. (December 2, 1839–January, 1840) and issues of Albany *Evening Journal, Argus,* and *National Intelligencer* for the same dates; Barnard, *Speech, December 4, 1839;* Adams, *Memoirs,* X, 145, 162, 167; Barnard to Weed, December 21, 1839, Francis Granger Papers, LC; Barnard to Weed, December 23, 1839, Weed Papers, University of Rochester.

7. *Globe,* 26th Congress, 1st sess. (March 16, 1840), 277.

8. *Globe,* 26th Congress, 1st sess. (February 13, 14, March 16, 23, 1840), 197, 199–200, 275–281; Barnard, *Speech, February 14, 1840;* Albany *Evening Journal,* March 20, April 7, July 29, 1840; Adams, *Memoirs,* X, 218.

9. *Globe,* 26th Congress, 1st sess. (March 24, 27, 1840), 285–288, 292–294; Barnard, *Speech, March 25, 1840;* Barnard to Lewis Benedict, Jr., March 26, 1840, Barnard Papers, NYSL; *National Intelligencer,* April 23, 1840. Barnard obtained the floor at approximately 11:00 P.M. and asked to be heard the next day as the House had been sitting for fifteen hours. The majority refused to adjourn and at 11:00 A.M. the next day (after twenty-three hours) Barnard rose and spoke for two and three-quarters hours.

10. *Globe,* 26th Congress, 1st sess. (June 11, 1840), 459; Barnard, *Speech, June 12, 1840;* Adams, *Memoirs,* X, 308; Barnard to Harriet Barnard, July 1, 1840, Barnard Family Papers, LC.

11. *National Intelligencer,* July 22, 23, 1840; Albany *Evening Journal,* July 23, 1840; Adams, *Memoirs,* X, 337.

12. Catharine Barnard to Harriet Barnard, January 8, 1840; Barnard to Harriet Barnard, July 1, 1840, both, Barnard Family Papers, LC.

13. *Unionist,* September 19, 1840; Howell and Tenney, *History of the County of Albany,* 367.

14. Albany *Evening Journal,* September 18, 22, October 2, 12, 24, 27, 28, 1840.

15. Albany *Evening Journal,* November 6, 7, 10, 11, 16, 19, 20, 1840; Albany *Argus,* October 12, November 11, 18, 1840; Barnard to John Taylor, October 26, 1840, Barnard Papers, NYSL.

16. Barnard to J. D. Dickenson, February 1, 1841, Barnard Papers, NYSL; Barnard to Weed, February 8, 1841; Millard Fillmore to Weed, February 6, 16, 1841, all in Weed Papers, University of Rochester.

17. Caleb Cushing to Barnard, April 6, 1841, Peltz Collection; Cushing to Barnard, April 17, 1841; Barnard to Cushing, April 10, 1841, last two, Cushing Papers, LC; Albany *Evening Journal,* April 12, 1841.

18. Warren, *Bankruptcy in United States History,* 69–71; *National Intelligencer,* May 14, 1840, August 3, 1841; Albany *Evening Journal,* February 29, March 18, June 19, 1840, July 17, 19, 1841.

19. See *Globe,* 27th Congress, 1st sess. (July–August, 1841), and issues of *National Intelligencer* and Albany *Evening Journal; House Reports,* No. 5, 27th Congress, 1st sess. (July 21, 1841); Warren, *Bankruptcy,* 69–74; Barnard, *Speech, August 10, and August 17, 1841.*

20. For discussion of the logroll see: Warren, *Bankruptcy,* 77–79; Van Deusen, *The Jacksonian Era,* 161–162; Adams, *Memoirs,* XI, 534. Barnard credited himself with much of the success in regard to

the bill. See, Barnard to Silas M. Stillwell, July 20, 1842, Ford Papers, NYPL. Barnard stated: "I have never had a moment of doubt in regard to our duty in regard to the bankrupt law . . . from facts of which the public knows nothing, rather than from any efforts of mine in the face of the public, I have some reason to flatter myself that my humble agency was at the time, essential to the success of this great moral measure." However, newspaper accounts at the time did not credit Barnard. Van Deusen sees Weed's as the paramount effort.

21. *Globe,* 27th Congress, 1st sess. (July 9, 1841), 175–176; Barnard, *Speech, July 9, 1841,* Albany *Evening Journal,* July 1, 2, 15, August 3, September 4, 16, 1841; *National Intelligencer,* July 13, 1841.

22. Barnard to Harriet Barnard, August 1, 1841, Barnard Family Papers, LC; Henry Clay to Barnard, October 17, 1841, Peltz Collection; Albany *Evening Journal,* September 13, 16, 1841.

23. Catharine Barnard to Harriet Barnard, June (n.d.) 1841; Barnard to Harriet Barnard, August 1, 1841, both, Barnard Family Papers, LC; Albany *Evening Journal,* September 25, 29, October 6, 7, 8, 1841.

24. Barnard to Leverett Saltonstall, October 24, 1841, Saltonstall Papers, MaHS.

25. *House Reports,* No. 931, 27th Congress, 2nd sess. (July 21, 1842); *National Intelligencer,* December 10, 15, 1842; Albany *Evening Journal,* December 21, 1842; *Globe,* 27th Congress, 2nd sess. (December 13, 20, 1842, January 16, 1843), 49, 65–72, 162–163; Warren, *Bankruptcy,* 84–85.

26. *Globe,* 27th Congress, 3rd sess. (January 16, 17, 1843), 162, 167–169; *National Intelligencer,* March 4, 1843; Albany *Evening Journal,* January 5, 7, 20, March 7, 1843.

27. Barnard, *Remarks, July 28, 1841.*

28. *House Reports,* No. 943, 27th Congress, 2nd sess. (July 23, 1842); *Globe,* 27th Congress, 2nd sess. (July 6, 23, 1842), 726, 782; Barnard, *Speech, July 6, 1842.*

29. *Globe,* 27th Congress, 2nd sess., (April 28, 1842), 453; Barnard, *Speech, April 28, 1842.*

30. Albany *Evening Journal,* June 24, July 1, September 6, 10, 12, October 8, 11, 26, 27, November 2, 5, 7, 8, 9, 10, 12, 23, 1842; Albany *Argus,* October 7, 10, November 2, 7, 10, 23, 1842.

31. Barnard, *Speech, February 20, 1843;* Albany *Evening Journal,* December 15, 1842, February 23, 1843; *National Intelligencer,* February 21, March 2, 1843.

32. Weed, *Autobiography,* I, 536.

33. Albany *Evening Journal,* March 17, 1843.

34. Daniel Webster to Barnard, August 27, 1842, Peltz Collection; Barnard, *Speech, August 31, 1841.*

35. Albany *Evening Journal,* July 14, August 2, 3, 11, 1843; *National Intelligencer,* August 9, 1843; Adams, *Memoirs,* XI, 402; *The Diary of John Quincy Adams,* 554–557.

36. *Globe,* 28th Congress, 1st sess. (December, 1843–February,

1844); House of Rep., *Journal* (December, 1843); *National Intelligencer,* December 5, 12, 18, 23, 1843; Albany *Evening Journal,* November 27, December 7, 8, 11, 15, 19, 1843, July 13, 1844; Adams, *Memoirs,* XI, 443.

37. Barnard, *Speech, February 13, 1844; National Intelligencer,* February 10, 13, 15, 17, 1844; Albany *Evening Journal,* July 13, 1844.

38. *Globe,* 28th Congress, 1st sess., House of Rep. (January 17, 1844), 160; Adams, *Memoirs,* XI, 487–488, XII, 19.

39. *National Intelligencer,* June 18, 1844; Albany *Evening Journal,* June 19, 1844; Adams, *Memoirs,* XII, 37.

40. Albany *Evening Journal,* July 13, 17, 27, August 3, 5, 1844—Barnard's letters to his constituents.

41. Albany *Evening Journal,* September 23, 1844; Barnard, *Speech, May 14, 1844;* Hamilton Fish to Barnard, October 16, 1844; Barnard to Fish, October 24, 1844, both, Fish Papers, LC; Barnard, *Speech, July 9, 1841.*

42. Barnard to Fish, October 24, November 13, 1844, Fish Papers, LC.

43. *National Intelligencer,* December 3, 10, 1844; Albany *Evening Journal,* December 6, 1844; *Globe,* 28th Congress, 2nd sess. (December 5, 9, 10, 12, 1844, February 27, 28, 1845), 12–25, 354–355: *National Intelligencer,* March 6, 1845.

44. For background on Texas see, Barker, "The Annexation of Texas"; Smith, *The Annexation of Texas,* 103–115, 138, 145, 191–192, 223, 277–280, 326, 333; Merk, "Dissent in the Mexican War"; Merk, *Manifest Destiny and Mission,* 40–48, 99–106.

45. Barnard, *Speech, January 24, 1845;* Adams, *Memoirs,* XII, 57.

46. For voting patterns see, Thomas Alexander, *Sectional Stress and Party Strength,* 31–56, 147–187; Silbey, *The Shrine of Party,* 53–61, 160–168.

CHAPTER VI

1. There is no comprehensive published work dealing exclusively with the New York Whig Party. However, helpful studies include: Van Deusen, "Some Aspects of Whig Thought and Theory," 307–315, *Thurlow Weed,* and *William Henry Seward;* Fox, "Economic Status of New York Whigs," 502–517; Benson, *The Concept of Jacksonian Democracy;* Donald, "Prelude to Civil War" (unpublished doctoral dissertation); Morris, "The New York State Whigs, 1834–1843" (unpublished doctoral dissertation); Warner, "The Silver Grays" (unpublished doctoral dissertation); Rayback, "The Silver Gray Revolt"; Carman and Luthin, "The Seward-Fillmore Feud." The New York Whig Party can roughly be divided into liberal and conservative wings. Barnard used the terms progressive, radical, liberal, and ultra interchangeably for the liberals. Conservatives were so called until the Whig split in 1850. Thereafter, conservatives also were dubbed Silver Grays and

the liberals within the party, the regular Whigs, were called Woolly Heads.

2. Barnard to Thurlow Weed, December 21, 1839, Granger Papers, LC; Barnard to Weed, December 23, 1839, Weed Papers, University of Rochester; Albany *Daily Advertiser,* November 13, December 13, 20, 31, 1838; Albany *Argus,* December 20, 1838; Albany *Evening Journal,* December 17, 1838, February 1, 2, 1839; Barnard to Millard Fillmore, November 19, 1847, Fillmore Papers, Oswego.

3. William H. Seward to Barnard, December 1, 1837, January 13, 1840, Peltz Collection; Seward to Hamilton Fish, December 4, 1849, Fish Papers, LC; Barnard to Seward, November 13, 1838, Simon Gratz Papers, PaHS.

4. Barnard, "The 'Anti-Rent' Movement" (December, 1845), 577–598; Albany *Evening Journal,* November 5, 9, December 9, 15, 1845, March 30, 1846, October 7, 1847; Barnard to Fillmore, November 19, 1847, Fillmore Papers, Oswego.

5. Barnard to Fish, February 26, November 17, 1846, February 3, 1847; Fish to Barnard, November 26, 1846 (draft), all in Fish Papers, LC.

6. Barnard, "The War with Mexico" (June, 1846), "The President and His Administration" (May, 1848), "Our Relations with Mexico" (July, 1846), "The President's Message: The War" (January, 1847), "The War: The New Issue" (February, 1848).

7. Barnard, "The Whigs and the War" (October, 1847), "The Whigs and Their Candidate" (September, 1848), "Mr. Slidell's Mission to Mexico" (April, 1847).

8. "President and His Administration," Barnard to Fish, April 5, 1847, Fish Papers, LC; Barnard to Robert Winthrop, October 24, 1847, Winthrop Papers, MaHS; Winthrop to Barnard, October 18, 1847, Peltz Collection.

9. Barnard to Fillmore, November 19, 1847, Fillmore Papers, Oswego.

10. Barnard to Fish, April 5, 1847, Fish Papers, LC.

11. Barnard, "Whigs and Their Candidate"; Albany *Evening Journal,* September 2, 1848.

12. Barnard, *Whig or Abolition?* (1849).

13. Albany *Evening Journal,* February 2, 1849; New York State Assembly *Journal,* February 6, 1849, 355–357; New York State Senate *Journal,* February 6, 1849, 167–169.

Assembly votes were:	William H. Seward	102
	John A. Dix	15
	Reuben Walworth	7
Senate votes were:	William H. Seward	19
	John A. Dix	6
	Daniel D. Barnard	2
	Reuben Walworth	2

14. Barnard to Fillmore, March 16, 1849 (private), Fillmore Papers, Oswego; Barnard to John M. Clayton, June 5, Clayton Papers, LC.

15. Teunis Van Vechten *et al.* to Zachary Taylor, March 5, 1849; Washington Hunt to Taylor, May 3, 1849, John A. Collier to Clayton, June (n.d.) 1849; Hunt to Clayton, May 3, December 3, 1849, all in Application and Recommendation Files, National Archives.

16. New York *Tribune,* September 27, 28, 1849. Votes were: Christopher Morgan, 80; Barnard, 41; Alvah Hunt, 1; Thomas Bond, 1.

17. Barnard to Fillmore, November 9, 1849, Fillmore Papers, Oswego; Fish to Taylor, November 29, 1849, Fish Papers, LC. For a different interpretation of the Whig losses, see Donald doctoral dissertation, 136–152.

18. Fish to Taylor, June 18, 1849, to Jacob Collamer, April 26, 1849, both, Fish Papers, LC.

19. Barnard to Fish, October 29, 1849, Fish to Taylor, November 29, 1849, Barnard to Fish, August 5, 1850 (private); Fish to Barnard, June 13, 1842; David B. Ogden to Fish, July 5, 1849, all in Fish Papers, LC.

20. Fish to Seward, November 29, 1849; Seward to Fish, December 4, 1849, both, Fish Papers, LC.

21. Barnard to Fillmore, December 15, 1849 (confidential), to Fillmore, December 17, 1849 (private), both, Fillmore Papers, BHS. By taking an average of the Whig votes cast for President 1840–1852, those designated as Whigs numbered approximately 228,000. If Barnard's estimate of 30,000 conservatives was correct, then conservatives constituted about thirteen percent of the party. Election figures are from Stanwood, *A History of Presidential Elections,* 138, 158, 176, 191.

22. Weed to Fish, January 12, 1850, Barnard to Fish, January 28, 1850, Weed to Fish, January 16, 1850 (confidential), all in Fish Papers, LC; Weed, *Life of Thurlow Weed,* I, 594–595; Barnard to Fillmore, January 31, 1850 (draft), Barnard Papers, NYSL; to Fillmore, January 31, 1850 (confidential), Fillmore Papers, BHS. Fish and Weed were on friendly terms throughout this period.

23. Fish to Seward, February 9, 1850, Fish Papers, LC.

24. Barnard to Fillmore, December 15, 1849 (confidential), to Fillmore, January 31, 1850 (confidential), both, Fillmore Papers, BHS; Albany *Evening Journal,* January 10, 17, February 15, 16, 1850; Barnard, Scrapbook, NYSL. Barnard's resolutions were similar to Webster's territorial plan. Barnard to Fillmore, February 25, 1850 (confidential), Fillmore Papers, BHS.

25. Barnard to Daniel Webster, April 10, 1850, Webster Papers, New Hampshire Historical Society; Barnard to Webster, July 11, 1850, Webster Papers, LC.

26. Barnard to Fillmore, February 25, 1850 (strictly private), Fillmore Papers, BHS. Further evidence of the split in the Whig ranks between Weed supporters and those of Fillmore can be found in issues of the Albany *State Register* (1850–52), a conservative Whig organ established by New York city merchants to give them a voice to rival Weed. See Warner doctoral dissertation, (65, 95, 332).

27. Barnard to Fillmore, July 10, 1850 (confidential), to Fillmore, August 26, 1850 (private), both, Fillmore Papers, BHS; Barnard to

Fish, August 5, 1850 (private), Fish Papers, LC; Barnard to Abbott Lawrence, July 5, 1850, Barnard Papers, NYSL.

28. Barnard to Fillmore, July 10, 1850 (confidential), Fillmore Papers, BHS.

29. Barnard to Webster, July 11, 1850, Webster Papers, LC.

30. Barnard to Fillmore, July 12, 1850 (confidential), Fillmore Papers, BHS.

31. Albany *Evening Journal,* July 19, 1850.

32. Barnard to Fish, August 5, 1850, Fish to Fillmore, July 22, 1850, Fish to Webster, August 8, 1850, all in Fish Papers, LC.

33. Barnard to Fillmore, August 12, 1850, Fillmore Papers, BHS; Barnard to Fish, August 15, 1850, Fish Papers, LC.

34. Barnard MS Diary, September 6, 8, 1850, Barnard Papers, NYSL; Albany *Evening Journal,* September 10, 1850.

35. Barnard to Fillmore, September 17, 30, 1850 (private), Jerome Fuller to Fillmore, September 20, 1850, Daniel Ullman to Fillmore, September 24, 1850 (private), all in Fillmore Papers, BHS. See, in addition, Warner doctoral dissertation, issues of Albany *Evening Journal* and New York *Tribune* for accounts of the convention.

36. Barnard to Fillmore, September 30, 1850 (private), to Fillmore, October 14, 1850 (private), both, Fillmore Papers, BHS. Granger, like Barnard, was a patrician in politics within the Whig party.

37. Edward Everett to Barnard, September 18, 1850, Everett Papers, MaHS; Barnard to Fillmore, October 13, 1850 (private), Barnard to Fillmore, October 4, 1850 (private), Barnard to Webster, October 4, 1850 (private), all in Barnard Papers, NYSL; Albany *Evening Journal,* October 17, 1850.

CHAPTER VII

1. Barnard MS Diary, October 16, November 1–December 3, 1850, Barnard Papers, NYSL; Barnard to Hamilton Fish, November 3, 1850, Fish Papers, LC; Barnard to E. Henry Barnard, January 5, 1851, Barnard Family Papers, LC.

2. Diary, December 1850, November 15, 1851; Barnard to Baron von Humboldt, December 17, 1850, both, Barnard Papers, NYSL; Baron Manteuffel to Barnard, December 9, 1850, Notes from the German Governments, II, National Archives; Barnard to Rev. Horatio Potter, April 15, 1851, Barnard Papers, NYSL.

3. Barnard to Millard Fillmore, December 23, 1850, Barnard Papers, NYSL.

4. Diary, January 4, 6, 8, 13, February 5, 12, 19, 26, March 3, 4, 6, 1851, January 4, 17, 21, 28, February 4, 6, 10, 22, 24, 1852, Barnard Papers, NYSL.

5. Barnard to Fish, April 22, 1851, Fish Papers, LC; Barnard to Ralph King, April 22, 1853; King to Barnard, June 14, December 8, December 18, 1851, all in Barnard Papers, NYSL.

6. Barnard to Fish, February 11, March 4, April 22, 1851; Fish

to Barnard, March 28, 1851; Fish to Barnard, November 24, 1852; Barnard to Fish, January 11, 1853; Barnard to Mrs. Fish, February 15, 1853, all in Barnard Papers, NYSL.

7. Barnard to Daniel Webster, Despatch No. 46, December 9, 1851, Despatch Book, Barnard Papers, NYSL; Webster to Barnard, Despatch No. 1, September 10, 1850, US. Dept. of State, Microcopy 77.

8. John V. L. Pruyn MS Journal, III, July 3, 6, 1851, 337–356, NYSL; Pruyn to Barnard, November 17, 1851; Barnard Diary, July 3, 1851, last two, Barnard Papers, NYSL.

9. Diary, June 10, 27, July 31, August 1–September 21, 25, 26, 1851, February 20, May 28, June 7, 1853; Barnard to Webster, December 23, 1850 (private); Theodore Fay to Barnard, February 5, 1853, all in Barnard Papers, NYSL.

10. Diary, June 10, August 27–September 14, October 19, 29, December 2, 5, 6, 1852, Barnard Papers, NYSL.

11. Fish to Barnard, November 10, 1851, Barnard Papers, NYSL; Fish to Fillmore, November 1, 1851, Fish Papers, LC; Barnard to Fish, April 22, 1851, Fish Papers, LC; Barnard to Fillmore, September 14, 1852 (private), to Potter, September 23, 1852, both, Barnard Papers, NYSL.

12. Barnard to Richard DeWitt, June 5, September 28, December 28, 1852, April 5, 1853, Barnard Papers, NYSL. DeWitt wrote that the tax bill was $30,000, but the letter does not include the period of time covered.

13. Barnard to Fish, July 22, 1851, Barnard Papers, NYSL.

14. Barnard to Webster, Despatch No. 12, February 25, 1851, Despatch Book, to Fillmore, March 11, 1851 (private); Baron Manteuffel to Barnard, February 8, 1851, Despatch Book, all in Barnard Papers, NYSL.

15. Barnard to John C. Spencer, February 11, 1851, to Fish, January 13, 1852, both, Barnard Papers, NYSL.

16. Diary, January 2, 1852; Barnard to Webster, Despatches Nos. 52, 60, 63, January 6, February 10, March 1, 1852, Despatch Book, all in Barnard Papers, NYSL.

17. Barnard to Webster, February 10, 1852 (private), Barnard Papers, NYSL.

18. Barnard to Webster, February 28, 1852 (private), Barnard Papers, NYSL.

19. Barnard to Webster, Despatch No. 43, November 25, 1851, Despatch Book, Barnard Papers, NYSL.

20. Barnard to Edward Everett, December 7, 1852, to Fish, January 11, 1853, to Timothy Barnard, January 27, 1852, to Webster, Despatch No. 90, October 19, 1852, Despatch Book, all in Barnard Papers, NYSL. In the letter to his brother Barnard does not give such a favorable view of Louis Napoleon and calls him a "Despot."

21. Ludwig Jacoby to Barnard, February 28, 1851, Despatch Book, Barnard Papers; NYSL; Barnard to Baron Schleintz, March 7, 1851, to Webster, Despatch No. 14, March 11, 1851, to Webster, Despatch No. 21, May 13, 1851, all in U.S. Dept. of State, Microcopy 44.

22. Barnard to James H. Duncan, June 29, 1852, Despatch Book, to Baron von Humboldt, October 18, 1852, to His Majesty the King of Prussia, January 16, 1853, to Everett, Despatch No. 102, January 31, 1853, Despatch Book, all in Barnard Papers, NYSL.

23. Barnard to Webster, Despatch No. 26, June 17, 1851, to Mr. Prokesch, June 12, 1851, to Charles McCurdy, June 29, 1851, all in Despatch Book, Barnard Papers, NYSL; Barnard to Abbott Lawrence, July 3, 1851, Barnard Papers, NYSL; *Senate Executive Documents,* No. 91, 32d Congress, 1st sess. (June 22, 1851); Webster to Barnard, Despatch No. 7, July 12, 1851, U.S. Dept. of State, Microcopy 77.

24. Barnard to Webster, Despatches Nos. 24, 27, 28, June 10, June 24, July 1, 1851, to Henry Sandt, June 17, 1851, to Baron Manteuffel, July 28, 1851, all in Despatch Book, Barnard Papers, NYSL; Manteuffel to Barnard, March 1, 1853, Notes from the German Governments, National Archives; Barnard to Everett, Despatch No. 115, March 8, 1853, Despatch Book, Barnard Papers, NYSL; Everett to Barnard, Despatch No. 23, January 14, 1853, U.S. Dept. of State, Microcopy 77.

25. Barnard to Manteuffel. July 3, 8, 1852, to Ralph King, July 5, 8, 1852, to Webster, Despatch No. 72, July 20, 1852, all in Despatch Book, Barnard Papers, NYSL; Barnard to Bernard Roelker, December 27, 1852, Barnard Papers, NYSL; *Senate Executive Documents,* No. 38, 36th Congress, 1st sess. (April 11, 1860).

26. Barnard to Fish, August 3 (private), October 16, 1852, Barnard Papers, NYSL.

27. Everett to Barnard (draft), January 14, 1853, Everett Papers MaHS; same letter, Despatch No. 23, January 14, 1853, U.S. Dept. of State, Microcopy 77.

28. Barnard to Everett, Despatch No. 106, February 8, 1853, Despatch Book, to Manteuffel, February 15, 1853, Despatch Book, both, Barnard Papers, NYSL; *Senate Executive Documents*, No. 60, 33rd Congress, 1st sess. (May 5, 1854).

29. Barnard to Samuel Bromberg, March 28, April 12, 1853, Barnard Papers, NYSL.

30. Malloy, *Treaties, etc.,* II, 1501–1503; Moore, *A Digest of International Law,* I, 358–362. By this treaty citizens of one country who became citizens of the other and resided there five years were to be treated as naturalized citizens of the latter.

31. Barnard to Fish, February 11, March 25, April 22, July 22, 1851, Barnard Papers, NYSL.

32. Barnard to John C. Spencer, February 11, 1851; Fish to Barnard, January 23, February 21, 1851, both, Barnard Papers, NYSL.

33. Barnard to Fish, March 25, 1851, Barnard Papers, NYSL.

34. Barnard to Fish, April 22, 1851, Barnard Papers, NYSL.

35. Barnard to Fish, October 28, 1851; Fish to Barnard, November 10, 1851, both, Barnard Papers, NYSL.

36. Barnard to Fish, March 8, June 7, December 14, 1852, Barnard Papers, NYSL; Van Deusen, *Thurlow Weed,* 189–190.

37. Fish to Weed, November 11, 1852, Fish Papers, LC; Fillmore to Weed, November 12, 1852, in Severance, *Millard Fillmore Papers,* II, 334; Albany *Evening Journal,* November 9, 13, 1852; Weed, *Life of Thurlow Weed,* I, 588; Fillmore to Fish, May 13, 1852, Fish Papers, LC; Fish to Barnard, January 23, 1851, November 24, 1852; Barnard to Fish, June 7, 15, 1852, all in Barnard Papers, NYSL; Fish to Barnard, May 17, 1852, Fish Papers, LC; Barnard to Abbott Lawrence, July 5, 1850, to Fillmore, June 15, 1852, to Fish, December 14, 1852, all in Barnard Papers, NYSL.

38. Albany *Evening Journal,* November 13, 20, 1852; Fish to Weed, November 11, 1852; Weed to Fish, November 13, 1852, both, ⌐ish Papers, LC.

39. Barnard to Webster, July 12, 1852 (private), to Abbott Lawrence, September 20, 1852 (private), both, Barnard Papers, NYSL.

40. Fish to Barnard, November 24, 1852, Barnard Papers, NYSL; Barnard to Fish, November 18, 1852, Fish Papers, LC; Barnard to Fish, January 11, May 23, 1853, Barnard Papers, NYSL.

41. Barnard to Fish, November 18, 1852, to Fish, January 11, 1853 (private), both, Fish Papers, LC; Barnard to President Franklin Pierce, February 15, 1853 (private), to Secretary of State, March 1, 1853, (confidential), both, Barnard Papers, NYSL.

42. Fish to William L. Marcy, March 14, 26, April 9, 1853, Fish Papers, LC.

43. Barnard to Fish, May 23, 1853, Barnard Papers, NYSL.

44. Barnard to DeWitt, March 8, May 24, June 14, 21, July 12, 19, 26, August 8, 1853, Barnard Papers, NYSL; Fish to DeWitt, October 26, 1853, Fish Papers, LC.

45. Barnard to Marcy, Despatch No. 129, June 21, 1853, Despatch Book, Barnard Papers, NYSL.

46. Barnard to Fish, October 12, November 12, 1853, both, Fish Papers, LC; Barnard to E. Henry Barnard, December 2, 1853, Barnard Family Papers, LC.

CHAPTER VIII

1. Albany *Evening Journal,* May 28, 1855.

2. Barnard to my beloved wife, November 15, 1857, Barnard Papers, NYSL.

3. Barnard, *Political Aspects, January 13, 1854.*

4. Barnard to Rev. Kip, July 11, 1855, Barnard Papers, NYSL; Barnard to E. Henry Barnard, November 24, 1855, December 22, 1856, September 30, 1858, Barnard Family Papers, LC.

5. Barnard to Mrs. Stevens, September 25, 1855, to Mrs. Spencer, March 7, 1854, both, Barnard Papers, NYSL.

6. Barnard to Mrs. Stevens, January 3, 1856, to Mrs. Forsyth, October 18, 1854, to Mrs. Thayer, January 6, 1857, all in Barnard Papers, NYSL.

7. Barnard to E. Henry Barnard, December 22, 1856, February 9, 1857, Barnard Family Papers, LC.

8. Barnard to Hamilton Fish, August 25, September 9, 15, 1854, Fish Papers, LC.

9. Barnard to Mrs. Fish, November 24, 1854, Barnard Papers, NYSL.

10. Barnard to Francis Granger, November 1, 1854, Barnard Papers, NYSL.

11. Albany *Evening Journal,* November 7, 28, 1854.

12. Barnard to Mrs. Fish, November 24, 1854, Barnard Papers, NYSL.

13. Barnard to Fish, December 21, 1854, Barnard Papers, NYSL. From 1855 to 1861 Barnard refers to the conservatives as the old-line Whigs, old school Whigs and Whigs of old. It is this group which he hopes to see reorganize as a national Whig party.

14. Barnard to Fish, June 15, 1855, Fish Papers, LC; Barnard to Fish, July 9, 1855, Barnard Papers, NYSL.

15. Barnard to Fish, February 27, July 9, 1855, to Kip, July 11, 1855, both, Barnard Papers, NYSL; Barnard to Fish, March 22, 1855, Fish Papers, LC.

16. Barnard to James Brooks *et al.,* October 10, 1855, to James Brooks (private), October 11, 1855, to Brooks (private), October 20, 1855, all in Barnard Papers, NYSL.

17. Barnard to James Brooks *et al.,* October 10, 1855, Barnard Papers, NYSL.

18. Albany *Evening Journal,* October 23, 24, 1855; New York *Tribune,* October 25, 1855; Barnard to Nathan Sargent, October 31, 1855, Barnard Papers, NYSL. Albany delegates were James Edwards, John Veeder, John Olmstead, and James Kidd.

19. Albany *Evening Journal,* October 31, November 1, 1855, February 25, 1860.

20. *Ibid.,* November 1, 2, 5, 1855.

21. *Ibid.,* November 8, 13, 1855; Samuel Ruggles to Barnard, November 5, 1855, Barnard Papers, NYSL; Barnard to Ruggles, November 15, 1855, Ruggles Papers, NYPL.

22. Barnard to James A. Hamilton, November 17, 1855, Barnard Papers, NYSL; Barnard to E. Henry Barnard, November 24, 1855, Barnard Family Papers, LC; Barnard to Fish, November 22, 1855, Barnard Papers, NYSL.

23. Barnard to Hamilton, November 23, 28, 1855, Barnard Papers, NYSL.

24. Barnard to Samuel Ruggles, November 15, 1855, Ruggles Papers, NYPL; Barnard to Hamilton, November 23, 28, December 3, 1855, Barnard Papers, NYSL; W. Anthon West to Fish, December 10, 1855, Fish Papers, LC; Barnard to West (private), December 13, 1855, Barnard Papers, NYSL.

25. Barnard to Hamilton, November 23, December 3, 1855, Barnard Papers, NYSL; West to Fish, December 10, 1855, Fish Papers, LC; West to Barnard, December 11, 1855, Barnard Papers, NYSL.

26. Barnard to Hamilton, December 17, 1855; Barnard, *Address to the National and Constitutional Whigs of the United States,* both, Barnard Papers, NYSL.

27. Barnard to Hamilton, December 13, 1855, to West (private), December 13, 1855, both, Barnard Papers, NYSL.

28. Fish to Barnard, December 15, 19, 1855, Fish Papers, LC.

29. Barnard to Fish, December 25, 1855, to Granger, December 27, 1855, to West, December 27, 1855, to Hamilton, December 24, 29, 1855, all in Barnard Papers, NYSL.

30. Barnard to Hamilton, January 2, 1855?, Barnard Papers, NYSL; West to Fish, January 9, 13, 1856; Fish to Washington Hunt, February 13, 1856; Hunt to Fish, April 2, 1856, all in Fish Papers, LC.

31. Barnard to Hamilton, January 2, February 7, 1856, Barnard Papers, NYSL; West to Fish, January 13, 1856, Fish Papers, LC.

32. Barnard to Fish, February 29, 1856, to Hamilton, March 1, 1856, both, Barnard Papers, NYSL; Hamilton to Fish, March 7, 1856, in Hamilton, *Reminiscences,* 410–411; Fish to Barnard, March 6, 1856, Fish Papers, LC; Fish to Hamilton, March 4, 1856 in *Reminiscences,* 409–410.

33. Barnard to Fish, May 26, April 28, 1856, Barnard Papers, NYSL.

34. Barnard to Hamilton, June 19, June 30, 1856, Barnard Papers, NYSL; Barnard to Millard Fillmore, June 25, 1856, Fillmore Papers, Oswego.

35. Barnard to Hamilton, July 17, 19, 1856, Barnard to Fillmore, July 26, 1856, all in Barnard Papers, NYSL.

36. Barnard, *Letter to Hamilton* (1856).

37. Barnard to E. Henry Barnard, December 22, 1856, Barnard Family Papers, LC; Barnard to Fish, August 4, 1856, Fish Papers, LC; Barnard to Luther Bradish, August 7, 1856, Bradish Papers, NYHS. Barnard wrote to his brother that 100,000 copies were sold.

38. New York *Tribune,* August 15, 1856; Barnard to Fish, September 23, 1856, Fish Papers, LC; Barnard to Hamilton, October 10, 1856, Barnard Papers, NYSL; Albany *Evening Journal,* October 8, 1856.

39. New York *Tribune,* September 13, 17, 22, 24, 1856; Albany *Evening Journal,* September 17, 23, 1856. Throughout this period other prime movers among the old-line Whigs, in addition to Barnard, were Luther Bradish, James and Erastus Brooks, Francis Granger, James A. Hamilton (before he turned to support of Fremont), Washington Hunt, Hiram Ketchum, J. P. Phoenix, Samuel Ruggles, Daniel Ullman, and R. A. West.

40. Barnard to E. Henry Barnard, December 22, 1856, Barnard Family Papers, LC; New York returns: Buchanan 195,866; Fremont 274,707; Fillmore 124,603.

41. Barnard to Fish, July 6, 1857, Fish Papers, LC; Barnard to Fish, September 26, October 12, 13, 1857, Barnard Papers, NYSL; Barnard to Fillmore, May 14, 1857, Fillmore Papers, Oswego; Barnard to Edward Everett, March 27, 1857, Barnard Papers, NYSL.

42. Barnard to Washington Hunt, December 30, 1857, Barnard Papers, NYSL.

43. Barnard to Fish, January 21, March 18, 1858, Fish Papers, LC; Barnard to Fish, May 25, 1858, Barnard Papers, NYSL.

44. Barnard to Fish, December 28, 1856, Barnard Papers, NYSL; to Fish, January 21, March 18, May 25, 1858, Fish Papers, LC; to Fish, August 30, 1858, Barnard Papers, NYSL.

45. Barnard to Washington Hunt, October 25, 1858, Barnard Papers, NYSL.

46. New York *Times,* January 19, 1859; Barnard to Fish, January 22, 1859, Barnard Papers, NYSL; to Fish, April 23, 1859, Fish Papers, LC; Edward Everett to Hiram Ketchum, March 28, 1859, Everett Papers, MaHS.

47. Barnard to J. Phillips Phoenix, *et al.,* February 28, 1859, Barnard Papers, NYSL.

48. Barnard, *Sovereignty of the States* (1860); Parker, *Landmarks of Albany County,* I, 99–100; Albany *Argus,* December 17, 1860; Barnard to Fish, January 23, 1860, Fish Papers, LC.

49. Barnard to Fish, January 23, 1860, Fish Papers, LC.

50. Barnard to D. C. Wigham, February 27, 1860, to Chauncey Moore, *et al.,* February 20, 1860, both, Barnard Papers, NYSL; Albany *Evening Journal,* February 25, 1860.

51. Albany *Evening Journal,* April 27, May 1, 3, 4, 9, 11, 18, 19, 26, 1860.

52. New York *Times,* July 19, 1860.

53. Barnard, *The Dangers of Disunion* (1860).

54. Albany *Evening Journal,* August 10, 15, 25, September 8, 15, 1860; Albany *Argus,* September 14, 1860.

55. Barnard to Fish, September 4, 1860, Fish Papers, LC; Hunt to John Bell, May 24, June 7, August 19, 1860, Bell Papers, LC.

56. Barnard to Fish, January 15, 1861, Barnard Papers, NYSL.

57. Albany *Evening Journal,* April 24, 1861; Albany *Argus,* April 26, 1861; Will of Daniel Dewey Barnard, Surrogate Court, Albany County. Barnard's wife, Catharine, lived on in Albany until her death in 1876. The daughter Cora was married in the summer of 1861 but had no children. The other daughter, Sarah, never married, so there were no direct descendants.

CHAPTER IX

1. Although many historians have ceased to refer to the period as the Age of Jackson, I have used the term as well as the age of egalitarianism because Barnard believed the rhetoric of the Jacksonians. He associated the Jackson party with radical reform ideas to a much greater extent than the Whigs, perhaps because he never tired of hoping that he could prevent the Whigs from out-Jacksoning the Jacksonians.

BIBLIOGRAPHY

PRIMARY MATERIALS

Barnard Manuscripts

Daniel Dewey Barnard Papers—NYSL
Barnard Collection in private possession of Mrs. John DeWitt Peltz
    of New York City
Barnard Family Bible Records—NYSL
Barnard Family Papers—LC
Barnard Papers—NYHS
Barnard Papers—NYPL
Miscellaneous Barnard Papers—Boston Public Library
Miscellaneous Barnard Papers—NYSHA
Miscellaneous Barnard Papers—PaHS
Miscellaneous Barnard Papers—Rochester Historical Society Library

Manuscripts of Other Persons

American Diplomats Collection—PaHS
American Lawyers Collections—PaHS
George Bancroft Papers—MaHS
John Bell Papers—LC
Luther Bradish Papers—NYHS
James Buchanan Papers—PaHS
Benjamin F. Butler Papers—NYSL
Cadwalader Collection, Richard Peters Correspondence—PaHS
Henry Clay Papers—LC
John M. Clayton Papers—LC
DeWitt Clinton Papers—NYSL
John A. Collier Papers—NYSL
Erastus Corning Papers—NYSL
John J. Crittenden Papers—LC

Caleb Cushing Papers—LC
Dreer Collection—PaHS
Edward Everett Papers—MaHS
Millard Fillmore Papers—BHS
Millard Fillmore Papers—NYSL
Millard Fillmore Papers—Oswego
Hamilton Fish Papers—LC
Hamilton Fish Miscellaneous Papers—NYSL
Ford Papers—NYPL
Jerome Fuller Papers—NYSL
Joshua Giddings Papers—LC
Francis Granger Papers—LC
Simon Gratz Papers—PaHS
Washington Hunt Papers—NYSL
John P. Kennedy Papers—LC
Hiram Ketchum Miscellaneous Papers—NYSL
James Kidd Papers—NYSL
William L. Marcy Papers—NYSL
James Monroe Miscellaneous Papers—NYSL
Thomas W. Olcott Papers—Columbia University Libraries
George Washington Patterson Papers—Rush Rhees Library, University
    of Rochester
John Van Schaick Lansing Pruyn Papers—NYSL
John Randolph Papers—LC
William C. Rives Papers—LC
Samuel Ruggles Papers—NYSL
Leverett Saltonstall Papers—MaHS
William Henry Seward Miscellaneous Papers—NYSL
William Henry Seward Papers—Rush Rhees Library, University of
    Rochester
Jared Sparks Papers—Harvard University Library
Jared Sparks Papers—MaHS
George Hume Stewart I and II Papers—Perkins Library, Duke University
John W. Taylor Papers—NYHS
G. C. Verplanck Papers—NYHS
Daniel Webster Papers—Dartmouth College
Daniel Webster Papers—LC
Daniel Webster Papers—New Hampshire Historical Society
Thurlow Weed Papers—LC
Thurlow Weed Papers—NYSL
Thurlow Weed Papers—Rush Rhees Library, University of Rochester
Thurlow Weed Papers—Union College
Robert C. Winthrop Papers—Harvard University Library
Robert C. Winthrop Papers—MaHS
John Young, Miscellaneous Papers—NYSL

Daniel Dewey Barnard: Published Speeches and Articles (in
chronological order)

Great Republican Meeting in Rochester (Rochester: n.p., 1827?).

Speech of Mr. Barnard of New York on the tariff bill, delivered in the House of Representatives, March 17, 1828 (Washington: Gales and Seaton, 1828).

An Address delivered September 6, 1831, before the Adelphic Union Society of Williams College; the evening preceding the Annual Commencement (Williamstown: Ridley Bannister, 1831).

Speech delivered in the National Republican Convention of the State of New York Held at Utica, July 26, 1832 (Utica: R. Northway, 1832).

An Introductory Address delivered before the Young Men's Association for Mutual Improvement, of the city of Albany, on the 7th of January, 1834 (Albany: Packard and Van Benthuysen, 1834).

An Address delivered before the Literary Societies of Geneva College, at the Annual Commencement of that Institution, August 6, 1834 (Albany: Packard and Van Benthuysen, 1834).

An oration delivered before the honorable the corporation and the military and civic societies of the city of Albany on the Fourth of July 1835 (Albany: E. W. and C. Skinner, 1835).

An Introductory lecture delivered before the Young Men's Association for Mutual Improvement in the city of Troy on the 17th of December, 1835 (Troy: N. Tuttle, 1835).

Annual Address, delivered before the Albany Institute, April 19, 1836 (Albany: Packard and Van Benthuysen, 1836).

Lecture on the Character and Services of James Madison delivered before the Young Men's Association for Mutual Improvement in the City of Albany, February 28, 1837 (Albany: Hoffman and White, 1837).

An Address delivered before the Philoclean and Peithessopian Societies of Rutgers, at the request of the Philoclean Society, July 18, 1837 (Albany: Hoffman and White, 1837).

A Discourse Pronounced at Schenectady before the New York Alpha of the Society of Phi Beta Kappa, July 25, 1837 (Albany: Hoffman and White, 1837).

A Discourse pronounced at Burlington before the Literary Societies of the University of Vermont, August 1, 1838, on the day of the Annual Commencement (Albany: Hoffman and White, 1838).

Speeches and Reports in the Assembly of New York, at the Annual Session of 1838 (Albany: Oliver Steele, 1838).

Mr. Barnard's Discourse on the Life and Services of Stephen Van Rensselaer with an Historical Sketch of the Colony and Manor of Rensselaerswyck delivered before the Albany Institute, April 15, 1839 (Albany: Hoffman and White, 1839).

"Commerce as Connected with the Progress of Civilization," *Hunt's Merchants' Magazine*, I (July, 1839), 3–20.

An Address delivered at Rochester before the Rochester Athenaeum and Young Men's Association, July 18, 1839 (Albany: Hoffman and White, 1839).

An Address delivered at Amherst, before the Literary Societies of Amherst College, August 27, 1839 (Albany: Hoffman and White, 1839).

Speech of Mr. Barnard of New York in relation to the contest for seats from the state of New Jersey, delivered before the House of Representatives, December 4, 1839 (Washington: Gales and Seaton, 1839).

Speech of Mr. Barnard of New York on proposition to refuse the oath to five members from New Jersey, delivered before the House of Representatives, the Twenty-Sixth Congress, December 18, 1839 (Washington: Gales and Seaton, 1839).

The Whigs and the Conservatives (Albany: Alfred Southwick, 1839).

Speech of Mr. Barnard of New York against Abandoning or Suspending the prosecution of works of internal improvement, delivered in the House of Representatives, February 14, 1840 (Washington: Gales and Seaton, 1840).

Speech of Mr. Barnard of New York on the Treasury Note bill, delivered in the House of Representatives, March 25, 1840 (Washington: Gales and Seaton, 1840).

Speech of Mr. Barnard of New York on the Sub-Treasury bill, delivered in the House of Representatives, June 12, 1840 (Washington: Gales and Seaton, 1840).

Speech of Mr. Barnard of New York on the Treasury Note bill, delivered in the House of Representatives, January 18, 1841 (Washington: n.p., 1841).

Speech of Mr. Barnard of New York on the loan bill, delivered in the House of Representatives, July 9, 1841 (Washington: National Intelligencer, 1841).

Remarks of Mr. Barnard of New York, on the bill in relation to duties and drawbacks, delivered in the House of Representatives, July 28, 1841 (Washington: National Intelligencer, 1841).

Speech of Mr. Barnard of New York, in opening the debate on the bankrupt bill in the House of Representatives, also his speech in reply on the same subject, delivered in the House of Representatives, August 10 and August 17, 1841 (Washington: National Intelligencer, 1841).

Speech of Mr. Barnard of New York in relation to the Destruction of the "Caroline" and the Case of McLeod, delivered in the House of Representatives, August 31, 1841 (Washington: National Intelligencer, 1841).,

Speech of Mr. Barnard of New York in favor of a uniform system of electing Representatives by districts throughout the United States, delivered in the House of Representatives, April 28, 1842 (Washington: National Intelligencer, 1842).

Speech of Mr. Barnard of New York on the veto of the provisional tariff bill, delivered in the House of Representatives, July 1, 1842 (Washington: National Intelligencer, 1842).

Speech of Mr. Barnard of New York on the policy of a protective tariff, delivered in the House of Representatives, July 6, 1842 (Washington: National Intelligencer, 1842).

Mr. Barnard's speech on the remedial justice bill (Washington: n.p., 1842).

Speech of Mr. Barnard of New York on the Executive plan for an exchequer, delivered in the House of Representatives, January 25, 1843 (Washington: National Intelligencer, 1843).

Speech of Mr. Barnard of New York on his provisional bill for supplying a national currency, delivered in the House of Representatives, February 20, 1843 (Washington: n.p., 1843).

A Discourse delivered before the Senate of Union College on the 24th day of July, 1843 (Albany: Weed and Parsons, 1843).

Anniversary Address, delivered before the American Institute at the Tabernacle, in New York on the 20th of October, 1843 (New York: James Van Norden and Co., 1843).

Speech of Mr. Barnard of New York on the bill to refund the fine imposed upon General Jackson, delivered in the House of Representatives, December 29, 1843 and January 2, 1844 (Washington: Gales and Seaton, 1844).

Speech of Mr. Barnard of New York on the report and resolutions of the Committee on Elections, relative to the elections by General Ticket in the four recusant states of New Hampshire, Georgia, Mississippi and Missouri, delivered in the House of Representatives, February 13, 1844 (Washington: J. and G. S. Gideon, 1844).

Speech of Mr. Barnard of New York on the tariff bill reported from the Committee of Ways and Means, delivered in the House of Representatives, May 14, 1844 (Washington: J. and G. S. Gideon, 1844).

Letter of the Honorable Daniel D. Barnard of New York in review of the report of the Committee of Ways and Means on the Finances and the Public Debt (Washington: Gideon's, 1844).

The Finances of the United States or the present situation of the National debt and the question as to the authors of such debt, clearly settled (Washington: National Intelligencer, 1844).

Daniel D. Barnard's letter in appendix of the Berkshire Jubilee celebrated at Pittsfield, Massachusetts, August 22, and 23, 1844 (Albany: Weare C. Little, 1845).

Address delivered at the Consecration of the Albany Cemetery on the 7th of October, 1844 (Albany: C. Van Benthuysen and Co., 1846).

Speech of Mr. Barnard of New York on the Annexation of Texas, delivered in the House of Representatives, January 24, 1845 (Washington: J. and G. S. Gideon, 1845).

A Plea for Social and Popular Repose, being an Address delivered before the Philomathean and Eucleian Societies of the University of the City of New York, July 1, 1845 (New York: Tribune, 1845).

"The 'Anti-Rent' Movement and Outbreak in New York," *American Whig Review*, II (December, 1845), 577–598.

The Anti-Rent Movement and Outbreak in New York (pamphlet; Albany: Weed and Parsons, 1846).

An Address to the Class of Graduates of the Albany Medical College, delivered at the Commencement, January 27, 1846 (Albany: C. Van Benthuysen and Co., 1846).

"The War with Mexico," *American Whig Review*, III (June 1846), 571–580.

"Our Relations with Mexico," *American Whig Review*, IV (July, 1846), 1–15.

Man and the State, Social and Political, an address delivered before the Connecticut Alpha of the Phi Beta Kappa at Yale College,

New Haven, August 19, 1846 (New Haven: B. L. Hamlen, 1846).
"The President's Message: The War," *American Whig Review*, V (January, 1847), 1–15.
"Mr. Slidell's Mission to Mexico," *American Whig Review*, V (April, 1847), 325–338.
"The Whigs and the War." *American Whig Review*, VI (October, 1847), 331–346.
"The War: The New Issue," *American Whig Review*, VII (February, 1848), 105–117.
"The President and His Administration," *American Whig Review*, VII (May, 1848), 437–452.
"The Administration: Its Treatment of General Scott," *American Whig Review*, VII (June, 1848), 553–572.
The Social System, an address pronounced before the House of Convocation of Trinity College, Hartford, August 2, 1848 (Hartford: S. Hanner, Jr., 1848).
"The Whigs and Their Candidate," *American Whig Review*, VIII (September, 1848), 221–234.
Whig or Abolition? That's the Question (Albany: n.p., 1849).
A Discourse on the Life, Character and Public Services of Ambrose Spencer, late Chief Justice of the Supreme Court of New York: Delivered by request before the Bar of the City of Albany, January 5, 1849 (Albany: W. C. Little and Company, 1849).
Daniel Webster: Speech of Mr. Barnard delivered at a meeting of Americans in Paris on the 16th of November, 1852 (Berlin: C. F. Unger, 1853).
Political Aspects and Prospects in Europe, a lecture delivered before the Young Men's Association in the city of Albany, January 31, 1854 (Albany: Weed, Parsons and Co., 1854).
Letter from the Honorable Daniel D. Barnard Addressed to James A. Hamilton on the Political Condition of the Country and the State of Parties and in favor of Millard Fillmore for President (Albany: J. Munsell, 1856).
A Letter from the Honorable Daniel D. Barnard Addressed to the Honorable Erastus Brooks, Senator, on the bill offered and pending in the Senate, as a substitute for the bill of the committee, in relation to Trinity Church (Albany: J. Munsell, 1857).
The Dangers of Disunion: A Letter from the Honorable Daniel D. Barnard of Albany (Albany: n.p., 1860).
Truths for the Times: Honorable Daniel D. Barnard on the Presidential Question (St. Louis: George Knapp and Company, 1860).
Truths for Voters: Addressed to the people (Albany: n.p., 1860).
Sovereignty of the States over their Navigable Waters; Argument of Daniel D. Barnard in Albany Bridge Case (Albany: Atlas and Argus, 1860).

Manuscript Official Records

Application and Recommendation Files, National Archives (1849–1850).

Assessment Records, Albany County, 1873.
MS Record New York State Canvas, 1838–1842, NYSL.
MS Record New York State Census, 1835, 1855, NYSL.
MS Record New York State — Civil Officers Elected by the People, 1828–1853, NYSL.
United States Legation, Berlin, Miscellaneous Correspondence, I–II, National Archives (1850–1853).
United States Legation, Berlin, Notes from the German Governments, National Archives (1850–1853).
Will of Daniel D. Barnard (1861), Surrogate Court, Albany County.
Will of Stephen Van Rensselaer (1839), Surrogate Court, Albany County.
Will of Dudley Walsh (1816), Surrogate Court, Albany County.

Other Manuscript Sources

Barnard Family Geneology, LC.
Daughters of the American Revolution, Bible Records, NYSL.
Daughters of the American Revolution, Cemetery Records, Rochester, Monroe County, NYSL.
Daughters of the American Revolution, Records of St. Luke's Episcopal Church, Rochester, Monroe County, NYSL.
Livingston Family Geneology, in private possession of Dr. James Livingston, Scotia, New York.
Records of St. Peter's Episcopal Church at Albany, New York, 1785–1855, NYSL.

Newspapers

Albany *Argus* (1826–1861).
Albany *Daily Advertiser* (1838).
Albany *Evening Journal* (1830–1861).
Albany *Freeholder* (1846).
Albany *State Register* (1851–1852).
Anti-Masonic Enquirer (Rochester, 1828–1830).
Anti-Renter (Albany, 1845–1846).
Monroe Republican (1825–1826).
National Intelligencer (Washington, 1839–1845).
National Republican (Rochester, 1832).
New York Colonization Journal (1850–1853).
New York *Times* (1851–1861).
New York *Tribune* (1843–1861).
Niles Weekly Register (1826–1829, 1838–1845).
Rochester *Daily Advertiser* (1826–1830).
Rochester *Republican* (1829–1832).
Rochester *Telegraph* (1824–1826).
Unionist (1840).

Periodicals

American Whig Review (1845–1852).
Hunt's Merchants' Magazine (1839–1861).
North American Review (1828–1850).

Other Published Primary Sources
—General

Adams, Charles Francis (ed.), *Memoirs of John Quincy Adams* (Philadelphia: J. B. Lippincott and Co., 1874–1877), 12 vols.
Adams, John Quincy, *The Diary of John Quincy Adams, 1794–1845,* Allan Nevins (ed.) (New York: Charles Scribner and Sons, 1951).
Address of the American party of New York adopted at the annual meeting of the State Council at Troy, February 24 & 25, 1857 (NP: n.p., 1857).
Address of the state convention of delegates from the several counties of New York on the subject of the presidential election, 1828 (Albany: Beach, Denis and Richards, 1828).
American Almanac and Repository of Useful Knowledge (Boston: Crosby, Nichols, Lee and Co., 1861).
Anti-Rent Controversy (London: Spottiswoods, Ballantyne and Co., 1865).
Beardsley, Levi, *Reminiscences* (New York: Charles Vinten, 1852).
Benton, Thomas Hart, *Abridgement of the Debates of Congress from 1789 to 1856* (New York: D. Appleton and Co., 1857–1861), 16 vols.
———, *Thirty Years' View* (New York: D. Appleton and Co., 1854–1856), 2 vols.
Boston Courier Report of the Union Meeting at Faneuil Hall, Thursday, December 8, 1859 (Boston: Clark, Fellows and Co., 1859).
Brown, Henry, *A Narrative of the Anti-Masonick Excitement in the Western Part of the State of New York, During the years 1826, 1827, 1828 and part of 1829* (New York: J. W. Leonard and Co., 1856).
Buckingham, Joseph T., *Personal Memoirs and Recollections of Editorial Life* (Boston: Ticknor, Reed and Fields, 1852).
Burr, Daniel, *An Atlas of the State of New York* (Ithaca: Stone and Clark, 1839).
Circular of the Whig Executive Committee of the Two Houses of Congress (Washington: Towers, 1848).
Correspondence between Honorable Hamilton Fish, United States Senator from New York and Honorable James A. Hamilton, son of Alexander Hamilton (NP: n.p., 1856).
Colton, Calvin (ed.), *The Private Correspondence of Henry Clay* (New York: A. S. Barnard and Co., 1856).
Dayton, Abram C., *Last Days of Knickerbocker Life* (New York: George Harlan, 1882).
Durfee, Calvin, *Williams Biographical Annals* (Boston: Lee and Shepard, 1871).
Everett, Edward, *Eulogy of Daniel Dewey Barnard* (Boston: n.p., 1861).

————, *Orations and Speeches* (Boston: Little, Brown and Co., 1850–1868), 4 vols.

Evening Journal Almanac (Albany: Weed, Parsons and Co., 1858).

Evening Journal Almanac (Albany: Weed, Parsons and Co., 1861).

Fitzpatrick, John C. (ed.), "Autobiography of Martin Van Buren," in *Annual Report of the American Historical Association, 1918,* II (Washington: Government Printing Office, 1920).

Francis, John W., *Old New York* (New York: Charles Roe, 1858).

Gazetteer of the State of New York, Thomas Gordon (ed.) (Philadelphia: T. K. and P. G. Collins, 1836).

Gazetteer of the State of New York (Albany: J. Disturnell, 1842).

Gazetteer of the State of New York, J. H. French (ed.) (New York: Ira J. Friedman, Inc., 1860).

Greeley, Horace, *Recollections of a Busy Life* (New York: J. B. Ford and Co., 1868).

Hamilton, James A., *Reminiscences of James A. Hamilton* (New York: Charles Scribner and Co., 1869).

Hammond, Jabez D., *The History of Political Parties in the State of New York* (Cooperstown: H. & E. Phinney, 1844), 2 vols.

Harvey, Peter, *Reminiscences of Daniel Webster* (Boston: Little, Brown, and Co., 1877).

Historical and Statistical Gazetteer of New York State (Syracuse: R. P. Smith, 1860).

Huntington, P. C., *The True History regarding the alleged connection of the order of ancient, Free and accepted Masons with the abduction of William Morgan in Western New York in 1826* (Chicago: C. H. Shaver, 1880).

Johnson, A. G., *A Chapter of History or the Progress of Judicial Usurpation* (Troy: n.p., 1863).

Kennedy, John P., *Defence of the Whigs* (New York: Harper and Brothers, 1844).

Latrobe, John H. B., *African Colonization: Its Principles and Aims* (Baltimore, John D. Fay, 1859).

Lee, John Hancock, *The Origins and Progress of the American Party in Politics* (rev. ed.; Freeport, New York: Books for Libraries Press, 1970).

McIntosh, W. H. *History of Monroe County* (Philadelphia: Everts, Ensign and Everts, 1877).

Mackey, Albert G., *The Mystic Tie or facts and opinions illustrative of the character and tendency of Free Masonry* (Louisville: W. M. Ellison, 1860).

March, Charles W., *Reminiscences of Congress* (New York: Charles Scribner, 1851).

Memorial of the Semi-Centennial Anniversary of the American Colonization Society (Washington: Colonization Society, 1867).

New York Annual Register, 1830–1845, Edwin Williams (ed.) (New York: Peter Hill, 1830–1845), 10 vols.

New York Colonization Society, First report read at the annual meeting, October 29, 1823 (New York: Seymour, 1823).

New York State Register for 1843, O. L. Holley (ed.) (Albany: J. Disturnell, 1843).

Ormsby, R. McKinley, *A History of the Whig Party* (Boston: Crosby Nichols, and Co., 1859).

Parker, Amasa, *Reports of Decisions in Criminal Cases* (Albany: Gould, Banks and Co., 1855–1863), 6 vols.

Proceedings of a State Convention of Delegates Friendly to the Election of William H. Harrison for President and Francis Granger for Vice-President (Albany: Hoffman and White, 1836).

Proceedings of the Union Meeting held at Castle Garden, October 30, 1850 (New York: Union Safety Committee, 1850).

Proceedings of the Whig State Convention of the State of New York assembled at Utica, September 14, 1848 (NP: n.p., 1848).

Proctor, L. B., *The Bench and Bar of New York* (New York: Diossy and Co., 1870).

Sargent, Nathan, *Public Men and Events* (Philadelphia: J. B. Lippincott and Co., 1875).

Savage, John, *Our Living Representative Men* (Philadelphia: Childs and Peterson, 1860).

Severance, Frank H. (ed.), *Millard Fillmore Papers* (Buffalo: Buffalo Historical Society, 1907), 2 vols.

Seward, Frederick W. (ed.), *Autobiography of William H. Seward, 1801–1834* (New York: D. Appleton and Co., 1877).

Slavery or Involuntary Servitude (Albany: Colvin and Bingham, 1863).

Smith, James H., *History of Livingston County* (Syracuse: D. Mason and Co., 1881).

Smith, Margaret Bayard, *The First Forty Years of Washington in the Family Letters of Margaret Bayard Smith*, Gaillard Hunt (ed.), (rev. ed.: New York: Frederick Ungar, 1965).

Speech of William H. Seward on the Compromise Bill delivered in the Senate of the United States (Washington: n.p., 1850).

Stanton, Henry B., *Random Recollections* (New York: Harper and Brothers, 1887).

Stebbins, G. B., *Facts and opinions touching the real origin, character, and influence of the American Colonization Society* (Boston: John P. Jewett and Co., 1853).

Taber, Azor, *Quarter Sales* (Albany: Weed, Parsons, and Co., 1850).

Thirtieth Annual Report of the American Colonization Society (Washington: C. Alexander, 1847).

Tocqueville, Alexis de, *Democracy in America* (Vintage ed.; New York: Alfred A. Knopf, 1945), 2 vols.

Trial of James Lackey, Issac Evertson, Chauncy H. Coe, Holloway Howard, Hiram Hubbard, John Butterfield, James Ganson, Asa Knowlen, Harris Seymour, Henry Howard and Moses Roberts at the Ontario General Sessions for Kidnapping Captain William Morgan (New York: n.p., 1827).

Tribune Almanac (New York: Tribune, 1856).

Tuckerman, Bayard (ed.), *The Diary of Philip Hone* (New York: Dodd, Mead and Co., 1910), 2 vols.

Van Tyne, C. H., *The Letters of Daniel Webster* (New York: McClure, Phillips and Co., 1902).

Weed, Harriet A. (ed.), *Life of Thurlow Weed: Including His Autobiography and a Memoir* (Boston: Houghton, Mifflin and Co. 1889), 2 vols.

Wendell, John L., *Report of Cases argued and determined at the Supreme Court of Judicature and in the Court for the Trial of Impeachments and the Correction of errors* (New York: Banks and Brothers, 1883), 4 vols.

Whig Almanac and United States Register, 1843–1856 (New York: H. Greeley, 1843–1856).

Whig Banner (Nashville: C. C. Norwell, F. K. Zollicoffer, 1843).

Whig Central Committee, *Notice to John H. Boyd of meeting at Stanwix Hall, Albany, July 24* (Albany: n.p., 1856).

Whig Portrait Gallery (New York: G. H. Colton, 1849).

Winthrop, Robert C. Jr., *A Memoir of Robert C. Winthrop* (Boston: Little, Brown & Co., 1897).

Local Histories and Directories

Albany Directories, Nos. 25–52 (Albany: Hoffman/Munsell,—1835–1860).

Steele's Albany Almanack (Albany: Oliver Steele, 1831).

Steele's Albany Almanack (Albany: C. Van Benthuysen, 1841).

Conway, Martin, *Index to Wills and to Letters of Administration* (Albany: James B. Lynn, 1895).

Howell, George Rogers and Jonathan Tenney, *History of the County of Albany, 1609–1886* (New York: W. W. Munsell and Co., 1886).

Mayo, A. D., *Symbols of the Capital* (New York: Thatcher and Hutchinson, 1859).

Munsell, Joel, *Annals of Albany* (Albany: Munsell, Rowland, 1850–1859), 10 vols.

———, *Collections on the History of Albany* (Albany: J. Munsell, 1865, 1867, 1870, 1871), 4 vols.

Parker, Amasa J., *Landmarks of Albany County* (Syracuse: D. Mason and Co., 1897), 2 vols.

Worth, Gorham A., *Random Recollections of Albany, 1800–1808* (Albany: J. Munsell, 1866).

—Federal Official Records and Documents

Bevans, Charles (comp.) *Treaties and other International Agreements of the United States of America, 1776–1949* (Washington: Department of State, 1968).

Biographical Directory of the American Congress, 1774–1949 (Washington: United States Government Printing Office, 1961).

Congressional Globe (Washington: 1839–1845).

Heads of Families at the First Census of the United States taken in 1790 (Washington: United States Government Printing Office, 1908).

House Executive Documents (Washington: 1851–1853).

Journal of the House of Representatives (Washington: 1839–1845).

Malloy, William M. (comp.), *Treaties, Conventions, International Acts, Protocols and Agreements between the United States of America and other powers, 1776–1909* (Washington: United States Government Printing Office, 1910), 2 vols.

Miller, Hunter (ed.), *Treaties and Other International Acts of the United States of America* (Washington: United States Government Printing Office, 1937), 8 vols.

Moore, John Bassett, *A Digest of International Law* (Washington: Government Printing Office, 1906), 8 vols.

Register of Debates in Congress (Washington: 1827–1831).

Richardson, James D. (comp.), *A Compilation of the Messages and Papers of the Presidents, 1789–1917* (New York: Bureau of National Literature and Art, 1904–1917), 20 vols.

Senate Executive Documents (Washington: 1844, 1852, 1854, 1860).

U. S. Department of State, *Despatches from the United States Ministers to the German States and Germany, 1799–1906* (Washington: National Archives, 1953), Microcopy 44.

U.S. Department of State, *Diplomatic Instructions of the Department of State, German States and Germany, 1801–1906* (Washington: National Archives, 1946), Microcopy 77.

—State Official Records and Documents

Lincoln, Charles (ed.), *Messages from the Governors, Comprising Executive Communications to the Legislature and other Papers, 1683–1906* (Albany: J. B. Lyon Co.,1909), 11 vols.

McKinney, William Mark, *McKinney's Consolidated Laws of New York: County Law* (Brooklyn: Edward Thompson Co., 1950).

New York (State), Assembly, *Committee on the Judiciary, No. 183* (Albany: E. Croswell, 1844).

New York (State), *Documents of the Assembly* (Albany: E. Croswell, 1838).

New York (State), *Journal of the Assembly of the State of New York* (Albany: E. Croswell, 1838).

New York (State), *Journal of the Senate of the State of New York* (Albany: E. Croswell, 1838).

SECONDARY MATERIALS

Books

Alexander, De Alva S., *History and Procedure of the House of Representatives* (Boston: Houghton, Mifflin Co., 1916).

———, *A Political History of the State of New York* (New York: Henry Holt and Co., 1906), 3 vols.

Alexander, Thomas B., *Sectional Stress and Party Strength: A Study of Roll Call Patterns in the United States House of Representatives, 1836–1860* (Nashville: Vanderbilt University Press, 1967).

Benson, Lee, *The Concept of Jacksonian Democracy: New York as a Test Case* (Princeton: Princeton University Press, 1961).

Binkley, Wilfred E., *American Political Parties* (New York: Alfred A. Knopf, 1958).

Blessing, Charles W. (ed.), *Albany Schools and Colleges Yesterday and Today* (Albany: Fort Orange Press, 1936).

Brauer, Kinley J., *Cotton versus Conscience: Massachusetts Whig Politics, and Southwestern Expansion, 1843–1848* (Louisville: University of Kentucky Press, 1967).

Carroll, E. Malcolm, *Origins of the Whig Party* (Durham: Duke University Press, 1925).

Chester, Alden, and Edwin Williams, *Courts and Lawyers of New York: a History, 1609–1905* (New York: American Historical Society, 1925).

Christman, Henry, *Tin Horns and Calico* (New York: Henry Holt and Co., 1945).

City of Albany (Portland: L.H. Nelson and Co., 1905).

Cole, Arthur Charles, *The Whig Party in the South* (New York: American Historical Association, 1914).

Coon, Horace, *Columbia: Colossus on the Hudson* (New York: E. P. Dutton and Co., 1947).

Crandall, John Riggs, *The Morgan Episode* (New York: Committee on Antiquities of the Grand Lodge of the State of New York, 1907).

Cross, Whitney, *The Burned-Over District: The Social and Intellectual History of Enthusiastic Religion in Western New York, 1800–1850* (New York: Harper and Row, 1950).

Current, Richard N., *Daniel Webster and the Rise of National Conservatism* (Boston: Little, Brown and Co., 1955).

Dangerfield, George, *The Awakening of American Nationalism* (New York: Harper and Row, 1965).

———, *The Era of Good Feelings* (New York: Harcourt, Brace, and World, Inc., 1952).

Davis, David Brion, *Slave Power Conspiracy and the Paranoid Style* (Baton Rouge: Louisiana State University Press, 1969).

Doherty, Herbert J., Jr., *The Whigs of Florida, 1845–1854* (Gainsville: University of Florida Press, 1959).

Eaton, Clement, *Henry Clay and the Art of American Politics* (Boston: Little, Brown and Co., 1957).

Ekirch, Arthur, Jr., *The Idea of Progress in America, 1815–1860* (New York: Peter Smith, 1951).

Ellis, David M., *Landlords and Farmers in the Hudson Mohawk Region, 1790–1850* (Ithaca: Cornell University Press, 1946).

Ellis, David M., *et al.*, *A History of New York State* (rev. ed.; Ithaca: Cornell University Press, 1967).

Esmond, Irwin, *Public Education in New York State* (Albany: New York State Teachers Association, 1937).

Flick, Alexander C., (ed.), *History of the State of New York* (New York: Columbia University Press, 1933–1937), 10 vols.

Foner, Philip S., *Business and Slavery* (Chapel Hill: University of North Carolina Press, 1941).

Foreman, Edward R. (comp.), *Centennial History of Rochester, New York* (Rochester: n.p., 1932).

Fox, Dixon Ryan, *The Decline of Aristocracy in the Politics of New York* (New York: Columbia University Press, 1919).

Fox, Early Lee, *The American Colonization Society, 1817–1842* (Baltimore: Johns Hopkins Press, 1919).

Fredrickson, George M., *The Inner Civil War: Northern Intellectuals and the Crisis of the Union* (New York: Harper and Row, 1965).

Freehling, William W., *Prelude to Civil War: The Nullification Controversy in South Carolina, 1816–1836* (New York: Harper and Row, 1965).

Fuess, Claude M., *The Life of Caleb Cushing* (New York: Harcourt, Brace and World, Inc., 1923), 2 vols.

Garraty, John A., *Silas Wright* (New York: Columbia University Press, 1949).

General Catalogue of the Officers, Graduates and Non-graduates of Williams College (Williamstown: Williams College, 1930).

Graves, Frank P., *History of the State Education Department* (New York: Columbia University Press, 1937).

Gregory, Winifred (ed.), *American Newspapers, 1821–1936* (New York: H. W. Wilson Co., 1937).

Griffen, C. S., *The Ferment of Reform, 1830–1860* (New York: Thomas Crowell, 1967).

Hamilton, Holman, *Prologue to Conflict: The Crisis and Compromise of 1850* (Louisville: University of Kentucky Press, 1964).

Harsha, David A., *Noted Living Albanians* (Albany: Weed, Parsons and Co., 1891).

Hislop, Codman, *Albany* (Albany: Argus Press, 1936).

Hofstadter, Richard, *The Idea of A Party System: The Rise of Legitimate Opposition in the United States, 1780–1840* (Berkeley: University of California Press, 1969).

Hooper, Rev. Joseph, *A History of Saint Peter's Church in the City of Albany* (Albany: Fort Orange Press, 1900).

Horner, Harlan H., *Education in New York State, 1784–1954* (Albany: State Education Department, 1954).

Hough, Franklin, *Historical and Statistical Record of the University of the State of New York* (Albany: Weed, Parson and Co., 1885).

Hudson, Frederick, *Journalism in the United States* (New York: Harper and Brothers, 1873).

Kimball, Francis P., *Albany: A Cradle of America* (Albany: Committee on the celebration of the 250th Anniversary of the granting of the Donegan Charter, 1936).

Lanier, Henry W., *A Century of Banking in New York, 1822–1922* (New York: The Gilliss Press, 1922).

Livingston, Edwin B., *The Livingstons of Livingston Manor* (New York: Knickerbocker Press, 1910).

McAdam, David, Henry Bischoff, *et al.* (eds.), *History of the Bench and Bar of New York* (New York: New York History Company, 1897), 2 vols.

McCormick, Richard, *The Second American Party System: Party Formation in the Jacksonian Era* (Chapel Hill: University of North Carolina Press, 1966).

McKelvey, Blake, *Rochester, the Water Power City, 1812–1854* (Cambridge: Harvard Univeristy Press, 1945).

Malone, Dumas (ed.), *Dictionary of American Biography* (New York: Charles Scribner's Sons, 1928–1937), 20 vols.

Mau, Clayton, *The Development of Central and Western New York* (Rochester: DuBois Press, 1944).

Merk, Frederick, *Manifest Destiny and Mission in American History: A Reinterpretation* (New York: Alfred A. Knopf, 1963).

Miller, Douglas T., *The Birth of Modern America, 1820–1850* (New York: Pegasus, 1970).

———, *Jacksonian Aristocracy: Class and Democracy in New York, 1830–1860* (New York: Oxford University Press, 1967).

Miller, Nathan, *The Enterprise of a Free People* (Ithaca: Cornell University Press, 1962).

Mock, Stanley U., *The Morgan Episode in American Free Masonry* (New York: Roycrofters, 1930).

Morgan, Robert J., *A Whig Embattled: The Presidency under John Tyler* (Lincoln: University of Nebraska Press, 1954).

Mott, Frank Luther, *American Journalism: A History, 1690–1960*, first ed., 1941 (3rd ed.; New York: Macmillan Co. 1962).

———, *A History of American Magazines, 1850–1865* (Cambridge: Harvard University Press, 1938), 2 vols.

Mueller, Henry R., *The Whig Party in Pennsylvania* (New York: Columbia University Press, 1922).

Murray, Paul, *The Whig Party in Georgia, 1825–1853* (Chapel Hill: University of North Carolina Press, 1948).

Nevins, Allan, *Hamilton Fish* (New York: Dodd, Mead and Co., 1936).

———, *Ordeal of Union* (New York: Charles Scribner's Sons, 1947), 2 vols.

North, Douglass, *Growth and Welfare in the American Past* (Englewood Cliffs: Prentice-Hall, Inc., 1966).

O'Connor, T. H.., *Lords of the Loom: The Cotton Whigs and the Coming of the Civil War* (New York: Charles Scribner's Sons, 1968).

Palmer, John C., *The Morgan Affair and Anti-Masonry* (Washington: Masonic Service Association, 1924).

Parker, Jenny Marsh, *Rochester* (Rochester: Scranton, Wetmore and Co., 1884).

Payne, George Henry, *History of Journalism in the United States* (New York: D. Appleton-Century Co., 1940).

Peck, William F., *History of the City of Rochester* (New York: Pioneer Publishing Co., 1908), 2 vols.

———, *History of Rochester and Monroe County* (New York: Pioneer Publishing Co., 1908), 2 vols.

Pessen, Edward, *Jacksonian America: Society, Personality, and Politics* (Homewood, Illinois: Dorsey Press, 1969).

———, *Most Uncommon Jacksonians: The Radical Leaders of the Early Labor Movement* (Albany: State University of New York Press, 1967).

Peterson, Svend, *A Statistical History of the American Presidential Elections* (New York: Frederick Ungar, 1963).

Poage, George Rawlings, *Henry Clay and the Whig Party* (Chapel Hill: University of North Carolina Press, 1936).

Porter, Kirk H., and Donald B. Johnson, *National Party Platforms, 1840–1956* (Urbana: University of Illinois, 1956).

Pratt, John W., *Religion, Politics and Diversity: The Church-State Theme in New York History* (Ithaca: Cornell University Press, 1967).

Prominent People of the Capital District (Albany: Fort Orange Recording Bureau, Inc., 1923).

Rayback, Robert J., *Millard Fillmore* (Buffalo: Henry Stewart, Inc., 1959).

Remini, Robert, *Andrew Jackson* (New York: Twayne, 1966).

Reynolds, Cuyler, *Hudson-Mohawk Genealogical and Family Memoirs* (New York: Lewis Historical Publishing Co., 1911), 4 vols.

Richards, Leonard L., *Gentlemen of Property and Standing: Anti-Abolition Mobs in Jacksonian America* (New York: Oxford University Press, 1970).

Rothman, David, *The Discovery of the Asylum: Social Order and Disorder in the New Republic* (Boston: Little, Brown & Co., 1971).

St. Peter's Church in the City of Albany (Albany: Fort Orange Press, 1907).

Savell, Isabelle K., *The Governor's Mansion in Albany* (Albany: Argus Greenwood, Inc., 1962).

Schlesinger, Arthur M., Jr., *The Age of Jackson* (Boston: Little, Brown and Co., 1945).

Scisco, Louis D., *Political Nativism in New York State* (New York: Columbia University Press, 1901).

Shaw, Ronald, *Erie Water West: A History of the Erie Canal, 1792–1854* (Lexington: University of Kentucky Press, 1966).

Silbey, Joel, *The Shrine of Party: Congressional Voting Behavior, 1841–1852* (Pittsburgh: University of Pittsburgh Press, 1967).

———, *The Transformation of American Politics, 1840–1866* (Englewood Cliffs: Prentice-Hall, 1967).

Sims, Henry H., *The Rise of the Whigs in Virginia, 1824–1840* (Richmond: William Byrd Press, Inc., 1929).

Smith, Justin, *The Annexation of Texas* (New York: Macmillan Co., 1911).

———, *The War with Mexico* (New York: Macmillan Co., 1919), 2 vols.

Stanwood, Edward, *A History of Presidential Elections* (Boston: James R. Osgood and Co., 1884).

Staudenraus, P. J., *The African Colonization Movement, 1816–1865* (New York: Columbia University Press, 1961).

Taussig, Frank W., *The Tariff History of the United States* (New York: Putnam's Sons, 1892).

Temin, Peter, *The Jacksonian Economy* (New York: W. W. Norton and Co., 1969).

Tyler, Alice Felt, *Freedom's Ferment* (Minneapolis: University of Minnesota Press, 1944).

Van Deusen, Glyndon G., *The Jacksonian Era, 1828–1848* (New York: Harper and Row, 1959).

———, *The Life of Henry Clay* (Boston: Little, Brown and Co., 1937).

———, *William Henry Seward* (New York: Oxford University Press, 1967).

————, *Thurlow Weed: Wizard of the Lobby* (Boston: Little, Brown and Co., 1947).

Warren, Charles, *Bankruptcy in United States History* (Cambridge: Harvard University Press, 1935).

Weber, Adna F., *Growth of Industry in New York* (Albany: State Department of Labor, 1904).

Weise, Arthur James, *The History of the City of Albany* (Albany: E. H. Bender, 1884).

Wiltse, Charles M., *The New Nation, 1800–1845* (New York: Hill and Wang, 1961).

Woodburn, James A., *Political Parties and Party Problems in the United States* (New York: G. P. Putnam's Sons, 1903).

Articles

Auchampaugh, Philip G., "Making Amendments in the Fifties: The Story of New York Factions in 1856," *Quarterly Journal of the New York State Historical Association*, VII (October, 1926), 304–317.

Barkan, Elliott R., "The Emergence of a Whig Persuasion: Conservatism, Democratism, and the New York State Whigs," *New York History*, LII (October, 1971), 367–395.

Barker, Eugene, "The Annexation of Texas," *Southwestern Historical Quarterly*, L (July, 1946), 49–74.

Carman, Harry J., and Reinhard H. Luthin, "The Seward-Fillmore Feud and the Crisis of 1850," *New York History*, XLI (April, 1943), 163–184.

————, "The Seward-Fillmore Feud and the Disruption of the Whig Party," *New York History*, XLI (July, 1943), 335–357.

————, "Some Aspects of the Know-Nothing Movement Reconsidered," *South Atlantic Quarterly*, XXXIX (April, 1940), 213–234.

Donald, Aida D., "The Decline of Whiggery and the Formation of the Republican Party in Rochester: 1848–1856," *Rochester History*, XX (July, 1958), 1–16.

Douglas, Harry S., "Pioneer Experiences in Western New York," *New York History*, XXXII (July, 1951), 259–274.

Ekirch, Arthur, Jr., "Daniel Dewey Barnard: Conservative Whig," *New York History*, XLV (October, 1947), 420–439.

Ellis, David M., "The Yankee Invasion of New York, 1783–1850," *New York History*, XXXII (January, 1951), 4–17.

Fox, Dixon Ryan, "The Economic Status of New York Whigs," *Political Science Quarterly*, XXXIII (1919), 501–518.

Fuller, John D., "The Slavery Question and the Movement to Acquire Mexico, 1846–1848," *Mississippi Valley Historical Review*, XXI (June, 1934), 31–48.

Grimsted, David, "Rioting in Its Jacksonian Setting," *American Historical Review*, LXXVII (April, 1972), 361–397.

Hammond, Bray, "Free Banks and Corporations: The New York Free Banking Act of 1838," *Journal of Political Economy*, XLIV (April, 1936), 184–209.

————, "Jackson, Biddle and the Bank of the United States," *Journal of Economic History,* VII (May, 1947), 1–23

Haun, Cheryl, "The Whig Abolitionists' Attitude Toward the Mexican War," *Journal of the West,* VIII (April, 1972), 260–272.

Hodder, F. H., "The Authorship of the Compromise of 1850," *Mississippi Valley Historical Review,* XXII (March, 1936), 525–536.

Krout, John A., "The Maine Law in New York Politics," *New York History,* XVII (July, 1936), 260–272.

McCarthy, Charles, "The Anti-Masonic Party: A Study of Political Anti-Masonry in the United States, 1827–1840," in *Annual Report of the American Historical Association,* I, 365–573.

Marshall, Lynn, "The Strange Stillbirth of the Whig Party," *American Historical Review,* LXXII (January, 1967), 445–468.

Merk, Frederick, "Dissent in the Mexican War," *Massachusetts Historical Society Proceedings,* LXXXI (December, 1969), 120–136.

Murray, David, "The Anti-rent Episode in the State of New York," *Annual report of the American Historical Association for 1896,* I, 139–173.

Pessen, Edward, "The Egalitarian Myth and the American Social Reality: Wealth, Mobility and Equality in the 'Era of the Common Man,' " *American Historical Review,* LXXVI (October, 1971), 989–1034.

————, "The Marital Theory and Practice of the Antebellum Elite," *New York History,* LIII (October, 1972), 389–410.

Rayback, Robert J., "The Silver Gray Revolt," *New York History,* XXX (April, 1949), 151–163.

Rowley, William E., "The Irish Aristocracy of Albany, 1798–1878," *New York History,* LII (July, 1971), 275–304.

Sears, Louis M., "New York and the Fusion Movement of 1860," *Journal of the Illinois State Historical Society,* XVI (April, 1923), 58–62.

Sellers, Charles, "Who Were the Southern Whigs?", *American Historical Review,* LIX (January, 1954), 335–346.

Stephenson, G. M., "Nativism in the Forties and Fifties," *Mississippi Valley Historical Review,* IX (December, 1922), 185–202.

Van Deusen, Glyndon G., "Some Aspects of Whig Thought and Theory in the Jacksonian Period," *American Historical Review,* LXIII (January, 1958), 305–322.

Wander, Philip C., "Salvation Through Separation: The Image of the Negro in the American Colonization Society," *Quarterly Journal of Speech,* LVII (February, 1971), 57–65.

Wilson, Major L., "The Ideological Fruits of Manifest Destiny," *Illinois State Historical Society Journal,* LXIII (Summer, 1970), 132–157.

————, "The Free Soil Concept of Progress and the Irrepressible Conflict," *American Quarterly* (Winter, 1970), 769–790.

Doctoral Dissertations (unpublished)

Donald, Aida D., "Prelude to Civil War: The Decline of the Whig Party in New York, 1848–1852," University of Rochester, 1961.

Fink, William B., "Stephen Van Rensselaer: The Last Patroon," Columbia University, 1950.

Fowler, Nolan, "The Anti-Expansionist Argument in the United States Prior to the Civil War," University of Kentucky, 1955.

Lichterman, Martin, "John Adams Dix, 1798–1879," Columbia University, 1952, 2 vols.

Morris, John David, "The New York State Whigs, 1834–1843: A Study of Political Organization," University of Rochester, 1970.

Warner, Lee H., "The Silver Grays: New York State Conservative Whigs, 1846–1856," University of Wisconsin, 1971.

INDEX

Adams, John Quincy, 7-8, 13-14, 69-72, 85-87, 90

Albany, 27-28, 30, 72, 91, 129, 133, 148, 151

Albany *Argus*, 30, 55, 83, 153

Albany Bridge case, 150

Albany *Daily Advertiser*, 68

Albany *Evening Journal*, 31, 63, 83-84, 87-88, 95, 100, 108, 123, 127, 133, 137, 140-141, 152-153

Albany Female Seminary, 51

Albany Medical School, 51

Albany Regency, 31

Albany *State Register*, 175

American party, 137-145

American Whig Review, 50, 96-99

anti-abolition, 46-48, 100-101, 152-153, 158

anti-Catholicism, 23-24, 41, 59

Anti-Masonic Enquirer, 17

Anti-Masonry, 15-18, 26, 88, 95, 157

anti-rent dispute, 49, 96-97, 103, 157

antislavery, 47, 99, 105, 136, 139, 151, 157

Austria, 24, 120

bankruptcy legislation, 74-77, 80, 171-172

bank (national), 29, 75, 78, 80, 83, 90

Barnard, Catharine (Walsh), 27, 69, 72, 79, 114, 133-134

Barnard, Cora, 7, 15, 28, 115, 134, 182

Barnard, Daniel Dewey (personal life), 3-5, 7, 8, 21, 27-29, 69, 72, 79, 91, 114-116, 129, 133-135, 147-148, 154, 157

Barnard, Ebenezer, Jr., 4, 5

Barnard, Ebenezer, Sr., 3

Barnard, Sarah (Livingston), 7, 15

Barnard, Sarah, 28, 134, 182

Barnard, Timothy, Jr., 117

Barnard, Timothy, Sr., 4

Bates, Edward, 142

Bell, John, 142, 152, 157

Berlin, 108, 113, 129, 133

Biddle, Richard, 69

Boston, 151

Bouck, William, 50

Brace, Charles, 121

Bradish, Luther, 56, 68, 94, 141-142, 146, 181

Breckinridge, John C., 152, 154

Brent, William, 10
Brooks, Erastus, 181
Brooks, James, 139-140, 153, 181
Brooks, Preston, 145
Buchanan, James, 145, 148

Calhoun, John C., 11
Childs, Timothy, 17-18
Choate, Rufus, 142
Clark, Myron, 136-137
Clay, Henry, 7, 25-26, 32, 37, 67, 69, 72-73, 75, 78, 83, 87-88, 99, 107, 127, 138, 149
Clayton, John M., 101-102, 104
Collier, John A., 102
colonization, 10, 46
Colquitt, Walter, 82
Columbia College (University), 102
Compromise of 1850, 105-107, 109, 127, 137, 146-147
Congress, (20th) 8-13, (26th) 69-70, (27th) 79, 83 (28th) 85, 88
Conscience Whigs, 94, 137
conservatism, 42, 157, see Chapter III
Constitutional Union party, 152-153
Cooper, James Fenimore, 50
Corning, Erastus, 47
Corwin, Thomas, 69
Cotton Whigs, 94, 104, 109, 126, 136-138
Crittenden, John J., 142
Cumberland Road, 13-14, 71
Cushing, Caleb, 75

D'Auterive, Marigny, 9
Democratic party, 26, 55, 58, 85, 94, 97, 128, 136-137, 140, 145-146, 148, 151
depression (1819), 6 (1837) 68, 75 (1857) 148
de Sandt, Henry, 122
deTocqueville, Alexis, 39
Dewey, Daniel, 3
Dewey, Phoebe, 4

De Witt, Richard, 110, 117, 129
distribution, 77, 82
District Election Law, 85-86
Dix, John A., 47
Douglas, Stephen A., 152, 154
Dred Scott case, 148
Dromgoole, George, 72
Duer, William, 153

education, 45, 59-61
Emerson, Ralph Waldo, 43
Erie Canal, 61-62
Everett, Edward, 8, 110, 122, 124, 142, 148, 152-153, 157
Exchequer, 83

Fay, Theodore, 116-117
Federalist party, 25
Fillmore, Millard, 30, 72, 94, 99-110, 114, 117-118, 124, 127, 133, 135, 142-147, 152
Fish, Hamilton, 69, 85, 88, 97, 99-104, 106-109, 113, 115, 117-118, 123-129, 133, 136-139, 142, 145, 147-154
Frederick, William IV, 113-114, 120-121
free soil, 99-100, 105
Frémont, John C., 145
French, James M., 74, 83
fugitive slave law, 107, 126, 136

gag rule, 70, 87, 89
Gallup, Albert, 68
General Banking bill, 57-58
Geneva College, 39
German Confederation, 118, 120, 124
Granger, Francis, 17, 26, 30, 32, 69, 94, 109, 136-137, 141-142, 144, 146, 181
Greeley, Horace, 94
Greig, John, 84
Griffin, William, 59

Hadley, Amos, 139
Hamilton, James A., 141-142, 144, 146-147, 149, 152, 181
Harrisburg Convention, 11

Harrison, William Henry, 32, 72, 74-75, 78, 99
Hunt, Washington, 28, 69, 85, 90, 102, 109, 113, 115, 141-142, 146, 148-149, 181
Hunter, Robert M. T., 70

Ingersoll, Jared, 84-85

Jackson, Andrew, 17-18, 25-26, 29, 32, 39, 55, 93, 158, 182

Kansas Nebraska bill, 136, 146-147
Kennedy, John P., 142
Ketchum, Hiram, 109, 149, 153, 181
Know-Nothings, 137-138, 140-143, 149
Kossuth, Louis, 119-120

labor, 48
Lansing, Gerrit, 31
Law, George, 142
Lawrence, Abbott, 127
Lecompton Constitution, 148
Lincoln, Abraham, 152-154
Livingston, Robert G., 7
Livingston, Sarah, 7
London, 117, 129
Louis Napoleon, 120
Louis Phillippe, 22-23

McCurdy, Charles, 121
Madison, James, 44
Maine law, 49
Mallary, Rollin, 11-12
Manteuffel, Baron, 118, 124
Marcy, William, 27, 31-32, 47, 56, 128-129
Maxwell, Hugh, 109
Mexican War, 44, 97-99
Miller, David, 16
Missouri Compromise, 136, 139, 154
Monroe, James (Col.), 105
Morgan, Christopher, 74, 102
Morgan, William, 15
Morse, Samuel F. B., 25

national bank, 29, 75, 78, 80, 83, 90
National Intelligencer, 83, 123
national power, 13-14, 44, 82, 86, 149-151
National Republican party, 19, 21, 25-26, 29
New York (city) 129, 142, 144, 147, 151
New York *Commercial Advertiser,* 140, 149
New York *Express,* 139
New York *Times,* 152
New York *Tribune,* 123
New York Whig party, 47, 55, 57, 67, 83, 90, 96-100, 102-103, 105-107, 109-110, 113, 125-126, 135-137, 147, 159
Niles Weekly Register, 12

old-line Whigs, 147, 180-181

Paris, 23, 129
Patrician politics, xiii, 6, 8, 17-18, 40, 41, 63, 67-68, 73, 95, 100, 104, 141, 159
penal reform, 48
Phi Beta Kappa, 39
Phoenix, J. Phillips, 149, 181
Pickens, Francis, 78
Pierce, Franklin, 127-128
Polk, James, 89
Pomeroy, Enos, 8
Potter, Horatio, 114
progress, 40, 42
prohibition, 48
Prokesch, Baron, 119
Pruyn, John V. L., 116
Prussia, 120-124, 130

Raynsford, Edmund, 55
reform, 43, 45-49, 51, 62, 158
Republican party, 137-142, 145-149, 153-154, 159
Rochester, 4-5, 8, 11, 24, 94
Rochester *Republican,* 22-23
Rome, 126

Ruggles, Samuel, 62, 142, 144, 181
Rutgers, 40

Saltonstall, Leverett, 69, 79
St. Peter's Episcopal Church, 51
Schmidt, Conrad, 124
Scott, Winfield, 72, 126-127
Settle, Paul, 55
Sergeant, John, 26
Sergeant, Nathan, 69
Seward, William Henry, 17, 30, 50, 68, 74, 94-96, 99-109, 125-126, 149, 159
Silver Grays, 109, 136-137
Slavery, 9-10, 15, 46-47, 62, 70, 89, 97-100, 105, 138-141, 145-146, 153-154, 158
Smith, Adam, 44
South, 14-15, 78, 82, 89, 138-140, 145-146, 148, 151, 154
Sparks, Jared, 21-22
Spencer, John C., 118, 124-125, 134
state sovereignty, 13-14, 79, 82, 86
Stilwell, Silas M., 172
sub-treasury, 57, 71
Sumner, Charles, 115, 148

Tallmadge, Nathaniel P., 68, 74, 95
Tariff, 10, 11, 77, 80-82
Taylor, Zachary, 99-107
Texas, 89-90, 97-98
Thompson, R. W., 142
Throop, Enos, 28
Trinity Church case, 150
Trinity College, 44
Tyler, John, 70, 72, 75-76, 78-83, 87

Ullman, Daniel, 181

Union, 139-140, 144-154, 158
Union College, 39
Unionist, 73
University of Vermont, 40

Van Buren, Martin, 25, 28, 32, 55-56, 67, 73
Van Rensselaer, Henry, 84
Van Rensselaer, Stephen, 49, 69, 157
von Humboldt, Baron, 114
von Ranke, Leopold, 114
Voorhees, Eliza, 117
Vroom, Peter, 129

Walsh, Catharine, 27
Walsh, Dudley, 27-28
Webster, Daniel, 69, 74, 85, 98-99, 102, 105, 107, 110, 115, 118-119, 122, 124, 126, 128, 138, 149
Weed, Thurlow, 7, 16-18, 30-31, 55, 63, 68, 72, 75, 84, 88, 94-96, 99-108, 125-127, 140, 149, 159
West, R. Anthon, 140, 142-44, 149, 181
Whig party, 19, 29, 40, 47, 55, 57, 62-63, 68, 70, 73, 75, 77-78, 83, 87, 90, 93, 97-98, 100, 102-103, 105, 107, 109, 113, 124-125, 128, 135-141, 143, 145, 147, 158-159, 173-175
Williams, College, 38
Williams, Sarah, 3
Wilmot Proviso, 47, 101
Winthrop, Robert, 69, 85, 90, 137, 142
Wirt, William, 27
Women's rights, 46
Wright, Silas, 9

Young, John, 97